NANCY NEVELOFF DUBLER
DAVID NIMMONS
ETHICS ON CALL

Nancy Neveloff Dubler joined the Montefiore Medical Center in 1975, several years after graduating from Harvard Law School. In 1978, she founded Montefiore's Law and Ethics Consultation Service, which she continues to direct. Dubler is also director of the Division of Legal and Ethical Issues in Health Care for the Department of Epidemiology and Social Medicine at Montefiore. She is a professor at the Albert Einstein College of Medicine. Dubler lectures and writes extensively on a number of topics in medical ethics, including termination of care, geriatrics, home care, and AIDS. She lives in New York City.

David Nimmons has coauthored seven books, three of which have become national best-sellers, including *Dr. Berger's Immune Power Diet*. Nimmons has contributed feature articles to magazines such as *Ladies' Home Journal, Parade, Playboy,* and *Families*. As an associate editor for *Playboy*, Nimmons covered issues in health, medicine, and politics. He lives in New York City.

ETHICS ON CALL

TAKING CHARGE OF
LIFE-AND-DEATH CHOICES IN TODAY'S
HEALTH CARE SYSTEM

NANCY NEVELOFF DUBLER
AND
DAVID NIMMONS

VINTAGE BOOKS · A DIVISION OF RANDOM HOUSE, INC. · NEW YORK

First Vintage Books Edition, May 1993

Copyright © 1992 by Nancy Neveloff Dubler and David Nimmons

All rights reserved under International and Pan-American Copyright
Conventions. Published in the United States by Vintage Books,
a division of Random House, Inc., New York, and simultaneously in
Canada by Random House of Canada Limited, Toronto. Originally
published in hardcover by Harmony Books, a division of Crown
Publishers, Inc., New York, in 1992.

Library of Congress Cataloging-in-Publication Data
Dubler, Nancy N.
Ethics on call: taking charge of life-and-death choices in today's
health care system / Nancy Neveloff Dubler and David Nimmons.
—1st Vintage Books ed.
p. cm.
Includes index.
ISBN 0-679-74538-6 (pbk.)
1. Medical ethics—Case studies.   2. Terminal care.
I. Nimmons, David.   II. Title.
R724.D78   1993
174′.24—dc20   92-50592
CIP

Manufactured in the United States of America
10 9 8 7 6 5 4 3 2 1

For the patients, families, and health-care providers at Montefiore Medical Center.

CONTENTS

ACKNOWLEDGMENTS

We are most grateful to Spencer Foreman, M.D., president of Montefiore Medical Center, who agreed to the writing and publication of this book with no requirement of prior review. We thank him for his trust, and we hope he agrees that the depth of concern portrayed here only adds luster to the reputation of the medical center.

Dr. Michael A. Alderman, chairperson of the Department of Epidemiology and Social Medicine, and Herbert Lukashok, vice-chairperson, arranged for the sabbatical leave that permitted Nancy to devote full time to this book. They have been unfailingly supportive and encouraging.

Many colleagues and friends were generous with their time and provided us with critical comments and expert advice. They are: John Arras, Paul Marantz, Peter Arno, Brian Regan, David Hammerman, Kenneth Schoenberg, Alan Fleischman, Louis Singer, Joanna Shulman, and Bettie Jackson. Three legal colleagues and friends, Edward Kornreich, Patty Lipschutz, and Connie Zuckerman provided critical counsel. Katheleen Powderly and Carol Levine offered valuable critique as did Arlene and Howard Eisenberg. Thanks to Alice Herb and Diane LaGamma, who, with the Montefiore Bioethics Committee, were primarily responsible for the value neutral living will in the appendix, and to Joan McIver Gibson, who permitted us to reprint her wonderful values history form.

Fenella Rouse, executive director of Choice In Dying, Inc.—the national council for the right to die, was extraordinarily generous, reviewed parts of the manuscript, and permitted us access to her organization's files for research. Choice In Dying, Inc., is also a major resource for readers in the future.

Amanda White was a dogged and effective research assistant. Walter, Ariela, and Joshua Dubler were good humored and comforting. Dave Fleischer, as always, was there with love, counsel, and support. Peter Guzzardi, editor extraordinaire, was patient, insightful, and offered numerous, excellent suggestions in pursuit of our shared goal—a book to empower patients and families in the complex world of modern medicine.

And most especially thanks to Nessa Rapoport who was midwife to this project, Daniel Kaufman who helped bring us together, and the wonderful Phyllis Wender, whose wisdom, advice, and enthusiasm make the complex world of book publishing feel so very much more human.

ETHICS
ON
CALL

INTRODUCTION

One winter evening my family and I spent dinner hashing over a particularly knotty case that had consumed me at work for the prior two days. It was the sort of heartrending situation that you just can't leave behind you at five o'clock. An infant boy had been born with the kind of grave multiple birth defects that virtually rule out survival. No treatment we could offer would help him thrive; at best, any intervention would only increase his suffering and prolong the inevitable process of dying. After extensive discussions between the parents and the neonatal care team, all agreed that the only possible compassionate solution was to keep him comfortable and in loving arms while he died. It was an agonizing decision for all of us—family, doctors, nurses, and me—the consulting ethicist called in to help sort through the issues. As we watched the infant, it became clear to us that a life of endless suffering was not a humane solution. But for my second child, perhaps identifying with this new person not so much younger than he was, the concept was a difficult one. "Mom, why would you ever let a baby die? This life is all the baby will ever have."

Not the average dinner table chat, perhaps. But when your mom happens to work as a clinical ethicist at a large urban hospital, you often find yourself grappling with intense and heartfelt discussions of some pretty hard issues. Indeed, such weighty discussions have been standard fare around the Dubler dinner table for a number of years. My children, now approaching adulthood, have grown up hearing about and pondering the sorts of issues that most of America considers beyond the realm of polite conversation: hopelessly imperiled infants, people in the prime of life reduced to dependency on machines, transplant organs needed by many and available only to a few, pregnant women unable to get prenatal care because they are too poor to pay for it. A few friends have suggested that it's a wonder my family doesn't have perpetual indigestion.

Obviously, such conversations are hard. They concern sickness, suffering, and death. But they are also immensely fascinating, offering glimpses into the very human dilemmas of people as they struggle to make the most important decisions of their lives and do right for those they love most. And to me, who spends every day at work having and leading such conversations, they are also hopeful. For they reveal the dawning awareness of individuals that they can have an impact upon, and even take control of, their lives—and deaths—in ways they never imagined.

For it is not just at my family's dinner table that talk about life, death, and medicine is gaining prominence. We hear such issues debated every day on the evening news, read them in the weekly magazines. Never has there been so much open and frank discussion about medical and ethical issues—abortion, transplantation, living wills, "pulling the plug," AIDS confidentiality, consenting to and refusing care. With all the discussion has come a growing realization that we need to do more than discuss these topics; we must understand them, because they can directly affect us and those we love most.

Over the last seventeen years of my career, I have been

privileged to find myself at the epicenter of this movement, part of the development of a new field of human inquiry called medical ethics. Today, if you should land in a hospital, you may find that the single most important person assuring you the care you want may not hold a medical degree. That person may be, as I am, trained as a lawyer; he or she may be a theologian or a philosopher, a social worker or a scientist. Whatever the background, that person will hold the title of "bioethicist," "clinical ethicist," or "medical ethicist."

As practitioners of medicine's newest subspecialty, we pose questions, offer arguments and analyses that affect your care and your very life itself. The bioethicist is concerned with how decisions get made in medicine, who makes them, and according to what principles. She is also concerned about the rights of patients and families in a setting where rights can often take second place to emergencies.

Let the doctors perform the death-defying acts of surgery and medicine that have won our hospital—Montefiore Medical Center—its reputation at the zenith of modern medicine; we work to keep in constant view the human values and social dilemmas in the nation's largest teaching hospital.

My job was perhaps most neatly defined by my colleague, philosopher Ruth Macklin: "to protect the rights and promote the interests of the patient"—to which I add, "and to support their families and loved ones." We ask the questions that reveal the options and clarify the players in any specific case. Ideally, those questions lay bare the uncertainty of medical diagnosis and prognosis, which places the profession somewhere between science and art, and reminds us that medical choices are ultimately based not only on science but on our personal histories and individual values.

Although patients are the ultimate beneficiaries of our discussions, my colleagues and I spend most of our time working with doctors, nurses, and social workers. We start where they get stuck, in the web of rights and responsibilities that ensnares all patients and caregivers. We get called in only when really baffling and more complex issues arise. In some ways, my team is an unlikely band: I am an attorney now working as a clinical ethicist; John Arras, a moral philosopher, also teaches at Barnard College; Alice Herb, for fifteen years a television producer with ABC News, has now returned to work in law and ethics; Diane LaGamma, an attorney, primarily serves our AIDS team; and Ruth Macklin, a bioethicist, spends most of her time at the Albert Einstein College of Medicine, our affiliated academic medical campus.

We work to help caregivers clarify the issues as they grapple to integrate technological advances and human desires with the infinitely human business of caring for the sick and dying. We sit with doctors and nurses, discuss and ask questions to clarify the issues, propose different ways to think about the situation, highlight the patients' rights, and work to give them the tools they need to deal with patients and families. For the nurses and doctors, social workers and physician's assistants, the medical students and house staff, we are there as teachers and as support for making the tough calls—a sort of ethics SWAT team.

Traditionally, the topic of ethics in health was the province of academics—moral and ethical philosophers, theologians, attorneys, and a few doctors and health-care advocates. Then, in the 1970s, these discussions began to move onto the wards and floors of our hospitals. In the almost two decades since, hospitals have begun to employ people like me to work full-time on ethical issues. As they are for the doctors we work with, our workdays are dictated by the changing needs of sick patients and anxious families. Our job is to ensure—despite the medical madness of any given day—that scrutiny and skepticism, wisdom and compassion are not lost in the crushing medical and monetary machinery of the modern hospital.

As with most people in this field, my path to this job was a bit circuitous. When I graduated from Harvard Law School in

1967, I knew I didn't want to spend my life augmenting the profits of corporations and wealthy individuals who could afford my services. So, for a decade, I practiced poverty law in some of New York's poorest and grimmest neighborhoods, defending delinquent kids, helping Bowery alcoholics, and setting up day-care centers. Then, in 1975, I joined the faculty of the Department of Epidemiology and Social Medicine at Montefiore Medical Center. My task was to think about law, ethics, and health care; the result was the creation of the Law and Ethics Consultation Service. Its mandate: to help medical students, nurses, doctors, and social workers grapple with the thorny decisions that arise as they care for human beings in the sprawling, roiling enterprise that is modern medicine.

Where once I defined the vulnerable as those caught in poverty, today I count as vulnerable any of us enmeshed in the health-care or hospital system. These systems are too intimidating, too distant, and too foreign to give the average patient or family member a fair chance to understand the options and affect the medical outcome.

What sustains me in this work, despite the cases that claw at my evening's calm and a workweek that routinely spills over into weekends, is my sense that the bioethicist's job is one of the newest ways of working for social reform. I remain an old egalitarian at heart, committed to the principle that all people should be provided with a level playing field. My work is one of the ways of weighting the patient's end.

I also do this work because I never forget that it could be me, or my family, in the next bed. Vulnerable humans in an inhospitable world, we all exist but a short ambulance ride away from medical mischance. Statistics tell us that we can virtually all expect, one day, to become an unwilling participant in a health-care drama—our own or someone else's. Whether you play the role of patient or relative, care for aging parents, ailing children, or beloved friends, it is virtually certain that you will at some point wander into the tangle of hospitals and doctors, the thickets of health agencies, insurance companies, and government bodies that today twine around illness in America. This book is written against that difficult day.

Fifty years ago, in the days of Marcus Welby medicine, there was little need for a book like this. Decisions were usually made in private, by patients, family, and doctors who knew each other, bound by shared values and common trust. House calls and family doctors existed and Health Maintenance Organizations didn't. In those days, as in most of human history, life, death, and medicine were straightforward: before dialysis, defibrillators, and ventilators existed, when your kidneys, heart, or breathing stopped, you were dead. In those decades, when pneumonia was known as "the old man's friend," people recognized death as an inevitable and acceptable, if sad, part of life.

Technology has changed all that. We now possess dozens of stratagems to beat death from the door: resuscitation to restart the heart and breathing in a body that has, in fact, already died; computer-driven respirators to breathe for us; pacemakers to quicken the failed heart; powerful drugs that artificially maintain not only blood pressure but the delicate chemical balance necessary to sustain life. Our technology now lets us confer several decades of healthy and productive life through procedures like cardiac catheterization or triple bypass surgery; yet it also lets us take a body with a massive brain hemorrhage, hook it up to a machine, and keep it nominally "alive," functioning organs on a bed, without hope of recovery.

Technology has opened new doors, certainly. Whether they lead to extended, healthy, and productive lives, or to dead ends that horribly prolong a painful death, that is often much harder to control. All too often, these technological changes create dilemmas that immobilize families and upset the expectations and agreements made by loving—if unsophisticated—relatives. I will never forget hearing a family told that they could not have the ventilator removed from their comatose ninety-three-year-old father because he had never left specific instructions for it, only to have them reply, "How could he have refused a machine he never even knew existed?"

With the technological changes have come legal ones. Over the last two decades, a vast codex of laws, state and federal regulations, policies, and scholarly legal commentaries has accumulated to provide guidance once sought in the experience and beliefs of families and the trusted family doctor. Decision-making power has gradually been shifting from patients, families, and doctors to legislators, regulators, bureaucrats, attorneys, and judges. Increasingly, such written policies and rules may directly conflict with what patients or families want; sometimes they frankly undercut their interests. As abstract rules and legal systems are imposed more widely, they can override individual plans, and disregard entirely the deepest values of those whose lives are at stake.

Those values lie at the heart of this book. The single most important idea in these pages is that, behind the objective medical facts on the chart, medical decisions always rest on somebody's value judgment. If you are aware and educated, the values will be yours; if not, they will be the values of others—good people but strangers. Whether you will be hospitalized or medicated; should an operation be performed and, if so, which one; will your mother be given CPR; can a bed be found for your child, experimental drugs for your lover, or a transplant for your uncle: these judgments are based as much on values as on medical knowledge and skill. But whose? The impersonal policies of institutions—hospitals, insurers, courts; the flesh-and-blood individual values shared among you and your family; the personal values of your doctors and nurses? Who, ultimately, will prevail—you or somebody else?

The most important change of all involves both your privacy and your power to decide. In the last decade, more and more matters traditionally viewed as private have come under the scrutiny of others. The bedside, once the private province of patient and family, now includes layers of administrators and bureaucrats, cost-cutters, lawyers, and legislators, reporters and insurers and political activists, all competing to control our most personal decisions when we are sick. Never before have so many players gathered at the bedside to push their own agendas forward.

Decisions our parents once made among loved ones with the support of the family doctor are now made by committees of strangers—all with their own agendas. The hospital may wish to avoid lawsuits, adverse publicity, regulatory sanction, and economic risk. The physician wants to avoid malpractice and preserve her position and status in the medical hierarchy; the insurer seeks to make money, the administrator works to limit your stay in this bed and preserve resources for its next occupant, and for the hospital's balance sheet. The reelection plans of a municipal judge, the dogma of the town church, even the passion of right-to-life activists—all can reverberate at the bedside, and affect your options and your care. Although you may never meet these players, their influence is felt in every aspect of your treatment.

Technology, legality, and cost containment. Together, they have forever changed the ground rules for how you are treated when you are sick. Together, they have made doctors' offices, hospitals, and clinics vastly different places from the comfortable world of solace and succor most of us envision. Amid all this complexity, in most places it is still true that if you don't stand up for your own values and rights, nobody else will.

My goal is to make that empowerment possible. This is a book about demystification. Its goal is to give you insight into the new, difficult and complex world of medical decision making. In these pages, you will eavesdrop on the discussions that have become commonplace among caregivers. You will attend debates among doctors and nurses, social workers, administrators, and managers in the back rooms of our hospitals. You will meet the players, hear about the issues and problems, and learn how decisions about real people get made. By the time you have finished reading this book you will know a great deal about the kinds of discussions that go on in hospitals and about the ethical dimensions of care. More important, you will learn how to analyze the problems and argue your case, how to make a difference in your care, and how, given the massive uncertainty in medicine, you can work to make things come out "right."

This is a book about predicaments and power. It is written for people who want to control their own medical care, to make decisions for themselves and participate in decisions for their loved ones, be they spouse, children, or parents, significant others or dear friends. It is a book about modern medicine, its triumphs and failures, and about the dilemmas that often surround its successes. At its conclusion, you will not yet be a clinical ethicist but you will have a variety of tools to argue your case and make sure the end result is something you can—quite literally—live with.

Knowing something of what I do as an ethicist offers a window on what any of us can expect when we find ourselves entering the maelstrom that is our medical system. Today, we can no longer leave it to the trusted family physician to know our families and "do what is best." Most physicians practice in systems that prevent their knowing very much about their patients; even if they did know us intimately, the choices these days are too many and too complicated to leave to the judgment of strangers, even our physicians. Today, only information about our medical options and choices permits us to take maximum control in the intricate, intimidating, and alien environment that is modern medicine. It is what allows us to use technology and medicine as part of, rather than an obstacle to, our own personal and moral values.

In the end, this book is a road map to autonomy, to show how you and your loved ones can penetrate the difficult and abstruse discussions that surround medical care. Ultimately, the goal is to give you and those you love a fighting chance, to help you make sure that your wishes and values are respected when it most counts.

In writing this book, my collaborator, David Nimmons, and I have followed some of the meetings and discussions occurring at Montefiore Medical Center. We have been privileged to observe some of the most intimate and private passages humans experience: the woman in silent tears coming to terms with removing her twenty-five-year-old son from a respirator; the young parents comforting their child who cannot understand why lifesaving surgery is needed; the tender compassion of an elderly woman seeking the best care for her husband of fifty-four years; the feisty humor of a young woman determined to beat her illness; such are the tales that make up this book.

The stories in these pages are true and their core ethical, medical, and human dimensions are presented unchanged. However, out of respect for the privacy and confidentiality of the many patients, families, doctors, nurses, social workers, house staff, and administrators, we have altered all identifying information so that they could not be recognized in any way. These reconstructions have been reviewed by the doctors involved to ensure that the medical issues remained unchanged and the patient identities obscured.

To the many patients and families who have opened their lives in the hope of helping the rest of us better face such moments in our own lives, we are deeply grateful. We are grateful, as well, to the doctors, nurses, and other care providers at Montefiore who have worked with us to make sure we get it all right. Their commitment to empowerment is no less than ours.

NANCY NEVELOFF DUBLER AND DAVID NIMMONS

I

THE KINDNESS OF STRANGERS

BEHIND THE SCENES AT THE MODERN HOSPITAL

Gene Patterson was seventy-six years old, having smoked for fifty-nine of those years, with a history of worsening emphysema. At first, his only symptom had been slight shortness of breath on his daily walks. But as his emphysema worsened, even the few short steps to the sidewalk from the apartment grew too demanding. For two months, he had scarcely left the home he shared with Elise, his wife of fifty-four years. He passed most of his days lying on the couch or bed, laboring to breathe, hardly moving or talking. Then, at 4:10 this morning, Elise had awakened to hear her husband gasping. Terrified, she dialed 911.

Now, her face was taut as she followed the gurney carrying her husband through the swinging doors of the ambulance bay. Instantly, three members of the emergency team converged on his inert form. As she turned to the emergency room attending physician, Dr. Selma Fuchs, the words caught in Elise Patterson's throat: "I know he's sick, Doctor. But he's . . . all I have. Please, will my husband be all right?" To Fuchs's skilled eye, the answer was all too clear. The contours of the man's face showed the classic one-sided droop that proclaimed a stroke; his skin had the gray-blue pallor of full respiratory arrest. Short of a miracle this man would not be all right; not even close, if she had to guess. But for now, her job was to get him breathing again; the rest would come later.

When they passed through the hospital's swinging doors, the Pattersons entered an alien world. Its assumptions, rules, and players have changed almost beyond recognition from what they were a few decades ago, and from what most of us might expect. The world we face when we are sick today is more complex, with many more rules, more decisions to make, and more parties trying to make them, than ever before.

My hospital, Montefiore Medical Center—"Mother Monte," as it is affectionately known—typifies the scale of modern medicine. It stretches in an archipelago of hospitals, clinics, and community-care centers across the entire borough of the Bronx. Its hospital units include the eight-story, 845-bed Henry and Lucy Moses Division (the original Montefiore Hospital) and the Jack D. Weiler Hospital of the Albert Einstein College of Medicine, a 430-bed acute-care facility on the medical school campus. Through an affiliation contract with the city of New York, the medical center provides faculty, house staff, and much of the professional staff to its municipal affiliate, the North Central Bronx Hospital, and shares a substantial amount of its faculty with the Bronx Municipal Hospital Center. The North Pavilion alone—just one of the six interconnected wings of the Moses complex—would cover eight acres stretched out on the ground.

Montefiore—with its staff of nine thousand—ranks among the nation's dozen largest medical centers: More than forty thousand patients will be admitted to the hospital and nine hundred thousand patients will pass through our combined outpatient facilities this year; twenty thousand operations will be performed in our operating rooms; and seventy-eight thousand people will, like Mr. Patterson, pass through our emergency room and intensive care units. We are also the nation's single largest teaching hospital system, training more physicians in medicine, surgery, pediatrics, ophthalmology, dentistry, and neurology than any other place in the country. Some of our divisions are world renowned; it was no surprise, for example, when the chairman of the Republican National Committee needed brain surgery in 1990 that the White House physicians chose Monte.

Over the next few days, the Pattersons would find themselves facing choices and decisions they could hardly anticipate. Like the Pattersons, most people who come into this hospital—or any hospital—do not understand how medical decisions get made by, for, and about them. Like them, most of us have no idea what happens when we, or those we love, get wheeled through the emergency room doors.

The emergency room (ER) team had been alerted by radio from the ambulance, and twenty seconds later the call blared from the hospital loudspeaker: "CAC in ER, clear the corridors! CAC in ER, clear the corridors!" CAC—cardiac arrest case—is the hospital signal to the "crash team" to converge on the ER. Instantly, the team of five specially trained doctors and nurses drop what they are doing. From wherever they are throughout the hospital—in the laboratory, in the cafeteria, conferring with a colleague or patient—they race to the ER, using special keys to commandeer the elevators. Every second counts: the team only has four minutes to start resuscitation and no more than eight minutes to attach advanced life support systems. If Mr. Patterson's heart and lungs are not pumping by then, he will suffer irreparable brain damage from lack of oxygen.

The resuscitation technique they are about to apply to him is one of modern medicine's miracles. The team is already moving into synchronized formation to apply the protocol they had been trained in—A-B-C-D: Airway, Breathing, Circulation,

Drugs. An anesthesiologist threaded a breathing tube down Mr. Patterson's throat to start the flow of oxygen directly into his empty lungs.

The lead physician, who is responsible for "running" the code, shouts "Stand away!" as she places two metal paddles on Patterson's bare chest. A high-voltage shock jolts through his body, making the old man's unconscious body stiffen and jump an inch from the table. To the uninitiated, it looks like torture; the team knows it is their only hope of jump-starting a human life.

A second doctor now cuts into his neck and inserts a widebore catheter, through which drugs can stimulate Mr. Patterson's failing heart. At times it may even be necessary to drive a three-quarter-inch needle through the chest wall into the heart muscle to inject the drugs directly. Someone else now crouches above the inert form to rhythmically compress the chest, bearing down with a pressure of 120 pounds. In an old and frail person like Gene Patterson, these compressions will almost certainly crack or break his ribs and sternum, and may even cause internal hemorrhage; those injuries are the price of bringing the dead back to life.

This brutal sequence—cardiopulmonary resuscitation, or CPR—was invented on the battlefields of the Second World War. It began as an emergency technique for soldiers who had suffered severe trauma, but were otherwise young and fit. If they could be kept alive long enough to reach a MASH hospital, and if their wounds weren't fatal, they could be patched up to live fifty more years. In those circumstances, with young and fit patients, resuscitation made clear sense. It may mean much less for a man like Mr. Patterson—seventy-six years old, debilitated from a progressive, fatal disease. In cases like his, CPR may only be the portal to a long, painful death.

For caregivers, however, the crisis atmosphere of the ER is no place to contemplate such nuances. Here, judgment calls must be made within seconds and existential questions have no place. This team presumes—medically and legally—that patients want to be treated, and it does so, often with stunning results. So, when Mr. Patterson arrived, to all intents a dead man, they set about dragging him back into life—all part of a day's work in the modern ER.

It is an open secret that the stunning medical advances of the late twentieth century have far outpaced our human judgment in applying them. Now that we possess the power to regularly cheat death, we find ourselves facing agonizingly complex ethical judgments on a daily basis. Our long march into medical technology—new machines, powerful drugs, daring surgical techniques—has carried us deep into uncharted moral territory.

Only twenty years ago, the first legal case concerning the removal of a ventilator had not yet made it into court; organ transplants were still novel enough to earn banner headlines; whole generations of drugs now used to treat life-threatening infections and heart attacks were still in the laboratories. Test-tube fertilization, microsurgery, and gene therapy had not yet emerged from the realm of science fiction; the AIDS epidemic would not even be named for another decade. And, when a day's hospital stay cost only $389, the specter that the government would one day ration health care, or that thirty-seven million Americans could afford no health insurance at all, was beyond credibility.

Six minutes after the ambulance pulled into the driveway, the ER team had Gene Patterson breathing, attached to a ventilator, and prepared for transfer to the intensive care unit for continued careful monitoring and further tests. Such sophisticated tests hardly seemed necessary, however, for the answers could easily be read in his physical signs: his pupils fixed and fully dilated, his limbs frozen into the classic asymmetrical posture, muscles relaxed and flaccid on one side and contracted on the other, his hand turned outward. All were the hallmarks of massive and irreversible neurological damage.

The neurologist's note in Patterson's chart summed up his diagnosis tersely: "L Decorticate, R Decerebrate. Probable PVS." That medical shorthand meant that on the entire left side of his brain, his higher cortical centers—where thought, memory, and language reside—were gone, billions of cells destroyed as surely as if they had been excised by a surgeon's scalpel. On his right side, destruction extended deep into the brain regions controlling motor function to the most basic part of the brain, the brain stem, which controls breathing and heartbeat. While his brain had been without oxygen its fragile cells had begun an irreversible cascade into chaos. In those few minutes, a human lifetime of memory and function flickered into permanent darkness. Gene Patterson was now adrift in a world nobody could share or reach. This man, this husband and father who only hours before had kissed his wife good night, now lay locked in what neurologists term a PVS, a persistent vegetative state.

If his mind had loosed its tethers to the world, his body was not so lucky. Lying on the bed, Gene Patterson looked like a frail bird snared in a web of tubes and wires. The web had been woven, strand by strand, over the seven decades of his own lifetime. The iron lung, crude ancestor of this computerized respirator, was invented for the polio epidemic of 1929. The bedside cardiac monitor where his heartbeat now spiked across a phosphorescent green screen came from technology developed for NASA astronauts. The intravenous infusion of the adrenaline-like chemical, dopamine, which maintained his blood pressure, was first developed in the 1960s. And the computer-enhanced MRI that provided the near-photographic image of his devastated brain was still being perfected. Of the dozen devices now yoking Gene Patterson to life, only one existed when he was born: the bed.

Machinery had wedged Mr. Patterson into an indeterminate niche between life and death. Here, he could be maintained for days, weeks, perhaps even years, a notion that would have been utterly inconceivable when Gene Patterson was born.

Then, as it had been throughout most of human history, medicine was largely a spectator science. The doctor could diagnose and comfort, but only in the rarest cases could he—the gender went with the occupation in those days—actually alter the course of events or effect a cure. The physician's prime tools were palliation, sympathy, and perhaps a bit of morphine at the end to ease the agony. Not until early in this century, when modern surgical techniques, reliable anesthetics, and sterilization were discovered, did the odds start improving. Indeed, not until the 1940s, with the discovery of penicillin antibiotics and sulfa drugs, did we enter what my colleague John Arras terms the "Pax Antibiotica"—the beginning of the modern medical era.

Predictably, new medical options begat new moral dilemmas. As physicians learned to defy death on a daily basis, we as a society found ourselves hard up against a set of perplexing questions. Often, such questions converge at the boundaries of life and death: What is the proper care for someone in a deep, irreversible coma, with no prognosis for return to a waking existence? Is there a responsibility to extend life in such a circumstance? If so, who has that responsibility? If not, who makes the decision to discontinue care: the family, the attending physician, a committee, a judge? If Mr. Patterson could not tell us what he wanted, who should? Can families and others direct that care be terminated? Should we permit suffering just to prolong life, or treat pain if it hastens death? Running through all of these is the most fundamental question of all: Who decides? And who decides who decides?

Such questions were far from the concerns of Dr. Tom Ferris as he stood at Gene Patterson's bedside the next afternoon. Tom was, in the parlance of the modern teaching hospital, a PGY-1. Montefiore, like many university medical centers, has abandoned the traditional schema of interns and residents in favor of the more descriptive term "PGY"—for "postgraduate year." Tom, a PGY-1, would once have been called an intern; a PGY-2 corresponds to a first-year resident and a PGY-3 to a second-year resident. They are, in the irreverent patois of the hospital, the "piggies." Behind their acronyms, these young doctors are here to receive on-the-job training. They will learn their trade as physicians always have, by listening to lectures, by following senior physicians on "rounds," by absorbing huge amounts of information, and, most of all, by practicing on sick people.

Mr. Patterson was one of those people, and he was just about as sick as they get. The emergency team had done its job, restarting his heart and breathing, then sent him to the ICU for monitoring and tests, which had lasted for several days. This morning, he had been transferred to Klau Pavilion, the medical wing of the hospital. In Mr. Patterson's case, the transfer to a regular Klau bed meant that the director of the ICU had decided that his patient could no longer benefit from the high-tech wizardry of intensive care. Such a decision might rest on an objective assessment of Mr. Patterson's medical condition and his poor prognosis, or it might involve balancing his medical needs against the needs of another patient who was waiting in the ER, in desperate need of the ICU bed that Mr. Patterson now filled.

Either way, Gene Patterson had run smack up against one of modern American medicine's most troubling trends. Skyrocketing costs are fast making medical care—particularly the kind of high-tech care that was keeping him "alive" in the ICU—an exercise in juggling scarce resources. Today, medical scarcities come in many varieties. Sometimes they are absolute: too few transplantable kidneys or corneas for the people who need them. Then, we face agonizing questions: who should get them—and who, in fact, does? Who gets to make that decision, and on what basis? Is it right that in our society the rich have access to transplants and the poor don't?

In this case, the scarcity Gene Patterson faced was man-made. Every hospital plans, builds, staffs, and maintains a limited number of expensive intensive care beds. In them, the brute force of medical technology can maintain gross organ functioning, the pure mechanics of life, for weeks, months, or years. But that comes at a very expensive price: not just in dollars—it costs $1,630 per day to stay in our ICU—but also in terms of the small number of beds. Gene Patterson lay in one of only ten beds in this ICU. If another patient, someone with a better shot at life, could benefit more from the high-tech ministrations of the ICU, the ICU director then faces a lifeboat calculus: with one too few places for one too many people, there may be no justification for this patient taking up the space that someone else needed more. Indeed, there are now whole departments in many hospitals, termed "quality assurance" or "utilization review" departments, charged with the delicate job of determining how the increasingly limited resources of the hospital are most fairly allocated among its needy charges.

Although the word "scarcity" was never uttered aloud, it was this hard administrative fact, coupled with his hopeless medical prognosis, that had resulted in Mr. Patterson's transfer to a regular medical floor. On this floor, without intensive monitoring, his vital systems would drift slowly out of synchrony until they could no longer sustain even this facsimile of life.

At the bedside, Dr. Ferris noticed that, somewhere along the way, this patient had undergone a tracheotomy, a procedure where a hole is cut in the neck to insert a breathing tube—"trache tube"—directly into the throat. Ferris didn't even have to look at the chart to know that, officially, it would note the procedure was done to prevent damaging his throat with the breathing tube, standard procedure in ventilator-dependent patients. Maybe that was the reason. But that, he mused, might be only half the truth. In fact, the tissue damage to his throat would take weeks to emerge, by which time this man would likely be dead. It was not impossible that the cause for the procedure might lie in the realities of a modern teaching hospital: some enterprising ear-nose-and-throat or surgical PGY-1 needed the opportunity to practice this basic surgical procedure. Such practice, after all, was vital, and you seize your cases where you find them—usually on the patients least likely to be harmed and the families least likely to object.

Such is the Faustian bargain of every teaching hospital. At a place like Montefiore, patients get the most sophisticated care from academic experts, the best professors of their time, brilliant diagnosticians and technicians with access to the most advanced machines and the finest professional resources. But these teachers are surrounded by their students, whose job it is to provide much of the routine care. And those students take their learning opportunities when and where they find them.

But, Ferris knew, the extra hole in his throat, whatever its origin, was the least of Gene Patterson's problems. Of greater concern was his temperature, which had spiked to 102.8 degrees the night before. The textbooks said that the right thing to do here was to search for a cause of the fever and prescribe appropriate antibiotics. But was that really the "right" thing? Looking down at the bed, Ferris imagined his own father, a few years younger than this man. If it were his dad lying there, what would he want done? Could he, as a loving and medically knowledgeable son, even presume to guess his father's wishes? What, for that matter, would Ferris himself want if he himself lay in this bed?

In Gene Patterson, Ferris saw both a metaphor for and a victim of the medicine he was being trained to dispense. For several days, in the ICU of one of the preeminent hospitals in the nation's largest city, the best medical science had done all it could for this man. It had "saved" this life, true, but for what? Mr. Patterson would never wake up; simply to pump antibiotics into his body, sentencing him to a few more days or weeks of unconscious immobility, seemed senseless, even cruel.

Yet for Ferris to do less would be to shirk the job he was trained to perform. His job was to help people; nowhere was he granted the power to arbitrate between life and death. Unfortunately, no one had yet devised a simple formula to calculate what constitutes "help" for a patient so clearly dying as Gene Patterson was. The young doctor knew that whether his patient got antibiotics might be a matter, not just of medical, but of legal, administrative, and even public relations concern. He wondered if he bore some legal obligation to treat, even if there was no really good medical reason. Omitting the basic medications that all students learned about in their first infectious-disease courses could open him, and perhaps the hospital, to criticism, bad publicity, or worse, a costly malpractice lawsuit. Letting this man go might be the most humane course, but the hospital counsel, and the office of risk management whose job it was to keep the hospital out of court, might not see it that way. Ferris had never even heard of risk managers when he had first started at the hospital, and he was sure the Pattersons had never heard of them, either. But the months of working on these floors had taught him that risk managers are powerful players at the bedside, for they speak with the full power of the hospital.

Looking at his patient's immobile form, chest rising in cadence with the wheezing machine next to the bed, Ferris sighed. The doctors had borrowed the time; now this patient was stuck living on it—if you could call it living. Gene Patterson's next step, he knew, would not require just their clinical skills. He made a note to call the Law and Ethics Consultation Service.

One half block south of Montefiore Hospital's main entrance lies a tidy, unprepossessing brick house. On its front doors, the sign proclaims that you have reached the Department of Epidemiology and Social Medicine. This modest structure is my office, where, on this particular day, I arrived to find the usual sheaf of "While You Were Out" pink slips, each from a different section of the hospital. One "URGENT" message bore the name of one of the senior surgeons. A male patient was refusing consent for a blood transfusion that would save his life because it conflicted with his beliefs as a Jehovah's Witness. Rifling through the pile, I glanced at the cases from the weekend: the head nurse in the cardiac care unit had called about an eighty-eight-year-old woman who wanted to be let die, but whose daughter was adamantly opposed. Could I stop by? And at the bottom of the pile, a PGY-1 named Ferris called about a Mr. Patterson.

After seventeen years at the hospital and fourteen years running a consultation service, I knew that these disparate cases shared a common element, something that distinguished them from the other eight hundred people occupying our beds on any particular day. They had popped out of the stream of routine decisions because somebody, somewhere, saw something and felt uncomfortable. Nine times out of ten, that means it is time for somebody to die.

Later that afternoon, I found myself sitting in a cramped nurses' station with a dozen members of the surgical unit team. I felt an edge of tension in the room as a surgeon began the case presentation. "John Morton is a married thirty-eight-year-old man with three children, ages eleven, fourteen, and twenty-one. Admitted for surgery for a mass in his colon . . ." He explained that the operation was a difficult one, often causing major blood loss and necessitating transfusion. And that was the rub: John Morton was a devout Jehovah's Witness, and adamantly refused to receive blood. In his view, and that of his church, a transfusion was a defilement of his body and an eternal pollution of his soul. To make his wishes crystal clear, he had signed a variety of hospital forms making his refusal absolutely clear prior to surgery. Indeed, recalled a resident, his last words before going under anesthesia were a plea asking his doctor to promise he would receive no transfusion.

That he was able to say that at all was a testament to other changes that have occurred in the medical system. Historically, Mr. Morton wouldn't have had a whole lot of influence on his care. Decisions were routinely made by the physician, with concern and knowledge, but often without discussing things with either patient or family. Those sorts of decisions are now referred to as "paternalistic," where the doctor plays the role of father, running the show.

Over the last three decades, however, the unwritten rule that "doctor knows best" has been challenged by patients, courts, and, more recently, by bioethicists. The result has been that patients like John Morton have been empowered to decide about their care, at the moment and in the future. Modern doctrines of informed consent and patients' rights to refuse care are based on the idea that patients have the right to determine what will happen to them. We now train caregivers to respect patients' and families' roles in making decisions, and to take patients' informed consents and refusals seriously. In Mr. Morton's case, however, it was not to be so easy.

No sooner was he asleep than other players began to see to it that his life became entangled in the law. In this case, those other players were members of his own family. They let it be known, in no uncertain terms, that we were to ignore his wishes and transfuse him if it became necessary. The operation went well, but as John Morton came out of surgery, as was expected, he began bleeding. The surgeon knew a transfusion was the only way to save his life, and ordered it. Our blood bank refused, citing their ethical and legal obligation to honor his clear wishes as expressed both in writing and orally. His wishes were amply documented and fully in accord with both law and common sense. If ever there was an ironclad refusal of care that we were ethically bound to respect, John Morton's was it.

At this point both his wife and his brother, neither of them Witnesses, turned up their pressure on the hospital to ignore Mr. Morton's wishes and give him blood. As he lay failing, they went to court. If we wouldn't listen to them, they knew, we would have to obey a judge. He could order the physicians to violate John Morton's wishes in order to save his life.

The notion that the legal system has a place in medicine is a peculiarly American notion, one unheard of by the family physician three decades ago and today still considered aberrant outside our country. But increasingly in recent years, law and medicine have collided, often in very public spectacles—and have propelled many ethical dilemmas into public consciousness. A stream of such legal cases has yielded household words, the case names a shorthand for complex moral issues: Karen Ann Quinlan and Nancy Cruzan, elucidating the right to die; Ryan White, embodying the rights of those with AIDS to fair treatment without discrimination; Mary Beth Whitehead, invoking the right of surrogate mothers to the babies they bear; the hopeless Baby Jane Doe, raising the right of newborns to treatment; the physicians Kervorkian and Quill, testing the limits of how and whether physicians may ethically help patients die.

A nation of voyeurs, we have watched these most intimate human tragedies played out in our morning newspapers and on the evening news. Like modern morality plays, these tales have captured our imaginations, driven us to anger and tears, challenged and frightened us. Most of all, they have forced us to rethink our collective assumptions about what it is to be human. Such very personal tragedies have helped mold our public policies.

As such, these cases represent the next logical step in an evolution that has been going on for a century: medicine has progressively become a more public undertaking. As people increasingly began and ended their lives within hospital walls, our most intimate and individual moments became public events. As these cases, and many others like them, have wound their way through our legal system, our options when we are sick have increasingly become matters of law. No longer do sickness and death revolve solely around patient, family, and doctor; now they may also involve judges and attorneys, hearings and regulations, statutes, and case law. Much of that effort has served to strengthen the right of individuals to make their own medical decisions. However, it has also brought many new players and an unprecedented level of legal complexity to the simple business of being ill.

In John Morton's case, law and ethics coincided. Ethically, Mr. Morton was our patient—not his wife, brother, or children. Before the operation, he was of perfectly "sound mind," making his decision known to us in a series of lucid, consistent, and rational discussions. Eminently capable of deciding for himself, he had discussed his wishes repeatedly with his doctors, and had even signed the formal "refusal of care" form that now lay in his chart. The team had no doubt that his refusal reflected his deepest, long-held beliefs; it was consistent with the pattern of who he was and how he behaved. Refusing blood lay at the core of his devout spirituality. That we, or his family, might disagree mattered little; his own wishes were 100 percent clear.

Donning my lawyer's hat, I pointed out that legally his refusal was also on solid ground. A landmark case, *Fosmire v. Nicoleau,* had clearly established the right of a woman—also a parent—to refuse blood. In that case, it was argued that her refusal and subsequent death would be an abandonment of her children, and so should limit her right to refuse; the trial judge agreed. The New York State Court of Appeals, the state's highest court, disagreed. New York State law was crystal clear: his refusal of care should be respected. Now John Morton's wife and brother adopted the same tack, arguing that his death would abandon his children, a state of affairs forbidden by New York family court law. Accordingly, they petitioned the Bronx Supreme Court judge to order transfusion. Where, hours before, this decision had been Mr. Morton's alone, now his family had propelled it to a court of law, where his fate would be decided by a stranger.

It fell to a fifty-one-year-old New York State judge, a man who seemed unfamiliar with the law, unschooled in the issues, and very skittish about letting this patient choose death. He faced the stark question: should a lifesaving transfusion be given against John Morton's express wishes? Or should an adult patient be permitted to refuse a treatment that will surely result in death? Because such questions are both emotionally and politically charged, they make judges enormously uncomfortable. This judge, like some of his peers, held his job through a political process of election or appointment, and never forgot that fact. Judges know that it is much less politically risky to prolong rather than terminate life. Even if doing so means overriding a person's own wishes, violating a judge's personal jurisprudential values; even if, as in this case, it means refusing to honor the very clear New York law; judges feel safer decreeing for life. John Morton's judge did just that. Granting the pleas of his wife and father, he signed a legal order requiring the hospital to give him blood. Although we knew it directly contravened his wishes, we had no choice but to do so.

It turned out to be the worst possible resolution. After fifteen hours of transfusion treatment, John Morton died despite these efforts. But it was not the death he had wanted. The judge's decision meant that his religious faith and the teachings of his church had been cast aside. In his final hours, in the view of his church and his commitment to a community of his faith, his eternal soul had been violated. Meanwhile, predictably, his wife and brother blamed it on the delay.

Medically, his was a preventable death; but at a human level, Mr. Morton was the victim of legal players entering the realm of personal medical decisions. Had we been able to keep the decision within the confines of the hospital, we could have honored his last wish. His family had prevented this. For a number of reasons, it decided it knew better for him than he did.

The care team was shattered by the experience. Our physicians and nurses try to take personal wishes very seriously, but in this case, forces beyond their control had undermined their solemn promise to their patient. They might not agree with his decision—indeed, none of the team would likely have made

John Morton's choice. But they knew he had made it, consistently and consciously, in accord with his faith. Knowing that, they had made a covenant with him, which they felt ethically bound to respect—and now felt they had broken. Too often, it is not only hard to know the right thing to do, but even harder to do it.

Not every case we get involves imminent death. Aaron and Donna posed a less urgent, but no less compelling, dilemma. Married for fourteen years, they both described their marriage as "happy." However, they had stopped having any sex at all after the first two years of marriage; now, wanting to have children, they had been seeing Dr. Ginny Chun, a physician in the family medicine clinic. For the last several months she had been working with them to resume their sexual relationship. The problem was that, from her private sessions with Aaron, Ginny knew something Donna did not: that Aaron had enjoyed a series of affairs—all with men.

Theirs was hardly the first such case Dr. Chun had counseled. Although statistics say that as many as 10 percent of American males are homosexual, her experience had taught her that the overwhelming majority of them, fearing censure from an intolerant society, lead deeply closeted sexual lives. Like Aaron, such men are often married, fathers of families, who conduct same-sex forays outside of their marriage. They may not even identify themselves as gay, considering themselves "bisexual" or even heterosexual. In her eight years in the clinic, Dr. Chun had seen a dozen Aarons, and knew the thorny ethical issues these behaviors could raise.

Those issues had only grown more complex with the advent of AIDS. Aaron lived in New York, the epicenter of the AIDS epidemic. He was, however, isolated from the organized gay community, and isolated as well from the intensive safe-sex education that has so dramatically reduced the spread of AIDS among gay men. He was, statistically, at higher risk than men whose acceptance of their sexuality permitted them access to risk reduction information. His sexual secret threatened to put not only him, but his wife, at risk.

Things were now at a critical juncture, as the couple told Dr. Chun they were considering resuming their sexual relationship. Dr. Chun was particularly worried in light of the "good news" Donna had shared that morning: they had booked a cruise for a second honeymoon, to rekindle their love life. It was then that Dr. Chun cornered me in front of the hospital coffee shop, as I clutched a tuna sandwich and a tepid cup of coffee. "I've got a doozy, Nancy. Can you stop by for a talk?"

A doozy, indeed. Dr. Chun had heard about Aaron's many sex partners in confidence, so she could not ethically tell Donna without breaching her duty of confidentiality to her patient. But Donna was her patient as well, and she could not allow her to be put at risk. Dr. Chun had been adamant with Aaron: before any sexual contact with his wife, Aaron had to be tested for any sexually transmitted diseases, especially to ascertain if he had been exposed to the HIV virus. "He told me he had, and it was 'all okay,' but I'm not sure I believe him. We're talking about two lives here, three if she gets pregnant." As a family doctor, she felt acutely her ethical, legal, and medical duty to both Donna and Aaron. Usually a physician has ethical obligations to one individual and those trump the hypothetical rights of others. But, in this case where both were her patients, was there an ethical way to resolve this tug-of-war—to protect the welfare and confidentiality of both? If not, what could be done?

In this case, I explained, common sense and ethics converged. Since Dr. Chun could not both protect Donna and respect Aaron's confidentiality, the "least worst" solution was to weigh the risks and benefits to each from either course of action and to choose that which seemed least harmful. To be sure, risks and benefits existed on both horns of this particular dilemma. By breaching Aaron's confidentiality, she would risk losing his trust and candor. He might even leave her care altogether. That, in turn, could harm him and could hurt the marriage without necessarily helping Donna.

The risks to Donna were more concrete: she could contract a sexually transmitted disease if Aaron had been exposed. Such infections could mean a minor annoyance, potential sterility—or, in the case of the HIV virus, her very life. That kind of risk-benefit analysis is a cornerstone of my work, one of the key operational principles that the clinical ethicist brings to every case. The risks and benefits here were clear. On one side of the balance was Aaron's desire to protect his privacy and control personal information about himself; on the other, the value to his wife of continued health and knowing what risks she was exposed to. Clearly, hers was the far greater risk, and the far stronger ethical claim. But was there a way to respect his privacy and her rights?

Such questions are central to what an ethicist does. We are, after all, not paid to be Solomon, nor do we possess a grab bag of neat solutions to tricky moral problems into which we reach for each case. Rather, we try to pose the right questions, to clarify, probe, and challenge. When it works well, we take heat and make light, so all involved can create a care plan that is ethically appropriate for each patient.

After much discussion, we settled on a clear course. Dr. Chun would have a frank talk with Aaron, explaining the risk-benefit analysis and her obligation to both of them as her patients. He could choose to be tested through her office so that she could be certain of his health status, or he could choose to fully explain his situation to Donna. That way, any decision Donna made would be based on her fully informed consent. If, however, Aaron refused, or if Dr. Chun was not satisfied that he had disclosed his situation candidly to Donna, then, and only then, she had a professional and ethical obligation to do it herself. In that event, she would also have to alert Aaron to her plan. The plan gave Aaron the first chance to explain. Dr. Chun would intervene only if she saw no other way to protect Donna's interests. As we wrapped up, Dr. Chun flashed me a wry smile. "Sometimes it's hard to know whether you're practicing medicine or being a referee. Let's just hope they didn't put a deposit down on those cruise tickets."

The day's last case was a success story, of a sort. Mary DeCarlo was eighty-eight years old, at the end of a long battle with progressive heart disease. When she was wheeled into the ER with congestive heart failure, she was alert, wide awake, seemingly in complete command of her faculties. She was also adamant: "Don't you go putting me on your boxes." She gestured to the bank of humming life-support monitors. "I'm an old woman, I've had a good life. And I won't spend my last time all hooked up to one of those darned machines!" The ER team did their job, stabilizing her and transferring her upstairs to the coronary care unit.

That meant the hard part fell to the medical service—as always. The ethos of the medical service is very different from the urgency of the ER seven floors below. In that setting, death is the ultimate defeat, to be postponed at all costs. But up here in the medical corridors, we deal in the larger arc of human life. Here, death is accepted as a familiar, if unwelcome, consort, the natural course for someone like Mary, with progressive, terminal disease. As soon as she met her new nurses in the cardiac care unit (CCU), Mary repeated her convictions: she would accept whatever medications she needed, but did not want to be put on a respirator—in her words, "punctured by machines."

Mrs. DeCarlo was responding to a perverse medical principle—what ethicists term the "technological imperative"—which demands that because a technology exists, it must be used, whether or not it will really benefit the patient. For a period, it had become all too easy for hospitals and doctors to prolong organ function without always knowing that treatment was actually making the person better. Sometimes, that sprang from real uncertainty about what might or might not help the patient; often it came from fears that families might sue doctors or hospitals for not "doing everything" for—and to—patients. The inevitable result was that families were traumatized by watching those they loved—usually older parents—end their lives among machines, pierced by a dozen needles and tubes, all in dehumanized settings among strangers. Starting about fifteen years ago, enough Americans had undergone the agony of watching family members die a prolonged death without dignity or control to know that this certainly wasn't what they wanted. There was a growing perception that it wasn't enough to have medical miracles—we needed, in the words of journalist Fred Friendly, to "manage our miracles." In tandem with technology that brought new medical options, we needed new stratagems to control them.

One of these is the do-not-resuscitate—"DNR"—order. These orders state clearly that when the lungs or heart "arrest" or stop pumping, the patient will not be subjected to an aggressive, often violent attempt to restart them. These orders are society's way of balancing the miracles of resuscitation with the compassion that has always been a part of doctoring. These documents, and others, have become powerful tools to make sure your wishes get heard in the high-tech tumult of treat-first-ask-later medicine. (DNR orders also make the care team's job much easier. For if Mary's heart or lungs failed, they could ethically and legally follow a simple, agreed-upon care plan, and avoid a panicked, draining argument about what to do.)

New York State law specifies that the patient (or the patient's family, if the patient is no longer able) can request a DNR order. Accordingly, the CCU nurses spoke to Mary at length about a DNR order, making sure they, as well as she, were aware of and comfortable with Mary's clear statements. They then recorded her wishes in her hospital chart, and her physician, after another discussion with Mary, wrote a DNR order.

The only problem was Mary's daughter, also a nurse. "I

know she really doesn't want to die. Mom is ambivalent—she's not herself," she proclaimed to whoever would listen. She denied knowing about her mother's wishes; late at night, in a tone of panic, she confided to one nurse's assistant that "I don't want her to die, I'm not ready." During the daughter's visit, the young and aggressive resident in charge of Mary's case came by. He also thought it appropriate that this patient be put on a ventilator if necessary, on the slim chance she could recover and eventually go home again.

In a series of hurried and confused discussions with the fast-weakening woman, daughter and doctor prevailed. Whether through ambivalence (nobody, after all, is unconflicted about dying), her fear of suffering, or simple exhaustion, Mary finally relented and agreed to be placed on the first level of ventilator support.

Over the next forty-eight hours, Mary was clearly miserable. Although the tube in her throat prevented her from speaking, she repeatedly wrote notes to her nurse, Lynn, asking to be taken off the machine, and stating that she was ready to die. But her daughter kept begging her to change her mind, alternately cajoling and badgering the nurses and doctor to disregard her mother's wishes and "do everything." Matters came to a head on the second day, when an air leak developed in the tube, necessitating that it be removed and replaced. At this juncture the medical staff, feeling caught in a dilemma, called me. That afternoon, I found myself sitting down with the CCU care team.

When you spend a lot of time, as I do, interacting with very sick, often very elderly people at the painful end of their lives, you learn that death is not necessarily the worst that life has to offer; there are worse states. And, in my personal view, Mary DeCarlo was in one.

This proud woman was now enduring at our hands precisely what she had most sought to avoid. She was clearly mentally intact, although deathly ill. I knew that ethically and legally, we were bound to respect the clearly stated wishes of a rational and lucid patient. Because Mary was alert and oriented, and clearly capable of making her wishes known, nobody had the right to come in and impose their preferences on hers—not a doctor, or us, not even her anxious daughter. The daughter could use her intellectual and emotional powers to sway her mother, but fundamentally, Mary was our patient and nobody had the right to interfere with her clear and consistent decision. And, I reminded the nurses, to impose treatment in clear violation of her wishes might be an assault and battery.

Moreover, these were not new wishes. The head nurse told me they had discovered a living will Mary had signed a year before, indicating that if she became unable to decide, she did not want to be resuscitated or maintained on a respirator. Couldn't we use that, one of the nurses asked? I reminded them we didn't even need to invoke that piece of paper. It was clear to the nurses that, despite her physical incapacity, Mary was still capable. She was consistent and forceful in her wishes to accept death. Every time a new person came into her room she snatched up her pad and wrote "I want this machine off; I am ready to die."

"It seems to me," I closed, "this patient has done everything right. She has told us what she wants, consistently and clearly, orally and in writing. Now our job is to be her advocate, and see that we respect her wishes." I looked around. "Is everybody comfortable that we're following her decision?"

One by one, the nurses nodded their heads. This is always a key factor, for nurses usually have the closest relationship with their patients, and will have to implement, or at least observe, policies that others decide on. One of the nurses, an Irish Catholic, seemed hesitant: "At first, I felt like we might be taking a ventilator away and causing her death. But after this discussion, I guess . . . this would not be my own decision, but if Mary wants it . . ." She nodded quietly.

Having decided to honor Mary's wishes, our next ethical

responsibility was to make sure she would not suffer. That meant her doctor would have to ensure that she would get morphine and Valium in sufficient doses to make her comfortable and spare her the agonies of gasping for breath.

That evening, the nurses and doctor sat down with Mary and her daughter to explain their ethical and legal obligation to follow Mary's wishes. As the daughter began to cry, Mary stroked her hand to comfort her daughter. When Mary understood that she would be sedated and feel no pain, she became very calm and stopped struggling with her leaky ventilator.

One by one her family members came to say good-bye to her. Each brought flowers—vases and bouquets of flowers. They explained that Mary had always grown flowers at the house, and had loved her garden, so this was how they wanted to say farewell. All the time, Mary was fully aware and knew what was happening, nodding her head, writing short notes, hugging and praying with family members one by one.

The next day, at 1:00 P.M., the daughter, her husband, and Mary's son came to her room. They put a bouquet of flowers in her hands and sat with her as the nurse sedated her. The doctor turned off the ventilator and, fifteen minutes later, Mary died. The family stayed for two hours, reminiscing and saying their good-byes.

Mary DeCarlo personified the irony of modern medicine: that documents like a DNR order and living will are now required to permit what once happened naturally—an unencumbered, peaceful, and relatively natural death. She knew about these tools and had used them to exercise her rights. Ideally, Mary and her daughter would have discussed matters, to help the younger woman comfortably accept her mother's wishes. Indeed, Mary said that she had tried but to no avail. Yet despite that lapse, we did our best to temper technology with humanity, to make sure medical competence did not stand in the way of compassion. It is rarely easy to grant someone the death they ask for—our job is to try.

It had been a long day, and it wasn't over yet. At 4:00 P.M. I sat behind the nurses' station listening to a young PGY-1 present the medical history of a Mr. Patterson: terminal emphysema, a hopeless neurological prognosis, a temperature suggesting infection. To me, the interesting facts at this juncture had less to do with the medical chart than with the family. Apparently, Mr. Patterson's wife and two grown daughters, ages twenty-nine and thirty-two, had tearfully asked Dr. Ferris what their father's chances of recovery were. Perhaps because the young doctor had little experience giving such grim news, perhaps in a misguided attempt to comfort them, he had hedged the harsh truth: "He has less than twenty percent chance of waking up."

Those words in the presentation sent eyebrows arching around the room; veterans of these corridors knew that the estimate was wildly overoptimistic. The extent of Gene Patterson's brain damage meant that there was simply no "him" to bring back. Recovery would be, quite simply, without precedent; this patient had exactly 0 percent chance of recovery, although ever-conservative medical practitioners rarely permit themselves such an absolute statement. This young doctor's well-intentioned euphemism had put them in a bind. For the family had focused their hope and denial on that seductive—and inaccurate—statistic.

Next to speak was one of the senior physicians, a wise man who has been practicing in these halls for three decades. "Tom, I know you were trying to be gentle, but euphemism doesn't do anybody any good here. This patient has no chance to wake up—not twenty percent, not five percent—none. I think we have to make sure the family hears that." PGY-1 Ferris nodded.

It was obvious to all of us that this family was extremely close and loving. Like most people, they were not highly educated or sophisticated in the complexities of modern medicine. Decent people thrown into the stressful and alien world of the hospital, they had taken a passive, hopeful, and compliant attitude, going along with the doctors at every turn. It was as if they had assumed there were rules of the hospital that we knew and they didn't, rules requiring continued treatment.

They were in obvious torment. The younger daughter and her mother were adamant that Mr. Patterson "never wanted to be like this." They recalled a discussion with him months before, when his emphysema had grown worse. When one of them had suggested that a stroke would be the worst thing, her father had shot back: "No, the worst thing would be if they brought you back." He then went on to describe his horror at a life as a "lump," as he called it.

This was the key we needed, for we could use his wishes as a beacon to a humane and responsible resolution. Neither law nor ethics demands that we treat where treatment is futile— where medicine cannot improve the person's condition or prognosis. This is particularly true when treatment prolongs suffering or extends a condition the patient had clearly indicated he would not have wanted.

The law in New York, among the most restrictive in the country along with Missouri, permits "prior explicit statements" of a patient to be used as the basis for discontinuing care. The conversation the family recalled was just that. Since our aggressive care was now only impeding Mr. Patterson's death, I suggested we discuss a DNR order with his wife and family. Our treatment had dragged him halfway back to life; now, a DNR order would give us the legal and ethical strength to stand back and let nature take its inevitable course.

Viewed in this light, the last remaining question of antibiotics answered itself. Did it make sense in the bigger picture of what the team was trying to do—to let him die in dignity and comfort? No drugs could bring him back to a meaningful state, they could only prolong his death. As caregivers, their ethical responsibility was not to prolong a patient's inevitable dying process.

The next step was theirs. Ferris, the attending physician,

and the social worker would talk to the family and explain clearly that not only did Mr. Patterson not have a 20 percent chance for recovery, he really had no chance. They would explain that his very explicit statements to his family meant they did not have to give antibiotics and prolong his death. They would ask his wife to consider a DNR order, and inquire whether he had made any specific statements that might support removing the ventilator, if that was what the family wanted. That way, the family and medical team would know we were doing our best to respect Mr. Patterson's values—as best we knew them.

The nurses and doctors were already drifting back to their stations. Gene Patterson was just one of several hundred cases to be decided on within these walls that day. Three days later, I learned that Gene Patterson had died. He never regained consciousness and the infection finally overwhelmed his weakened lungs. His wife and one daughter were with him when he died. All too often, even in this world-renowned medical center, the better part of compassion is simply the wisdom to know when to quit.

Few of us are doctors or nurses, but many of us will one day be patients; as such, we are likely to become the participants in—or the subjects of—such discussions. Although we all hope for health, Gene Patterson or Mary DeCarlo could be our spouses or parents, John Morton our husband or son, Aaron and Donna our friends. Like them, we could find ourselves confronting an entire hospital full of policies and procedures, and phalanxes of well-meaning but intrusive people, some of whom think they know better for us than we do.

When that day comes, it is essential that we understand what these discussions are, and how they work, if we are to safeguard our rights to decide for ourselves. The changes overtaking medicine, and the myriad new players involved in decisions, make it more important than ever that we protect our own values and those of our loved ones. Whether you are involved as patient, parent, family member, lover, or friend, you can increase the odds that your experience will be respectful, dignified, and appropriate for you. Caring for ourselves or a loved one, we can never be dispassionate, nor should we be. But we must be informed. We should know what the issues and discussions are about, understand when and how they are likely to arise, and know how they will affect us.

Always, at their root, health-care decisions are by and about people, decisions that reverberate deep into our lives to the values we hold most dear. Remember: practitioners like me may be the experts on ethics, and those people in the white coats may be the experts on medicine. But you are always the expert on your values, and good medical care demands all three.

Also note that on December 1, 1991, a new federal law, the Patient Self-Determination Act, went into effect. It requires all hospitals, nursing homes, and health maintenance organizations (HMOs), to inquire on admission whether or not a patient has a living will or a proxy and if so to note its provisions in the patient's chart. They must also inform new admissions about the applicable law in each state regarding advance directives. Finally, they must offer the patient the opportunity to sign either a living will or a proxy if he has not yet and chooses to do so.

By knowing the issues we are likely to face, thinking about questions ahead of time, taking steps to educate ourselves and our families, and, most of all, by discussing our preferences and documenting our wishes—by doing that, then none of us need ever depend on the uncertain kindness of strangers.

2

PHANTOMS
AT
THE BEDSIDE

Slightly over a century ago, the English artist Luke Fildes painted a tableau called *The Country Doctor*. In the bed lies a young patient; behind him, half in shadow, his concerned parents keep vigil at the bedside. On the left sits the physician, the only non–family member in the tableau. In those days, the sickroom was a simpler place. For the great majority of people, illness and death transpired in private and familiar places, usually at home. Those in attendance knew the patient intimately and shared his history and values.

Although he stood in the background, the physician was in one sense the most powerful person in the picture. Despite his lack of effective medical treatments, he decided, almost alone, the medical path the patient would take. Patient and family both received instructions rather than participating in the process of making decisions. Only in the last thirty years has the movement for patients' rights, based on medical consumerism, legal rights, and medical ethics, truly placed the patient at the center of the tableau.

Today, we paint our modern medical scenes on flickering

canvases of video and film, and the basic setting has changed dramatically. Heart monitors now beep at the bedside, IV tubes and bottles hang where linen drapes once did, and the cast of characters has grown to include eminent medical specialists and a small army of highly trained nurses. And, in the Hollywood version, it is still the closest circles of patient, family, and intimates who ask the questions, call the shots, and run the show.

In real life, however, there are many more characters with whom to contend. Today, more than ever before, new strangers have inserted themselves into the process of making our medical decisions. Were Fildes's painting *The Country Doctor* in the modern medical center, he might well include a host of figures, floating just beyond sight, their presence felt rather than seen. They are the phantoms at our bedsides, and in modern medicine they shape what happens to us when we are sick to a far greater degree than you probably know. I know, because I am one.

These phantoms assume many different guises. Some, like a bioethicist or an ethics committee, are assumed to act as independent guardian angels, safeguarding your rights so you are presented with options to choose the most appropriate care. Other phantoms bring agendas that may or may not coincide with yours: the risk managers, paid to protect the hospital from lawsuits; the DRG (diagnosis related groups) system that determines what the hospital is paid to take care of you; the Utilization Review team, making sure that the hospital's limited resources are used where they will do the most good; and the discharge planner (usually a social worker), who helps plan your move from the hospital. Still other phantoms don't belong to the medical system at all, but to the legal system. The municipal judge hearing a case about a patient may truly be a just person, concerned to craft an equitable decision; he may also be a politician, worried about reelection. The most dangerous phantoms have nothing to do with either law or medicine, and may be frankly hostile to your interests. The local journalist on the trail of a hot story or, worse, the religious activist or ideologue ("Roving Stranger") who views you as a pawn to further a particular political agenda—all can change your care, even your life.

Whether they act with your interests in mind or not, all phantoms have two things in common. First, they are strangers, interlopers in the personal domain of illness, pain, preference, and death. They always have the option of leaving your life and walking out the door when the clock strikes five o'clock. They may be immensely compassionate, caring, and heartfelt, but their interest in you is professional. Second, phantoms seek to affect what happens to you, whether you know they are there or not, whether you want them there or not. That such players come uninvited is certain; you would probably not invite strangers to attend your most difficult moments, much less cede them a pivotal role. Yet they have taken to themselves that role, and today wield increasing power, often behind the scenes. Sometimes phantoms are involved in your care without your even knowing they are there. Others come wearing the ubiquitous white coat, looking indistinguishable from the stream of doctors that poke, prod, and question you from dawn till midnight in the average teaching hospital. (I find such subterfuge completely unacceptable; neither I nor my team ever wear white coats, and I make it a point to introduce myself as a lawyer and clinical ethicist—after all, you have the right to know who is visiting you.) But whether they are visible or not, these phantoms are soldiers in a struggle being waged in hospitals and doctors' offices across the country. Ultimately, the balance of power among them will determine who can decide about such personal matters as your health, freedom, life, and death.

With so many powerful, confusing, and contradictory new players in health care, each year makes it more likely that you or those you love could become enmeshed in an administrative-regulatory-legal web of their devising. What happens then may have more to do with their values and purposes than with your own. At stake is nothing less than your right—or the right of your family on your behalf—to make your most human decisions in your most vulnerable moments. All of us owe it to ourselves and to those we love to understand who these new players are and what they do.

The First Phantom: Me

Let me start with the phantom I know best: myself. As a bioethicist, I represent one of the newest players on the medical scene, one who is profoundly reshaping the decisions you will have to make in the hospital and your doctor's office. Even more important, we are changing the decisions being made by you, around you, and about you when you fall ill.

My discipline of clinical bioethics evolved gradually from the halls of academia. In the beginning, theologians, lawyers, and philosophers working on moral and legal problems in medicine were careful to separate their scholarly commentary from the real world of taking care of patients. Then, in the late 1970s, a few academics began to serve in hospitals, on newly formed ethics committees. Increasingly, in the 1980s, major teaching hospitals saw the need to create room for the formal ethics consultant. Given the tricky ethical questions posed by new technologies, the increased public participation in and scrutiny of medical decisions, and the enormous explosion of medical, ethical, and legal literature on ethics, they saw that these questions were too important to be left to the occasional administrator or well-intentioned physician. Someone had to take responsibility for digesting these new ideas and making them a regular part of patient care, so teaching hospitals began to budget time for discussions of the ethics of care.

But all of this was just beginning in 1978, when I formed the Law and Ethics Consultation Service at Montefiore. My task was not only to create a think tank for academics, but to integrate new modes of thinking into patient care. If I were to make a difference in the rough-and-tumble world of this big-

city teaching hospital, I felt that I needed to be a bedside clini-
cian as well as a teacher. So Montefiore became one of the
nation's first teaching hospitals to marry the adjective *clinical* to
the noun *ethicist*. This new function was designed to be available
at the call of physicians, nurses, social workers, or medical
students, to help sort through and analyze particularly difficult
cases as they were developing.

Most people who do this sort of work are paid by university departments or special academic bioethics centers. It is less
common, although a growing trend, for us to be paid directly
by a hospital. Whether we are paid by hospitals or medical
centers, our job is to be "nettlesome." Given who writes our
paychecks, patients might wonder if there is not the ever-
present danger that we would become co-opted by our employ-
ers; there is. Ethicists all recognize this and try to stand vigilant.
We know that independence and advocacy are the guiding standards for our actions. We must always stand ready to challenge,
confront, and criticize in pursuit of clear thinking and in support of patients' rights. Although our paychecks come from our
hospitals, we try never to forget that our primary constituents
are the people in the beds.

Clinical ethicists, now more common, work alongside the
doctors and nurses in the intensive care units and the medical
floors. Nonetheless, we are not immune from the sorts of institutional pressures that affect other employees of the hospital.
The chairperson of a powerful hospital department once told
me that she didn't care about the law—she was not willing to
discuss decision-making issues with patients. In such circumstances, I have to weigh an aggressive and public reaction
against my general effectiveness as a teacher and social reformer.
When you work in an institution, you pick some fights and
avoid others. If you alienate powerful figures, they will work to
exclude these concerns and analyses from the curriculum, to the
detriment of the patients. The goal of empowering patients and
families proceeds slowly. So are bioethicists always fierce ad-

vocates? Certainly not. Are they always objective? Probably not. Do they contest violations of ethical norms? Yes and no. Have they made a difference in the institutions in which they work? Yes.

Through give-and-take with caregivers and careful analysis, we clarify the underlying values, assumptions, and trade-offs of each particular case. We use a step-by-step calculus to sort out the facts, options, and principles raised by each case. We are concerned to determine the "right" solution—or the range of "right" solutions—to the questions of a particular medical case. Often, this is a woefully difficult and complicated matter, because there are elements of the right answer—what ancient philosophers termed "the good"—in various possible paths. This is what creates the bioethical dilemmas we read about in the morning papers, situations where two possibly worthy goals are mutually incompatible, and where the "right" solution depends on which legal and moral principles you hold most dear.

When I visit the hospital floor, I am armed with the basic bioethicist's toolkit of philosophical and legal principles:

◆ The principle of "beneficence"—that the goal of medicine is to promote the well-being of the patient.

◆ The principle of "proportionality"—that if a patient may either be harmed or helped by a treatment then the treatment should only be offered if the benefit outweighs the burden.

◆ The principle of "respect for persons"—that patients should be treated as autonomous beings and those patients who cannot make choices for themselves should be protected by others.

◆ The principle of "justice"—that all persons who are equal should be treated equally.

◆ The legal principle of "self-determination"—that adults capable of making decisions have the right to consent to or refuse care, even if the result of that refusal is death.

◆ The legal principle of "best interest"—that those who cannot decide have the right to have decisions made that maximize their welfare.

Like the doctors we work with, we never know in advance just what issues will arise with the patient in the next bed. Practicing physicians must be able to diagnose and treat any one of hundreds of diseases, syndromes, or injuries in their subspecialty. They must keep a reference library of symptoms, diagnoses, and treatments in mind for instant retrieval. Similarly, ethicists must have a ready working familiarity with a broad storehouse of ethical and legal principles, rules, analyses, cases, and examples. We must know the thinkers and arguments in the fields of moral philosophy, bioethics, and religion. We must have read legal cases and commentaries—local, state, and national—on topics ranging from statutory definitions of insanity to nursing home regulations to newborn rights. We must know the ethical consensus that national panels of medical experts, jurists, and philosophers have developed on scores of major issues, from neonatal care to confidentiality about HIV infection in a sexually active gay man.

My colleagues and I, however, bring more than just factual knowledge and analytic skill to our discussions with the care teams. We sometimes bring welcome neutrality and freedom from internecine turf battles. We can be the only participants in a discussion with no predetermined stake in a particular outcome. We have not cared for this tragically imperiled infant for five months, we have no frustrating history with a demanding or dishonest patient, we are not mired in the egos, politics, or economics of the departments of medicine, surgery, or pediatrics. But we are committed to ideas of the "good" and to modes of analysis. In that sense we are, too, the products of our training and discipline. Our biases are different, but not absent, and we all have an overriding theme—the protection of patients' rights.

The clinical bioethicist, at least in my model, does not make decisions, but rather helps doctors, nurses, social workers, medical students, and the house staff understand the facts, identify the core principles, and apply larger principles to the very specific people they are treating. Sometimes this leads to a clear and unambiguous care plan on which all can agree. Unfortunately, as I tell my students, "principles are clear and patients are messy," so discussion often leads to a series of options, none of which seems perfect to the staff. It then falls to the doctors and nurses to discuss the options with the patient and family—although we will help them do that if they ask us to.

In the controlled chaos that is the hospital, our cases seem to find us rather than the other way around. If somebody on the care team has a significant concern about a patient, we can expect to be called at the office, buttonholed in the hospital lobby, or waylaid on the elevators or in the halls. It may be a physician's assistant or a PGY-1 unclear of her ethical or legal responsibility, a nurse or social worker worried that she isn't doing the right thing for a patient, or a call from an attending physician with a case that raises challenging or troubling issues.

In addition to consulting on specific cases, we are also teachers. In that, clinical ethicists follow a long tradition of roaming moral instructors. Like Aristotelian moral philosophers, who taught in the Lyceum of ancient Athens in the fourth century B.C., we move from bedside to nursing station to intensive care unit, meeting with caregivers and administrators and, when asked, with patients and families themselves. Like the Casuist philosophers of the seventeenth century, we build our intellectual ramparts from the mortar of real-world particulars, always working to tease out the abiding principles of right and wrong from the specifics of each individual case. One might even trace our intellectual roots back to Socrates himself, for we take our most valuable tool from the method that bears his name: the well-honed question. Indeed, were the father of Western philosophy himself reincarnated in the Bronx in 1992, he might well find himself posing moral questions to doctors and nurses in our ICU.

The best way we can help tomorrow's caregivers understand the rights of patients and the ethics of care is to give them the chance to think their way through the issues they meet in real practice, where the questions arise—on the floors and in the units. So my philosopher-colleague John Arras and I regularly lead scheduled ethics teaching rounds on a dozen different services within the hospital: the children's critical care unit, the adolescent AIDS team, the newborn intensive care unit, geriatric and coronary care units among them.

Our classrooms are the floors, the medical units, and the bedsides. There, in monthly rounds, doctors, nurses, and support staff gather to present a case from their unit for ethical analysis and observations. These rounds have become part of the regular teaching program for the medical students and house staff. Every year, about half of the eight hundred medical students and house staff who come through Montefiore attend some of these rounds. There they learn the specific terms and ways of thinking to help them consciously, systematically apply theories of rights and moral values in their chosen profession of doctoring.

Our ground rules are simple: we ask that each case be discussed in plain English, as if they were speaking to a patient's family. A decade and a half of such discussions have taught me that it helps to shed the efficient clinical jargon in which caregivers routinely cloak medicine's more appalling details. We want everybody—from the distinguished attending physicians to the youngest medical student on her first rotation—to let down her guard and ask for help in thinking through the ethical and human implications of what to do. All can participate; all opinions are respected; there is no such thing as a dumb question. These discussions permit people the rare luxury of acknowledging feelings in a profession that generally requires its practitioners to check their emotions at the door. Because discussions of ethics are really about values, we welcome worries and fears, anger and opinions, for the real role these play in the human side of this most human calling.

Sometimes, our teaching demonstrates that even knowledgeable and experienced professionals can disagree about the most compelling argument or the best solution. Our colleagues take particular pleasure when John Arras and I disagree—which happens often. We are like an old vaudeville comedy team: "Nancy, you miserable creature . . . John, you useless rogue . . . How can you possibly argue that this poor confused patient is telling us what he really wants? How could you possibly deny that this statement is consistent with all he has ever stood for and should therefore be honored?" Over the years we have come close to submitting some of our intellectual disputes to binding arbitration, except neither of us would accept the resolution of a stranger.

Sometimes, our discussions simply help the care team find consensus and comfort in a decision they knew was inevitable. In the words of Rachel Fall, a veteran nurse in the pediatric ICU: "It's easier to watch a baby die when you know you've done all you could, and when you can all let your hair down and admit how much it hurts."

These sessions give staff and students an opportunity they get in few other places. In the crushing day-and-night rotations that make up the frantic rhythm of the modern American teaching hospital, it is often impossible to take time out for reflection. If we expect medical practitioners to take ethical issues seriously—and Montefiore does—then we must teach these principles, just as we teach surgical procedures or medical diagnosis. Our goal is to give medical students and new doctors the tools to integrate the principles and reasoning of bioethics into their regular practice, so that the doctors and nurses of tomorrow will carry these concerns with them as they minister to all of us. After all, I am training the generation of doctors who will take care of my kids, and theirs.

Watching Out for Your Interests:
Ethics Committees

The next phantom is also concerned with ethics, and goes by the august title of the ethics committee. It, too, is a relative newcomer on the hospital scene, having been born only in the last decade and a half. It works to sort out the thorny issues that get raised each day by our newest medical advances.

These committees have become medicine's newest boom industry. In 1983, a survey by the President's Commission for the Study of Ethical Problems in Medicine and Biomedical and Behavioral Research counted thirty-seven such committees nationwide; today that number has grown nearly a hundredfold, to more than thirty-five hundred such committees across the nation. Currently, bioethics committees exist in hospitals large and small, in teaching and research, community, private, and religious institutions. They have spawned their own symposia and networks, published their own journals and convened conferences, and provided a focus for the concerns of caregivers about the terrible dilemmas that they face daily.

These committees play at least three different roles, and can vary enormously from one institution to the next. Sometimes, they are mainly teaching bodies, working to educate hospital staffs about ethical issues. If these committees analyze cases, they do so in retrospect, as teaching aids. Other ethics committees work primarily to develop hospital policy on ethical issues like treatment of newborns or terminating care. In both of these roles, of course, they can affect your care, but they do so indirectly.

However, it is in their third role that this phantom can affect you far more immediately. In many hospitals, ethics committees serve as invisible consultants on actual patients. Challenging cases are taken before the committee for discussion and consultation. While your doctor has the ultimate responsibility for a care plan, an ethics committee's conclusion can have a tremendous impact on the directions things take, and the options you are offered.

Behind their impressive label, ethics committees vary enormously in power, scope, expertise, wisdom, and competence. At their best, these committees bring together people who are thoughtful, trained, and knowledgeable in such decisions. They include doctors, nurses, social workers, attorneys, ethicists, administrators; even, sometimes, local community representatives. At their best, these committees provide an interdisciplinary forum to present information and views about a case and air many different perspectives. They create an open, nonlegal, deliberative process where people can and must argue their positions and be challenged. The committee forces them to think through the facts of the case, articulate principles, and defend their position in front of their peers. In this setting, a physician, attorney, or administrator cannot, by simple virtue of rank, personality, vocabulary, or expertise, dominate or manipulate the discussion.

But this phantom is only as good as its members. With little standardization and no regulation, ethics committees may—and often do—contain people with scant real knowledge about the issues. They may be composed of whoever most wants to attend, people sometimes unencumbered by knowledge of the relevant medical, legal, and philosophical issues and facts. At worst, such forums can amount to little more than a bunch of well-intentioned folks getting together and trading hunches about what's "right." They may engage in a sort of intuitive, untrained, seat-of-the-pants thinking, with little attempt at systematic analysis of issues. They may be dominated by strong personalities who seek to impose their will on the group.

Worse, in some places they are stacked with institutional players—lawyers, administrators—whose agenda is to shape the committee's decisions to safeguard the institution, rather than to find the most ethical solution to safeguard patients' and families' interests. When hospital attorneys, for example, sit on an ethics committee, they should not be there to play their usual roles. After all, the committee exists to forge consensus on the ethical principles in a particular case and to find possible solutions that fit those principles. The best ethics committees function freely, their deliberations uncontaminated by hospital interests. Later the hospital may choose to accept or reject its views for its own reasons—but those views should be allowed to develop independently.

An ethics committee is a classic phantom, because in most places it operates behind a veil of institutional silence. It is standard practice for its consultation in a case to occur without either the family or the patient knowing it. Most patients never meet, or even see, the members of the ethics committee whose opinion may carry so much weight in shaping what could happen to them. Just because you are not told that your case is being brought up before such a committee doesn't mean it hasn't been.

When discussions about you, your family, and your case occur without your knowing about them, substantial decisions can be affected in that secretive forum. Usually, decisions reached by that body can take on their own momentum. Once a half dozen hospital players have fixed their collective view of what is best, it becomes harder for you as patient or family to change it.

Sometimes, however, you can use this phantom as an ally. When, as patient or family, you find yourself facing a tough situation, you may benefit by asking that it be brought to an ethics committee. That may accomplish several things. First, a committee can offer you one way to clarify your own position and thinking, and understand the often complex available options surrounding medical decisions. Second, if you find yourself frustrated in your attempts to interact with caregivers, or if you have found them inaccessible or elusive, this is a tool to encourage caregivers to engage with you, to explain their views and clarify their suggestions.

To make use of this decision-making tool you must first ask if a bioethics committee exists at your hospital. If you are dealing with any major urban hospital, regional center, or teaching-and-research hospital, the answer will probably be yes. Even most medium-size community hospitals are likely to have such a deliberative body. Some places, particularly academic medical centers, have several. At Montefiore and its associated hospitals, for example, I sit on four such committees.

Major teaching hospitals often have a separate pediatric or neonatal ethics committee. We have one Infant Bioethics Review Committee covering all four of our affiliated institutions and another separate Pediatric Ethics Committee to consult on particularly difficult cases. At the other end of life, more and more nursing homes are adding ethics committees, but it's unlikely you will encounter one of these. When they do exist in that setting, these committees are far more likely to be controlled by institutional interests, reflecting the hierarchical way these places work.

If the ethics committee is to truly play fair, families and their patients must know that they exist (as they should know about me). If an ethics committee is called to consult on a case involving you or your family, where its decision could affect the outcome, you have every right to be involved. You are well within your rights to ask if the committee is discussing your case and ask to have a chance to address it or to meet with caregivers to give your perspective of events. If the meeting has already happened, you have the right to be told what the recommendation of the ethics committee was and why.

Among the questions you should feel free to pose are:

- Does this institution have an active ethics committee?
- Who sits on the committee? Who is the chairperson?
- When does the committee meet?
- Will its members be discussing my case, and if so, when?
- Is there a way I can request that it consider my case?
- Can I be present for that discussion?

- If not, how can I be certain my views will be presented to the committee?
- What happens if my case comes before it?
- What is its role in my case?
- What does its recommendation mean to me?

Your doctor will almost certainly know about these committees; complex issues cannot be discussed at a committee without your own physician being there. If your doctor doesn't know or is unavailable, you can pose these questions to a patient representative, nursing supervisor, or the administrator on call.

They may well be startled at your questions, because care providers and ethics committees are not in the habit of disclosing their activities. At Montefiore, the Neonatal Ethics Committee on which I sit makes it a practice to alert the family when we are discussing their child's case—but that seems the exception. Accordingly, you can expect a wide range of reactions, much as you would whenever you exert your right to be an informed patient. Even raising the issue of an ethics committee will establish you as a sophisticated and savvy medical consumer, which in turn can affect how you are treated. Remember: the clinical ethicist and ethics committee are phantoms that may also, and ideally should, be friends—but only if you know they are available to you.

Risk Managers: The Phantom of Institutional Fear

Now we come to the phantoms whose roles are somewhat more ambiguous and problematic. Their recommendations, decisions, and actions may reflect what you would want to have happen, or may not. But the thing that distinguishes these phantoms is that they are serving a master different from your personal interests.

The first such phantom is called the office of risk management and its task is straightforward: to keep the hospital out of court and free of potential liability that could bankrupt it. In the long run, that is a good thing for everybody: bankrupt hospitals cannot stay in the business of providing essential care. But the risk to the hospital is not only economic. Even a lawsuit that does not succeed in a court of law costs the hospital dearly in the court of public opinion and damaged community relations, in the ill will and bad feelings it generates, in anxiety and distress for employees and potential patients, and in time lost from the business of caring for the sick. That is why risk management works very hard to make sure the hospital avoids all lawsuits—those that they could win as well as those that they could not.

Risk managers have the institution's interest at heart. This does not mean that their efforts don't help individual patients; they may do so, for example, by insisting that discussions about your case be held openly, according to certain protocols. But their discussions center not around your health and well-being, but rather around potential legal actions by you or your care partners. They figure, plan, and advise all the hospital's branches on how to lower that risk, generally and in your specific case. And their advice carries a lot of clout.

Risk managers were created in the 1980s as a way to improve care. In those years, as costs were rising, hospitals started to turn a critical eye on their own efforts. They combed past patient records to unearth patterns of error so they could improve care. If, over three years, two dozen septuagenarians broke their hips rolling out of bed, the hospital would note it and install bedrails. (In Great Britain, they solved this particular problem more sensibly—they lowered the beds.) If a surgeon had been successfully sued ten times they would scrutinize that doctor's performance closely. Stopping preventable and unnecessary medical mishaps at their source meant better care. It also meant fewer lawsuits and, ultimately, lower costs for hospitals, insurers, and medical consumers alike. Who could argue with that reasonable goal? So hospitals across the country began studying the patterns of what they termed "negative incidents" within their walls, to learn from their past errors to make a safer future.

But as hundreds of hospitals rushed to establish risk management departments, other changes in the medical system were to overtake them. In the late 1950s courts and legislatures began to focus on how medical care decisions should be made. Courts in every state started to require physicians to provide patients not just with good care, but with the information necessary for patients to make informed, voluntary, and personally appropriate decisions. This new idea—termed "informed consent"—meant that many long-standing medical traditions such as the assumption that doctor knows best, the tendency to treat now and tell later, the paternal approach to patients, had to change.

As they did, so did the risk manager's job. For if patients were to be informed, educated, instructed, and included, the hospital could be held responsible for neglecting any of that. Doctors and hospitals could now be held liable for failures in decision making and communication, as well as for the usual medical reasons, and with lawsuits on the upswing, risk managers could no longer simply catalogue mistakes after the fact. Decisions were like those extra bedrails: it made sense to stop the damage before it happened, at their source, on the floors where decisions were made. So risk managers would have to monitor not just incisions, but decisions; not merely what was performed, but who was informed. And where once they looked at what *had* happened, they were now concerned with what *should* happen. So during the 1980s, new faces began attending case discussions on hospital floors from Burlington to Burbank.

That represented a major change. Now, for the first time, bedside discussions about real people included risk managers—players motivated by institutional concerns and loyalties. Suddenly, it seemed, they had a voice in all sorts of questions: Should Mrs. Lopez be offered natural childbirth or be steered to have a C-section? What if she refuses? Can we operate against her will? Should fifteen-year-old Irene be given birth control? Did her parents need to consent? Should they remove ninety-two-year-old Mr. Willis, permanently comatose, from his respirator? Would they make the same decision if no family were around to sue?

Risk managers bring noticeable improvements: they are definitely a force for better care; they often design streamlined procedures for informing patients; they require better documentation of the patient's care; and they sometimes help all of the various parts of the team to communicate more effectively. Yet, what began as an effort to improve care added a new player to the health-care drama, a stranger's voice shaping decisions about the people in the beds.

Today, in offices of risk management, all of us are at risk of losing the rights we have fought for in the courts over the last decades. In some hospitals, for example, mainly public hospitals serving the poor and people of color, risk managers routinely allow, indeed urge, obstetricians to perform cesarean section deliveries—invasive surgery posing real risks and requiring anesthetic—over a woman's clear refusal and without a court order. They do this to protect the baby when obstetricians fear a risk from a natural delivery. Doctors are instructed to create a paper trail demonstrating medical need and then perform the operation even over active refusal.

From a risk management perspective, that may be viewed as an "appropriate" solution. Juries, they know, don't like to punish hospitals for saving lives, so the hospital runs greater risk by having to explain why it didn't do a C-section than it does by forcing surgery on an unwilling, but alive, woman—especially if the baby has birth defects. And there is the real possibility, in some cases, that a C-section might have avoided the birth defect. A handicapped baby is a fearsome thing to the risk manager, both because it is emotional dynamite and because courts set damages by lost potential earnings. A baby's lifetime of lost earnings will cost the hospital a pile of money. If there is a poor outcome, it seems safer to have tried one's best to save the baby than to respect the mother's wishes. Even if the infant's handicap is unaffected by the delivery, risk managers know that juries are more sympathetic to a hospital that "did everything"—even if it means riding roughshod over the rights of women. Better a resentful adult, they calculate, than an imperiled baby.

Were the patient an eighty-eight-year-old woman on a ventilator, the risk manager might apply the reverse formula. Our courts value seniors' lives less highly, due to their low future earning power, so fewer lawsuits are brought on their behalf. But pain and suffering is, in the lingo of the profession, a "big-ticket item." Balanced against that, the odds of a lawsuit shrink when there are no close relatives apt to hire lawyers. But even for the patient without family, there is always the possibility of the disaffected employee or Roving Stranger happening onto the scene to challenge care. Back and forth goes the calculus of the risk managers, doing precisely what they are paid to do, being consummately, vigilantly, risk averse.

In human terms, unfortunately, their imperative to protect the institution can conflict with your wishes—your fear of surgery or desire for natural childbirth, your freedom to die without being attached to a respirator. What happens then depends on who they are, who you are, and how you protect yourself.

Risk managers, like salespeople and United States presidents, possess widely varying intelligence, knowledge, beliefs, and integrity. The best of them—in which I count my colleagues—try to help patients and families reach the decisions that patients think best. They believe that informed patients, open consensus, and clear cooperation are the institution's best insurance against lawsuit. When an informed, capable patient makes a decision, they try to honor it.

But not all risk managers are so enlightened. Some are comfortable ignoring patient or family wishes to better cover the institutional backside. They may also have a wide range of training. At many hospitals, mine included, they are mainly former nurses. Occasionally, risk managers are lawyers, or non-lawyers who consult with lawyers on a regular basis. Some of them take seriously their role as conveyors of the law, and feel a duty to uphold patients' rights. Others may tend to see a potential plaintiff in every bed and treat him like a legal adversary. Attorneys, whose milieu is conflict, often harbor inflated fears about what the local district attorney might do, how the local newspaper will write up the incident, or how the family members might change their minds and sue.

But no matter a risk manager's training or competence, they all share one thing: a lot of power. They possess the wherewithal to shape decisions and, increasingly, to alter significantly what happens to you or a family member in their institution.

This phantom is here to stay. More than four thousand of our nation's hospitals have departments devoted to risk management. They exist in every major teaching hospital, more and more in community hospitals, and new ones are sprouting every year. Risk managers read their own journals, convene national conferences, and have their own association (with its unlikely acronym, ASHRM), the American Society For Healthcare Risk Management. For medical consumers, that means that any time you are involved in hospitals over the next decade, whether as patient or family, it is possible that a phantom risk manager may shape decisions about your care—decisions that touch on your deepest values, perhaps on your life itself.

If you land in the hospital, the large likelihood is that you will never trigger a risk management review. But if risk managers do get called into your case, there are some things to keep in mind. First, you are most likely to get involved with risk managers if you or your family attempt to refuse a treatment or procedure. Refusals rend the fabric of consensus that surrounds medicine. Your decision may come from religious conviction, like the Jehovah's Witness whose faith prevents him from accepting blood transfusions, or from personal fears or values like not wanting to die attached to a machine, or even from delusional psychosis if you hear inner voices telling you not to go under the knife. But your refusal jams the gears of the medical machine, calling into question the basis of what the whole system exists to do: provide care. In some cases, saying no can be the first step toward someone deciding they know better than you do.

Patients and families may not know when risk management has been called in. If you have any doubt, and particularly if you or your loved ones are refusing care, it is perfectly appropriate to ask the person at your bedside if the office of risk management is involved in your case. You will, I guarantee you, be the first patient they have ever had ask.

Here are three questions you may want to ask:

- Does this hospital have an office of risk management?
- If so, have they been consulted in my case?
- Is part of your recommendation about my care in any way based on risk management recommendations?

Affirmative answers don't mean anything ominous, they merely open a dialogue about what phantoms are involved in decisions about you. They also mark you as someone informed and vigilant about your own rights to make decisions. You are entitled—indeed, you owe it to yourself—to know if this particular phantom is at your bedside.

Quicker and Sicker: DRG's and Bedside Bureaucrats

Our next phantom comes direct to you from Washington, D.C. It involves the long arm of Uncle Sam, reaching right into your sickroom, affecting your care from the moment you enter the hospital.

Uncle Sam cares what happens when you get sick because

for many of us, he picks up at least part of our bills. If you are over age sixty-five—as are many of the patients in our hospitals—your bills are generally paid by Medicare. If you are one American in seven—about thirty-seven million in all—with no health insurance, and you are poor, your medical bills might be split between Uncle Sam and your own state under Medicaid. Veterans often receive care directly from the government through Veterans Administration hospitals. One way or another, Uncle Sam is knee-deep in the business of health care. In 1990 the nation's spending on health reached 666.2 billion, of which the government funded 42.2 percent.

Federal and state governments, and all of us who pay taxes, have a very legitimate interest in containing the cost of medical care, and making sure that our money is spent wisely and carefully. Given the gargantuan rise in health-care costs, the federal government is justly concerned. Accordingly, Washington has some very firm ideas about what should happen to us when we are sick: how long we can stay in the hospital, what treatments we can receive, when we can leave the hospital, even where we go next. Those ideas get imposed through something called a DRG—the "diagnosis related group."

DRG's begin, like many phantoms, with money. Each year, we spend a larger chunk of the federal budget on health care. The U.S. Department of Health and Human Services reported that health spending in 1990 increased 10.5 percent, more than twice as fast as the GNP. We've all seen it. A day's stay in Montefiore, which cost $389 in 1970, cost $1,038 twenty years later—an increase of 267 percent. By 1990, those costs added up to a total health-care bill of the previously noted $666 billion, or $2,664 for every man, woman, and child in America. Put another way, in 1990 our nation spent almost twelve cents of every dollar of our total GNP on health care, approximately 10 percent more than the previous year—which, in turn, had increased 11 percent from the year before that. (Most galling of all, approximately 20–24 percent went to administration—at a time when tens of millions of Americans went without care altogether. Canada, by comparison, spends between 8 and 11 percent of its health-care dollar on paperwork.)

A prime cause of this escalation can be found in how we have traditionally paid for doctors and hospital care: the more they did, the more they earned. In the past, every hospital, clinic, and physician in the nation charged by the test, procedure, or exam; more of those tests, procedures, and exams meant more money for somebody. Some procedures might be needless or, worse, dangerous, but all were profitable. Because patients, by and large, weren't paying themselves, they had no incentive to cut costs. Physicians and institutions weren't complaining, for they made money while protecting themselves against possible malpractice claims of having missed a diagnosis or treatment. Taken together, the system of "profit-motive medicine" was structured to give every incentive to provide more care.

By the late 1970s, things were starting to break down. Insurers, institutions, and the government were getting worried about who would foot astronomical health bills. Clearly, something had to be done to bring spending under control. Partially in response, Congress created the Health Care Financing Administration, charging it to find ways to cut medical costs.

For several years, flocks of earnest cost counters sorted, chewed up, and spat out millions of health statistics. They looked at hospitals and how long people stayed in them. In the end, bureaucrats came up with the idea that the best way to save money was to provide precisely the amount of care you needed—no less, and certainly no more. They looked specifically at one of the biggest-ticket items, days spent in a hospital. If those could be reduced, costs would dwindle. Thus was born the DRG, three small letters that would bring seismic changes to the landscape of American health care.

Diagnosis related groups were invented as a statistical tool—a diagnostic categorization—a way to gather information and classify information for health economists. They simply assigned a given length of hospital days to a given medical condition. They told us that people with a total mastectomy for breast malignancy will, on average, require a mean time of 5 days in the hospital. If you have chest pain, your mean stay time will be 2.8 days; gallstones, 3.4 days; an appendectomy, 4.2 days; and so on through every ill that can befall the human body. These are, of course, mean values, statistical artifacts. Some people with good healing powers and no complications go home sooner; others, especially the old and infirm, tend to convalesce more slowly. In health economics, such numeric means made sense. DRG's, after all, were simply a convenient analytic fiction, a way to analyze health-care expenditures. They were never intended to describe real people in the real world any more than any American family really has 2.3 children. Unfortunately, as concern grew over mounting Medicare bills, that fact got obscured.

In 1983, government cost counters decided that this abstract statistical creation could be used to assign pathology a price tag. Knowing the mean length of hospital stay for most problems, they could now establish how much federal money should go to the hospital for each case. DRG's permitted a lump-sum payment, based on diagnosis, for most of the ills that can befall us. Under DRG's, the hospital gets paid for a specified number of days, no more and no less. So if your aged mother's hip fracture mends well and she leaves before her allotted 8.2 days, the hospital keeps the extra money from Medicare. But if she takes longer to heal than this allotted time, the hospital gets stuck with the bill. Either way, the Feds are off the hook.

The DRG system has, to be sure, accomplished much good. It has made us pay attention to people staying in hospital beds too long. Yet its paint-by-numbers approach to illness also has some serious flaws. For one, although broad age categories are often used in DRG's, they are not adequately weighted for

all important age distinctions. How we recover at age eighty-
five from hip surgery is very different from how we would have
recovered twenty years earlier. Yet patients in both categories
"earn" the same rate. For another, DRG classifications may not
fully take into account the nuances of disease and injury that
affect recovery. Due to preexisting complications, two people's
medical conditions may differ greatly, yet they can earn identical DRG's on paper. Another key problem with DRG's is that
they do not weight the socioeconomic states of the patient or
any patient's unique physiology and medical history. If a patient
is poor, has had inadequate health care, and insufficient nutri-
tious food, the patient will be less healthy on admission, will
respond less quickly to care, and will be more difficult to discharge to a safe environment.

Lastly, your DRG is based on the diagnosis that on discharge was responsible for admission. So if you come in for a
hernia operation, have a heart attack during the repair surgery,
then get an infection that takes six weeks to clear, the hospital's
payment is based on the 5.1-day stay for the hernia. It seems fair
to say that DRG's have become just what one might expect
when we allowed statisticians in the sickroom: the bluntest of
instruments, one that fails to take into account the realities of
how people actually get sick and get better.

They have also brought a sea change in how we pay for
medicine. For the first time, hospitals are paid, not for what
they *have* done, but for what they *will* do—a system called
"prospective payment." Today, that fundamental shift has
brought a host of new and unseen pressures on patients, pressures that affect you quite directly. Through DRG's, federal and
state regulation increasingly limits our medical options. What
began as an index of length of stay is now exerting its effect on
what care you have available to you. DRG's can affect how care
is provided, what information you are given, which options are
presented to you, what choices you are told that you have a
right to make.

Nowhere is this clearer than in surgery. DRG's have been the engine driving the move toward outpatient surgery. When I came to Montefiore fifteen years ago, removing a cataract was routinely a three-day hospital event: you came in the day before the operation and healed for two days before going home. But when Medicare stopped reimbursing the hospital for those three days, hospitals had to adapt to handling cataracts as a one-day, outpatient procedure. Now patients were told to come in for the procedure, spend a few hours recovering, and go home that same day.

For cataracts, as for scores of other procedures, hospitals now champion the virtues of ambulatory surgery. They have an incentive to get you out ASAP—not just for your own good, but because shorter bed stays mean more money for them. This is decidedly a mixed blessing. Nobody should be in the hospital unnecessarily. Hospitals are disorienting, expensive, impersonal places where you risk dangerous infections and medical mishaps. But for some people, in some cases, this change is not a salubrious one. It means added pressure is being brought to bear to move you out of the hospital—whether you are medically or mentally ready or not.

The DRG system has put a new player at the bedside; a phantom whose interests aren't exactly the same as the patient's enters into the calculus of care. DRG's, born as a statistical shortcut for health analysts, have today expanded from Medicare to Medicaid, and more and more private insurance companies use similar schemes to set your length of stay in advance. All of us do well to keep this in mind when we interact with a hospital or clinic, an insurance company, even with our own family physician. Prospective payment has become a fundamental operating principle in the management of the hospital, a basic fact of economic life—and you'd best know it is at work.

During your discussions with caregivers, you can certainly ask directly:

- Are there any federal or state regulations that color, determine or structure how you have discussed this issue with me?
- How many hospital days are covered by my payment plan?
- What happens then? What if I have to stay longer?

Your best defense is always to ask questions and know your rights. If you are a Medicare patient, you have several explicit rights:

- The right to all hospital care necessary for your proper diagnosis and treatment. Specifically, your discharge date must be determined solely by your medical needs—not DRG or Medicare payments.
- The right to be fully informed about decisions affecting your Medicare coverage and payment, both while you are in the hospital and afterward.
- The right to be given written notice if Medicare is about to stop paying for your care.
- The right to have your discharge reviewed by independent doctors—called PRO's, or peer review organizations—or by a Medicare intermediary. If you still disagree with their finding, you have the right to ask it be reconsidered, and appeal it to an administrative or federal judge. After any or all of those steps, you can still refuse to be discharged, but then expect to pay the bills yourself, starting one day after the PRO review.

Getting Out: Utilization Review, Discharge Planning, and Social Workers

DRG's exist only on paper. They are brought to life by the next phantom: the department of utilization review, or, as it may be termed, "quality assurance." This phantom's job is to keep tabs on the financial course of its patients' illness. These departments, staffed by medically trained people like nurses or doctors, work to answer one question: Is this person in this bed using the hospital's resources appropriately? Given that any hospital has a finite number of intensive care beds or dialysis units, the utilization review department must make sure they are used in the best way. This is not only a proper task but, given our health-care costs, a necessary one. As we struggle with rising health costs, more and more decisions focus on not just what a patient needs, but on the hard facts of how we can stretch our limited resources to do the most good.

The utilization review department examines admissions from the first moment you enter the hospital, deciding if your condition warranted admission in the first place, tracking the number of tests and procedures you get and how long you stay. Its job is to ensure that patients receive what they need, but no more. It has a strong incentive to eliminate costly but unnecessary tests, reduce procedures, and control physicians or departments whose patients routinely overstay their DRG-imposed welcome. Utilization review also keeps constantly vigilant to make sure patients move out as soon as possible, to free hospital resources for the next person. Given the tragic overcrowding in many of our hospitals—especially urban ones—and the fact that there is always somebody waiting for a given bed, this has become a necessary part of American medical practice.

You aren't likely ever to see anybody sporting a badge saying "Department of Utilization Review." This staff works primarily behind the scenes, reviewing your medical chart, checking lab test results, and conferring with the doctors. The job of actually moving patients out of their beds has been handed to an old player in health care: the social worker—in a new role—the discharge planner.

Social workers hardly seem like phantoms; they are, after all, quite visible, and usually very friendly. But their role, and their agenda, is a bit more complex than it might at first seem. Once upon a time these people were the therapists and soft shoulders of medicine: they arranged support services, made sure patient and family were taken care of, listened and talked to everyone about the problems of being sick. But that job has changed drastically in the last few years as costs, and regulations, have escalated. The change has caused tremendous pain to social workers who were trained under the old rules. They remember the times they acted as advocate, therapist, and friend to patients and families. But, more and more in the modern teaching hospital, and increasingly in community hospitals, social workers serve a primary role: helping to set a discharge plan that can get you out on or before your DRG limit. Their name tags may read "social worker," but truth in advertising might require them to be called "discharge planners," which some hospitals do, and which is often how they are known to the hospital staff.

You may be visited by someone wearing the same white coat and beeper as practically every other person you have seen since admission. The social worker may start by asking how you are feeling, and how the hospital is treating you. The discussion will soon come around to your plans for leaving: how you will manage, how much help you have. If you need home care, will there be anyone to provide it? Who might look after you and cook for you—are there family, friends, or neighbors to help?

This is more than just a concerned chat; the discharge planner's job is to identify patients who could overstay their DRG-mandated welcome. Someone who is confused or disabled, living alone, or without family or friends to support him, whose condition precludes returning home immediately—these people are likely to get special attention. In such cases, it is common practice that a social worker appear early in the hospital stay.

Most hospitals are required by law to discharge you to safe and suitable surroundings. A bed-bound or enfeebled patient cannot be sent home to fend for herself without help. That is an important protection for patients, who are often weak and disabled. It falls to the discharge planner to create a safe transition between life in the hospital and life outside. He must make sure you have a safe place to go and an adequate support system when you get there. He knows where to turn to arrange help for nurses and home care. By keeping you safe, he keeps the hospital safe as well.

Whatever the source of the social worker's concern as an educated medical consumer you need to know that the compassionate face at the foot of your bed is both your ally and the agent of your eventual dismissal. He brings several agendas: to get you out quickly (which you probably want as much as he does); to open your bed for the next paying patient; and to live up to the hospital's legal obligations.

Occasionally that creates conflicts. This person must balance the twin imperatives of a speedy and safe discharge. The patient, however, may have different concerns. For you as patient, safety may be only one of many considerations, even a minor one at that. You may be more concerned about your autonomy and independence, and want strongly to be among familiar surroundings. You may fear the strange hospital, fiercely covet your privacy and independence, or want more than anything to get back to put affairs in order at home. Such personal wishes and needs are important to you—but they may be lost in the discharge planner's professional and institutional calculus.

Sometimes, the discharge planner is caught in a tug of wills between competing phantoms. The hospital's DRG mechanism, the utilization review department, and the discharge planner may all be exerting pressures to propel you out the door. Yet they may be in conflict with the professional opinions of the care team who may believe that you are not ready—mentally or physically—to leave. Often, social workers or the care team can foresee personal disaster at home better than the hopeful or disoriented patient can. Commonly, patients or families are inexperienced in managing care at home, unrealistic about their ability to cope, and unaware of the resources available. Conversely, it is my experience that medical professionals and social workers regularly overestimate the care a patient will need once discharged. In other words, doctors act like doctors and patients act like patients.

Other people, like family, may have their own agendas. A family may want the patient at home so they and not an institution can receive the Social Security check—despite the fact that they cannot truly care for the patient's needs adequately. Conversely, they may want the person off their hands and in the safekeeping of a hospital. It is the job of the discharge planner to resolve these conflicting pulls and devise a safe and reasonable plan. It is a job that demands the wisdom of Solomon and the patience of Job.

Already, the bedside seems crowded. But the cast is only half-filled, for the phantoms so far are simply those that the hospital itself has put there. Several of the most powerful phantoms do not inhabit the medical system at all. Indeed, the single most powerful phantom affecting your care wears the august robes of our legal system.

Barristers at the Bedside: The Phantom of the Law

More than ever before, your options when you are sick have become matters of law, involving judges and attorneys, regulated by statute, regulation, and case law. The modern commingling of law and medicine began in the late 1950s when courts began to consider whether patients had the right to consent to, or refuse, care. Having decided that they did, the courts began to develop rules about how that right could be enforced. They decided that patients who had the ability to make decisions about their care could consent or refuse—even if the result of that refusal was death.

Matters changed dramatically on April 15, 1975. On that date, a twenty-one-year-old New Jersey college student collapsed at the home of friends. During the next hour, she apparently stopped breathing twice, each time for about fifteen minutes. At the hospital, in respiratory arrest, she was put on a ventilator. But the damage was already done. Lack of oxygen had destroyed a significant portion of her brain, leaving her in what physicians term a "persistent vegetative state," or PVS. This young woman would spend the rest of her life suspended between life and death. Her name was Karen Ann Quinlan.

She lay in the hospital, silent and unresponsive, breathing with the aid of a machine. Her body was curled in the "decorticate" posture characteristic of patients whose higher brain centers are destroyed, her arms drawn into her chest and her legs contracted in the fetal position. She was not brain dead—she appeared to have sleep-wake cycles and sometimes seemed to follow people with her eyes—yet she remained totally unaware of anything or anyone around her.

No one in her condition had ever recovered. In court, her doctors testified that "her chances for return of discriminative functioning are remote." Others bluntly termed it "nonexistent" and, knowing of no treatment to reverse her condition, stated that "Karen will not return to a level of cognitive function." In plain English, she would never again awaken, think, or relate to others. But physicians refused to speak in absolutes, or to testify that there was *absolutely, positively* no hope. They could not categorically rule out the possibility of some, albeit miraculous, improvement from her present condition. At best, they agreed, her continued existence off the respirator would be "uncertain."

After months of watching this near-lifeless young woman suffer, and after long discussions with their parish priest, her family decided to remove Karen from the machine and end her suffering. The question was how, for the hospital was unwilling to remove her respirator and let nature take its course.

Because Karen was legally an adult, and therefore responsible for her own decisions, her father petitioned the New Jersey Superior Court to be appointed her guardian in order to discontinue the machines. The court refused, citing its "obedience to the dictates of morality and conscience," and duty to "aid and protect Karen Quinlan and act in her best interests." To this judge, the issues at stake included necessary legal protection for the incapacitated and the sanctity of life.

The Quinlans appealed the decision to the New Jersey Supreme Court. There, the judges addressed themselves to Karen's constitutional "right to privacy." They said that this included her right to refuse care if she were alert. As she was not, someone else—her father—could exercise this right on her behalf.

After weighing the absolute protection of life—or at least continued organ function—against Karen's personal privacy, the court threw Karen's case back to the hospital, but with very clear guidelines. "If the physicians could conclude," they wrote, "that there was no reasonable possibility of her emerging from her comatose condition to a cognitive, sapient state," and if they could agree that her prognosis was hopeless, they could withdraw the life-support systems.

The court relied on the legal doctrine of "substituted judgment," which asks: "What would this patient want if she could tell us?" Its analysis wrested the decision from the exclusively medical realm and put it squarely in the domain of individual rights and values. It established no absolute principle, nor any rigid concept of "state interest" requiring the state to preserve every human life at all costs. In short order, her father was appointed guardian, the procedure was followed, and he arranged for her ventilator to be turned off.

Ironically, her family's struggle to help her to die failed even as it succeeded. Karen Quinlan lived nine more years with a feeding tube providing her sustenance, finally dying in 1985, without regaining consciousness. Her long struggle was over; for the rest of us, it had just begun.

For now something fundamental had changed. The Quinlan case made our most personal passages of life and death a matter of public discourse. Our most private matters were now discussed on talk shows and headlines. Across the country, in hospitals, universities, and legislatures, America had opened a great national debate: What are the ethics of care? Do we have a "right" to die? Who decides when the patient cannot?

To answer the vexing questions that began to arise, a complex set of notions and rules emerged in state courts and legislatures around the nation. In California, as Karen Quinlan lay in the hospital, the California Natural Death Act gave people the right—under certain narrowly defined circumstances—to leave instructions to prevent caregivers from continuing treatment. It was the first formal, legal protection to halt the use of technology when the patient could no longer cry halt himself.

Legislatures, which had always been considered irrelevant to individual decisions about life and death, were now taking actions that affected events at the bedside. These decisions were issuing from legislatures composed of our elected representatives—that is to say, politicians—with all their competing agendas and motivations.

Where there is law, of course, there are lawyers. Some drew up regulations interpreting the statutes and advised their clients—patients, families, and hospitals—how to retain their power and authority and lower the odds for personal or financial loss. They also fanned fears of liability among doctors. Outside of their very specific role in helping formulate and articulate the rules, barristers rarely bring benefits to the bedside. But they have arrived there nonetheless, in growing numbers.

Predictably, many of these discussions ended up in court, propelled by torrents of petitions, court briefs, and adversary arguments. By the 1980s, judges faced a growing docket of cases relating to people like Karen Quinlan, people whose very lives were debated, dissected, and decided on in a public court of law. They were ordinary people whose lives derailed into medical mischance and then into court. They were named Claire Conroy and Brother Joseph Fox, Shirley Dinnerstein and John Storar, thrown into the public spotlight as legal and moral questions were raised about their care. All were incapable of deciding about their own care; each raised issues of who should decide, on what basis, with what safeguards. Each came down to the same question: Can we allow some people to choose death for others?

Their cases became object lessons in the need for rules that were fair, just, and equitable to help us reflect the values and mores of our society. Claire Conroy, an eighty-four-year-old bedridden woman, had serious and irreversible physical and mental impairments and a nephew who wanted to remove the feeding tube keeping her alive. Brother Joseph Fox had been in perfect health, went in for hernia surgery, had a heart attack during surgery, and wound up in a deep and irreversible coma. Shirley Dinnerstein was a sixty-seven-year-old woman suffering from end-stage Alzheimer's disease whose family sought to spare her the pain and suffering of futile resuscitation; John Storar, whose mental abilities were those of a toddler, had lived since adulthood in a state facility for the mentally retarded. He now suffered from terminal bladder cancer, requiring treatment by blood transfusions that scared and distressed him, causing him great pain and anxiety. Because he could not understand enough to be comforted, his mother asked to stop treatment on the grounds that it was torturing her retarded son.

Today, the spirits of these people and others attend unseen at our bedsides. Decisions made by courts in every state affect all our lives since they set precedents that others will follow in the future. In some cases, rulings brought new protections from discrimination by those who think that some lives—those of the retarded or disabled, for example—are less worthy of care. Other rulings erected barriers that prevent loving family members from ending what they see as an inhuman purgatory.

What has emerged from this decade of statutes, regulations, and case law is a legal patchwork. When it comes to the question of allowing someone to die, for example, in New Jersey the law looks to the constitutional right to privacy and allows a guardian to discontinue life supports under certain circumstances. Across the river in New York, courts instead require people to have an explicit directive proved by "clear and convincing evidence" before care can be withdrawn, or to have executed a "proxy" appointment. But across the country in Washington, a guardian can refuse care for another person. In Kentucky and Wisconsin, you cannot refuse life-sustaining tube feedings at all with a living will, but in California you can. In a myriad of different ways in as many different states, the law controls issues of life, death, dignity, and privacy. Sometimes, it seems, we need to be legal specialists to understand how we—and those we love—may live or die.

Anyone who has spent much time in our legal system knows that our nation's courtrooms are staffed by judges of widely varying degrees of wisdom, compassion, courage, and intelligence. Even the best of them may lack familiarity with the latest in bioethics and health law. Many judges are political appointees, susceptible to political and public pressures. No wonder there have been some magnificent decisions—and some shoddy ones.

By definition, judges walk a careful line, at one moment standing squarely within societal values and at the next leading us to new levels of interpretation and understanding of social dilemmas. But most of them, most of the time, remain firmly within the confines of the established order. The case law they produce is, in the words of Supreme Court Justice Oliver Wendell Holmes, "at best, and at bottom . . . a response to the unconscious preferences of society." Rare indeed is the judge who will bravely stake a claim at the far end of conventional thought.

Judges themselves are often uncomfortable at having such cases come before them. Recently, St. Louis Probate Judge Louis Kohn found himself facing a case where the father of a young woman in a persistent vegetative state wanted to remove his daughter from a respirator. As the neurologist in the case described how such decisions are best made by the family and physician, Judge Kohn noted, "He didn't say one word about the courts. I think that's the way it should be . . . the way it has been since time immemorial."

That consensus is shared among most medical ethicists. We have seen that these more formal settings of courtrooms, far removed from patients and families, are not the best places to make personal decisions. Instead such decisions should generally be made by families cooperating with caregivers, in the context of the medical establishment, and never taken to court at all.

The move from sickroom to courtroom also changed the tenor of discussions. Family decisions always concern a specific, identifiable individual: What is to be done for Aunt Bea? But when moved to the public forum, those personal claims now compete against a farrago of abstractions: Societal Interest. The Common Good. Inalienable Rights. Privacy. Equity. Not just what was good for Aunt Bea, but what would be good for all the Aunt Beas of the world. With each new regulation and written ruling handed down, it came to matter less and less if these rules reflected any particular person's individual desires. For now they carried the full force of law. As such, they can be imposed on any of us, overriding our own values and beliefs and those of our family.

In principle, the discussion of such cases ought to be based on values shared by everyone in society: that there is a legitimate interest in protecting life, that people should be able to make their own decisions where possible, that the helpless should be protected. In practice, opening these personal decisions to the law brought a dizzying set of agendas, biases, and opinions. We had laws written by legislators, mindful of polls and constituents, fretting over reelection; cases brought by district attorneys before judges, both of whom watch headlines and also fret over reelection; hearings argued by lawyers, thinking of fees and reputations, who themselves look to their own futures as legislators, judges, and district attorneys.

Unfortunately, in this morass of competing interests, any one of us can be put in the position of fighting the entire legal/medical system to keep decisions in our own hands. As a patient, you may find yourself in a situation where no one tells you about your rights, so you'd better know them, if you are to have any hope that you and yours keep control of what happens to you.

Medicine by Media

When we threw open the doors of the sickroom to the scrutiny of courts, several other phantom players sneaked in uninvited. The first of these was the press. Inevitably, the most disturbing cases came into the klieg-light glare of media attention: Karen Ann Quinlan and Nancy Cruzan, lost in their persistent vegetative states, never to awaken; Baby Faye, who received a baboon's heart transplant in Loma Linda, California; the desperate families in Chicago, Brooklyn, Florida, and California who, taking matters into their own hands, killed comatose babies and relatives as medical staff looked on.

Such stories sell papers and boost ratings. They include very sensational elements: drugs and blood, machines and needles, tender babies, helpless and suffering patients, doctors in white coats "playing God." Such tales stand at the irresistible confluence of mortality and power. Given such eminently juicy copy, one can hardly expect reporters to resist—and they don't.

In the best cases, reason, respect, and fact inform media discussions, allowing them to bring these inestimably delicate issues to us all for reflection and consideration. More often, people's traumas of personal choice and private agony are spattered across the newsstands in thirty-six-point headlines: "BABY KILLERS FREED," "SUICIDE DOC NABBED"— the ghoulish gospel according to the tabloids. These are the stories physicians and administrators fear.

They worry, and rightfully so, that medicine's increasingly public nature has brought the tabloids to join the phantoms at the bedside. Not in person—that isn't necessary. This phantom works through the hearts and minds of the other players involved. Nurses and physicians ("MODERN MENGELE KILLS GRANDMA"); hospital administrators and risk managers ("HOSPITAL REFUSES CARE, BABY DIES"); judges and prosecutors and lawyers ("JUDGE FREES BABY KILLER DOC"): each in his own way, each from her own perspective, cannot help but keep a wary eye on the sensational press. Or, more accurately, on the least common denominator of its most sensational practitioners. However small a role it plays, however seriously professionals take their roles, the press forces most of these players to weigh decisions with at least a backward glance.

If they don't, there is another phantom who does, for whom thinking about the press *is* her professional role. It is now standard operating procedure at virtually every major hospital, when a patient's case is brought to court for whatever reason, that the department of public affairs/public relations is informed. These people, again doing their job, are yet other players serving institutional, not individual, interests. As a general rule, the further removed any given player is from personal contact with patient and family, the more heavily press and public relations considerations weigh on them.

Minding Other People's Business: The Roving Stranger

The blurring of sickroom and newsroom brought the final, and by far the most disturbing, phantom onto the medical stage. This phantom, the one most feared by the hospital and doctors, is the "Roving Stranger." Roving Strangers are third parties: not patients, family, or physicians. They have no legitimate decision-making role, no caregiving responsibility, and no real knowledge of the patient. Their target: anyone with whom they disagree. To them, health-care decisions are political, not personal issues. Born in the struggle over abortion and reproductive choice, the Roving Stranger has become a self-anointed crusader in a holy war against personal autonomy.

The first important Roving Stranger case occurred in Boston in 1975. There, a seventeen-year-old unwed mother in her fifth or sixth month of pregnancy made the painful decision to have an abortion. She went to Boston City Hospital, where Dr. Kenneth C. Edelin gave her a surgical abortion called a hysterotomy. The fetus that emerged might have looked to the untrained eye like a premature baby; the medical professionals knew that survival at that length of gestation was unprecedented and, accordingly, made no attempt to resuscitate. But despite the fact that the abortion was requested by the woman in a confidential relationship with her physician, a third party—in this case a band of right-to-life activists visiting the hospital a full two months after the procedure took place—were outraged. They convinced a local prosecutor, a man with strong conservative sympathies, to indict the doctor for manslaughter. The physician was convicted, appealed, and was finally acquitted on appeal.

In 1983, another Roving Stranger case occurred in New York, in an episode that made national headlines. Baby Jane Doe was born at St. Charles Hospital on Long Island with a half dozen terrible birth defects: very severe spina bifida, a birth defect where the spinal cord and brain fail to develop properly; hydrocephalus, where excess fluid compresses the brain; microcephaly, an abnormally small head; and serious malformations in the deepest part of her brain, the brain stem. Her combined impairment was at the gravest end of the spectrum. She could neither close her eyes nor suck; her upper limbs were severely spastic; and her thumb was entirely encased within her fist. Her mother, twenty-three, and father, thirty, consulted a dozen pediatric surgeons and specialists who agreed that their little girl faced overwhelming odds; her deformities, they said, were all but incompatible with life. At the very best, she would have to

endure several long and painful surgeries that would not necessarily work. Even if they all were successful she would be
profoundly mentally retarded, epileptic, and immobile and was
unlikely to live past age twenty. Without surgery, she would
certainly die.

After spending several days weighing their daughter's suffering, talking with clergy and family and doctors, the young
parents finally came to the most wrenching decision a couple
can ever make: they would let nature take its course. Sorrow-
fully, they asked the physicians not to proceed with painful
treatment. These young parents wanted only to relieve the
baby's suffering and mourn their loss. It was not to be so easy.

Local right-to-life activists contacted Lawrence Washburn,
a right-to-life attorney in Vermont. He went to court to force
the doctors to treat the child, claiming that they were infringing
the rights of a handicapped person—the baby. Overnight, this
Roving Stranger had turned personal tragedy into political tug-
of-war. After several months, the case wound up in federal
court in Washington, D.C. There, attorneys from the Reagan
administration's Justice Department weighed in with the right-
to-life Roving Stranger, arguing against parents' rights to
choose or refuse treatment for their severely handicapped newborn child. One can scarcely imagine what it must have felt like
for these anguished young parents to read the legal papers de-
scribing themselves and the hospital as adversaries of "the
United States of America."

The judges finally ruled that the government had no
grounds to interfere, although government advocates and physicians subsequently agreed on regulations. But it was a hollow
victory for the family. In the interim they had been under constant public scrutiny. Their baby's condition had swung up and
down with dramatic swings and spiking fevers. She had been
treated and, as the doctors had predicted, had survived.

Long before the case ended, before the court had told him
in no uncertain terms to mind his own business, the roving

right-to-life activist had returned to Vermont to practice law. He would bear no legal or financial responsibility to the family for his intrusion. But that young family on Long Island will grapple for the rest of their lives with the results of a hit-and-run Roving Stranger.

How far Roving Strangers will go was seen six years later, in the town of Manhasset, New York. There a thirty-two-year-old woman, two months pregnant, lay in a coma, the victim of a serious highway accident. The combined effects of her serious injuries and her pregnancy were putting such strain on her body that her doctors saw scant chance for recovery. The only hope to save her life, they felt, was an abortion, to relieve the extra stress on her body. She was, of course, unable to grant permission, but her husband, desperate to save his wife's life, did so immediately. The surgery was what he thought she would have wanted, and was certainly what he wanted, so he gave his permission.

Unfortunately, a right-to-life hospital nurse thought differently, and alerted a Roving Stranger. He went to court to prevent the surgery, citing his role as an advocate for the well-being of the fetus. Even if it meant forfeiting the young woman's life, even flouting her husband's wishes, the Roving Stranger tried to stop the procedure. Again, the judge supported the husband's decision to authorize the operation. The woman eventually regained consciousness and the couple is now struggling to rebuild their lives.

These Roving Strangers won't go away. They are a part of the endless ebb and flow of sectarian interests seeking to impose moral and religious beliefs on others. As such, they are nothing new. What is new, and what may hold ominous implications for all of us, is that the Roving Stranger has changed his strategy.

Right-to-life activists, formerly focused on birth and contraception, are now attempting to apply their absolute moral doctrines to our decisions at the other end of life. Across the country, they are seeking to move out from the delivery rooms and women's clinics to the geriatric floors and the intensive care units in our hospitals. If abortion was their battle in the 1980s, terminal-care decisions have been added to their agenda for the 1990s. They bring to this discussion the same zeal and guerrilla tactics that they brought to the abortion debate. In a half dozen communities across the country, this vocal minority has intervened to turn people's private dilemmas into public spectacles.

On December 14, 1990, Nancy Cruzan lay in a persistent vegetative state in the Missouri Rehabilitation Center in Mount Vernon, Missouri. After an eight-year legal fight all the way up to the United States Supreme Court and back again, her parents had finally gotten permission to remove the feeding tube maintaining organ function in their daughter's body. One might well have thought that the Cruzan family had at last earned the right to the dignity and privacy of this sorrow as they watched their thirty-three-year-old daughter and sister finally die.

Again, Roving Strangers knew better. Despite the family's own wishes; despite the considered judgment of the Missouri court, in accord with the rules set down by the United States Supreme Court; despite several trials where all the evidence was considered; this band of strangers descended on the private hospital in Mount Vernon, Missouri. In the days after the feeding tube was removed, as Nancy Cruzan's organs slowed and stopped, carloads of religious activists converged from as far away as Florida and Georgia. For days, they camped in parking lots and held prayer vigils on the hospital steps. On the fifth day, they tried to force their way into the hospital to physically reattach her feeding tube. Nineteen were arrested and taken before a judge who sternly reprimanded them that they had no business in this case. Implacable to the end, they remained unshaken in their conviction that they knew better for the Cruzans than did the family themselves, and the courts that supported the family's decision.

To conservative and fundamentalist theologians—be they Catholic or Jewish or Protestant—it may seem to be in their theological interest to draw clear lines around death to protect their view of the sanctity of life. In this absolutist, or "vitalist," view, life is most easily grasped in terms of stark black and white. It starts at conception and ends, apparently, when it can no longer be supported by any conceivable means available. To the vitalist, organ function—a beating heart, pumping lungs, any brain activity whatsoever—is life. Never mind that the heart beats with the aid of pacemaker and drugs, the breathing is forced by a ventilator, or the brain activity is so minimal as to forever preclude consciousness. Horrified that doctors might "play God" by removing a respirator, they seem unconcerned when physicians do just that by turning these machines on in the first place.

Most of all, they don't care that the person in the bed, or her spouse, closest intimates, and family, may wish to allow death in peace, comfort, and dignity. Roving Strangers are convinced that they know what's right, at life's end as at its advent, and do not hesitate to impose their views on the rest of us. In seeking to restrict our decisions about terminal care, they would put the state at the bedside to police our most private passages. The legal power of the state could force all of us to endure a prolonged, undignified death—in the name of one absolutist view of life. Happily, for the moment, other courts in New York and Washington have held that Roving Strangers have no standing to interfere with other people's most intimate decisions.

But although they have not generally won in court and although they surface only sporadically, Roving Strangers have left an indelible mark on the practice of medicine. As much fantasy as fact, they nonetheless cast a shadow on behavior. They have become the bogeyman of the modern medical center, giving administrators bad dreams at night for fear that the next Roving Stranger will be a right-to-life nurse or an overzealous medical student on their staff. Now, each time a hospital physician and family agree to turn down the respirator on a permanently vegetative ninety-four-year-old, they cannot help look over their shoulders. What if a nurse's aid disagrees and calls the district attorney? Will some hospital technician decide this constitutes patient abuse and report it to the authorities?

As bizarre as these scenarios seem, one of them has already happened. At one point in the Baby Jane Doe litigation there was a brief period when neonatal nurseries around the nation were indeed required to post an 800 number that could be called by anyone who thought that a child was being "abused." The object of the regulators was to put Big Brother among the bassinets: to prevent any decisions to forgo treatments, and enlist all staff and visitors in ad hoc morality squads, scrutinizing any decisions by anyone about any baby. Fortunately, those regulations were struck down by the court although some states still post numbers to call.

Unfortunately for all of us, the Roving Stranger, whether we like it or not, has become a presence at the bedside. You can only hope that the next case in which he takes an interest won't be yours.

Standing Up to the Phantoms

The artist who painted *The Country Doctor* would scarcely recognize the modern bedside, crowded with so many new faces. Ethicists and committees, administrators and risk managers; legions of lawyers, judges, legislators, and politicians; reporters and right-to-lifers: never before has being sick been such a committee affair.

Somewhere in all of this we must face up to the basic question: What about the person in the bed? What if, as will happen at some stage, that person is you or someone in your family? What if you are lying sick, unable to communicate your wishes or caught in the grip of technology? How can you keep your right to determine what happens to you? With so many invisible and powerful players uninvited at the bedside, it has never been so important to keep personal control.

The good news is that by thinking about these issues ahead of time, and doing the right kinds of advance planning, you can put the odds on your side when you or someone you love is the patient. You have now met many of the players involved in illness today, so you need not meet them for the first time when you are least ready to deal with them. But knowing such players exist is only the first step. The rest of this book is geared to the specifics of demystifying what happens in our health-care system, and showing you how to keep control of decisions vital to you and your family.

By knowing the players and knowing your rights, knowing where your options lie and how discussions about medical ethics get conducted, you can help return these ancillary strangers to the background where Fildes painted them. As you do, you shift the focus back to where it has always belonged: on the people in the beds, and all of us who love them.

3

WHO GETS
TO
DECIDE?

UNDERSTANDING

INFORMED

CONSENT

Decisions are the very mortar of medicine. They come in a thousand forms: Which patient will get a transplant or a respirator? Must we act to save a mother or a fetus? Can we treat this person against her wishes? Will we resuscitate the next? Is a third eligible for an experimental drug? Although each situation may look different, behind all of them lie two fundamental questions: Who will ultimately decide, and on what basis? Will the choice of care rest with the sick person, with family, loved ones, or friends? Or will it rest with someone else—a physician, an administrator, or some other stranger? If it does, how do they know that they are doing the right thing?

In one form or another, the question of "who gets to decide" beats at the heart of almost all difficult medical situations. In most of the cases that I and my bioethical colleagues discuss on the hospital floors, *who* gets to decide shapes *what* will be decided. Indeed, many problems that at first seem like knotty ethical dilemmas reduce to this same fundamental question: whose values and wishes will, ultimately, be respected?

The inescapable fact is that decisions will always be made—by someone. As pathology follows its own inexorable course, it creates its own schedule and demands for action. So, too, do the logistical demands of a modern hospital. Hospitals are active places. They abhor a person or a process in stasis; either care must move forward on some recognizable course or the patient must be discharged. The forward momentum of the place demands decisions.

What happens then will reflect either your own desires and values, or those of others. Ideally, whenever we are caught up in the health-care system, our goal must always be to hear and heed the voice of the person in the bed. That person's values, wishes, and desires must always be at the center of our thinking. Sometimes, however, it takes real work to make that happen.

Wendy was thirty-two years of age, in her third pregnancy after two earlier miscarriages. Perhaps because of that history or perhaps because of her naturally anxious personality, Wendy was apprehensive about each detail of her pregnancy: her diet, her every physical movement, her job, her husband's work environment, her medical care. In the shared opinion of her obstetrician, pediatrician, and midwife, Wendy's anxiety extended far beyond the bounds of healthy maternal concern. Given Wendy's previous tendency to hypertension, the care team watched vigilantly for signs that the constant stress caused by her anxiety might elevate stress hormones and blood pressure, and so actually harm her fetus.

By her fifth month, when all seemed to be going well, a prenatal sonogram detected that the fetus might have a cleft lip—a condition that can be associated with more serious defects, but isn't usually. In this case, the doctor felt it was likely to be a very minor problem, in all likelihood one easily corrected by surgery after birth. Given her patient's emotional instability, she was very reluctant to tell Wendy. In her best medical judgment, the chances were significant that Wendy would be unduly upset by the news, which might bring harm to her and the baby.

Weighing the potential damage of Wendy's intense anxiety against the damage of learning about the correctable condition after birth, the physician decided it would be better for all concerned not to divulge the sonogram results. In doing so, she was invoking a notion called "physician privilege," which states that if a doctor believes her patient will experience "direct and immediate harm" from hearing the truth, she may withhold some information. As a notion, physician privilege is vague and ill defined: it is not clear how long a physician can continue not to disclose, or whether she is obliged to approach a close family member or significant other in place of the patient. In my experience, physician privilege is usually applied as an escape hatch without proper justification. Because it is so nebulous, many responsible physicians are reluctant to invoke it at all, and a small number of physicians tend to abuse it.

But in this case, it was clear Wendy's obstetrician had agonized over the decision. As a woman, a physician, and a mother, she felt immensely torn. She trusted the professional judgment she had honed over twenty-six years of caring for pregnant women, and she believed that telling Wendy would be likely to cause real harm to her and perhaps to the fetus. Did not, she asked, her duty of beneficence—to do what she thought would best help her patient—override the abstract principle of full disclosure? Several younger residents in the obstetrics unit thought not, arguing that the mother had a right to know this information, even if it might hurt her or the baby. Stuck, they called to schedule an ethics round later that week.

Not so long ago, this question would not even have come up. From its roots with Hippocrates twenty-five hundred years ago, Western medicine had considered it an axiom that patients could not be trusted with information about their diseases and care. The oath that bears his name fairly rings with the notion that doctors know what's best for their patients. For two and a half millennia after that oath was written, the doctor played God and patriarch. Medical practitioners were expected to do what they thought best; patients expected—and had—little say in what happened to them. By definition, the physician was thought to be acting in the patient's best interests.

Under those rules, the professional's opinions counted far more than the patient's. If your physician thought it wise to perform a medical procedure—a sterilization, say, or a mastectomy or even a lobotomy—all he had to do was inform you: "Well, Mrs. Jones, I am now going to remove a part of your brain." Even if he only gave you one possible treatment option—"We must remove your breast"—if you said yes, he was off the legal hook. He was not required even to mention possible alternative treatments like chemotherapy, surgery, or radiation. Nor was he required to make sure you understood the procedure or its consequences. His task was defined as acting in your best interests simply because he was using his skill, wisdom, and expertise to select and follow the best plan of care for you.

If you disagreed with the doctor, you had little recourse. Because medicine involved touching, one could file a complaint against a doctor for unconsented touching of one's person— assault and battery. But that was after the fact—the damage had been done—and besides, you weren't likely to win. Given the context of the times, judges and juries shared the view that doctors knew best. Treatment was then a tautology; if you were being treated, it was assumed that you needed to be. It was hardly surprising that juries rarely found in favor of patients.

Then, beginning in the late nineteenth century, and more specifically during the last forty years, a new standard began to develop in legal and ethical thought. Starting in the late 1950s, a series of legal cases in California and the District of Columbia forever changed our vision of the doctor-patient relationship. One case in California involved a young woman who received radiation therapy to heal a large wound, the result of a prior mastectomy. Instead of shrinking, her wound grew. She sued, claiming her doctor had never explained that possibility to her—had not, in fact, adequately explained the overall risks of the large doses of cobalt radiation she had received. The doctor argued that the woman had consented, but the court held that unless such a consent was fully informed and the patient actually understood the risks of the procedure, the doctor was not protected from later liability.

The D.C. case involved a seventeen-year-old who needed back surgery. He was still a minor, so the surgeon telephoned his mother for permission. When she asked how risky this surgery might be, the physician answered that it was no more risky than any other surgery. After a series of postsurgical complications, the young man was left paralyzed from the waist down and incontinent. In that case the judge decided that the physician bore "a duty to warn of the dangers lurking in the proposed treatment." In his words, "True consent to what happens to one's self is the informed exercise of choice, and that entails an opportunity to evaluate knowledgeably the options available and the risks attendant upon each." The judge continued that informed consent should include information about "inherent and potential hazards of the proposed treatment, the alternatives, and the results likely if the patient remains untreated."

These cases were among the first in which courts said clearly that the physician's duty went beyond using his physical and intellectual skills to provide treatment and medications. He must also give patients enough information to weigh the risks and decide among the medical options at hand. Increasingly, from that time on, courts said that doctors were expected to use their greater knowledge to provide information to help patients choose. With that, our modern legal notion of "informed consent" was born.

The issue soon became what kind of information and how much—just how "informed" must consent be? Some argued that a physician only had to tell patients as much as the "standard practice" of other physicians in that community. Other courts argued that patients should be entitled to all information that was "material" or "relevant" to their decision, no matter what other doctors did.

Along with this notion came the idea of patient "autonomy," a principle that has become a touchstone of all medical ethics. My favorite definition is that of Dr. Bart Collopy, a philosopher at Fordham University, who calls it "a cluster of notions—self-determination, freedom, independence, liberty of choice and action, control of decision making and activity—by the individual. It is human agency free of outside intervention and outside interference." Autonomy involves the exercise of your sense of values, independence, personal history, life, principles of behavior—who you are and how you live.

For the last three decades, American courts and state legislatures have built on these pillars of informed consent, autonomy, and self-determination to expand our national consensus regarding a patient's rights, a change that shifted the practice of medicine from a thoroughgoing paternalism to the process of consent. Informed consent and patient autonomy have become accepted features of the medical landscape, something some physicians now practice without even thinking about it. When you go to your doctor, when you seek a second opinion, when you ask what's going on with your health or care, when you sit and talk with your doctor during your physical, you are becoming an informed patient, so as to best protect your autonomy.

In a few short years, talk has become a key tool in the doctor's black bag. As information joined medication as a requisite part of adequate medical care, it meant that a physician could be found negligent for not providing enough of it. If the doctor did not share information with the patient, if she just went ahead and acted, she could risk being sued not only for battery—unconsented touching—but also for negligence in not living up to the accepted standards of professional performance.

This heralded a sea change in the medical relationship. For the first time in more than two millennia of medical history, patients and families are seen as having the right to information with which to decide what should happen to them. Physicians are expected to tell patients what is wrong (diagnosis), what is likely to happen (prognosis), and what the available treatment options are, including not doing anything at all. As patients, all of us now have the explicit legal right not only to consent to or refuse care, but to give our "informed consent" about the medical issues and options. For the first time, we possess the right to the information with which to make up our own minds. Legal and ethical thought now recognize that the person in the bed is an active participant in, not simply the passive object of, medical care.

From this perspective, I pointed out, our duty to Wendy was clear: whatever information the doctor has *about* the patient should be shared *with* the patient. In Wendy's case, we had to stand for the principle of personal autonomy over that of physician paternalism. For her, that meant that whatever decisions lay ahead, whether to operate, terminate the pregnancy, or do nothing, she should have the right to weigh options and choose what was appropriate medical care for her—as uncomfortable as that might be for her and her caregivers alike.

As things are rarely so straightforward, however, I asked the team whether they would see it differently if Wendy had been beyond the twenty-fourth week of her pregnancy, and therefore unable to choose an abortion. Perhaps at that point an absolute position on truth telling might have been more properly balanced against any benefit to her in concealing the information. Some of the team took solace in that possibility, but most remained convinced that the best ethical course still lay in full disclosure.

It is amazing how often physician discomfort plays a real role in such circumstances. It is not uncommon to hear "I can't discuss this with patient so-and-so because he will get so upset/he can't tolerate stress in his condition/it might make him anxious." Sometimes this is true, sometimes not. Often the "too sick" argument is used as a way to exclude the patient from decisions rather than as a real reflection of a person's physical or mental capacity. The reasons physicians give for not informing people of bad news abound, may well be valid, or at least seem valid to the doctor. But also at work may be the doctor's simple inability or unwillingness to deal with emotions—hers or the patient's. In a very understandable, human way, physicians may not be eager to have difficult, tearful, even angry conversations, if they can avoid them.

As in Wendy's case, when and what to tell patients can be complicated. Generally, physicians walk a delicate line between unduly alarming patients on the one hand, and shielding them excessively on the other. A doctor must tell you all of the facts that are necessary and relevant to deciding, without overwhelming you, causing you to suffer, prejudicing your decision, or just plain being insensitive.

Every physician has heard of cases where a patient has actually been harmed psychologically or physically by being given information inappropriately. One of the cruelest medical events I ever witnessed involved watching a senior neurosurgeon at another hospital some decades ago compel a nineteen-year-old man with a brain tumor to copy in laborious longhand seven pages of fine print from a neurosurgery textbook, detailing all of the possible gruesome risks and complications of the brain surgery the young man was about to face. No possible medical event was too ghastly, no chance too remote for the youth not to be forced to write it down. I never knew if this doctor really believed this heartless exercise was his best protection against a lawsuit or whether he was simply indulging a fit of pique at the legal requirement to fully inform his patient. Whatever the case, this physician had clearly not made peace with the idea of a truly humane informed consent.

In Wendy's case, I pointed out that the physician could not

predict with certainty that the pregnant woman's response would actually injure her or her fetus. I knew this physician was a caring and sensitive person, and felt confident that her discussion with Wendy would more than likely be able to provide the information in its proper context. In the final analysis, we all agreed that the larger principle of informed consent dictated that Wendy had a right to be told. Ethically and professionally, her care team's job was to support her in dealing with whatever consequences that decision brought. In Wendy's case the consequences were minimal, her upset easily managed, and her baby, happily, fine.

Informed Consent: The Cornerstone of Care

Today, whenever you are sick, the cornerstone of your care rests on the very basic and simple premise that you have the right to choose what will be done from a range of suggested medical options and you will be given enough information to decide what is the most appropriate for you. It is the single most important tool you have to keep control of what happens to you, and the decisions made about you, when you fall ill.

But having a right, of course, is just the beginning. It is all well and good that individuals have the right to act autonomously, exercise self-determination, and give or withhold their "informed consent." But until we understand the ways in which medical-care decisions are made, those rights will stay, dusty and unused, on the shelf. So to make your rights become reality, we have to resolve one basic question: just who is the decider? Whose "informed consent" are we talking about? And what makes a consent or refusal of care truly "informed"?

At first, it might seem that the ones who are most informed, by definition, are the doctors. Your physicians have spent a decade or more in rigorous training, giving them vast collective and individual experience around diseases in general, and your condition in particular. Theirs are the most well formed and researched opinions based on the deepest understanding of our various treatment options. As the agents our society has designated to understand the ways of illness, aren't they the most appropriate players to tell us what to do, to chart our course from illness back to health? Why shouldn't they be the ones to decide?

There are two good reasons why not. First, ours is a culture that celebrates the individual. Independence and freedom are central to the American soul. In our careers and our lifestyles, in our expression and our worship, in every corner of our character, we are individuals. Our medical culture is only recently shedding its paternalistic past and coming to reflect the same consistent commitment to self-determination. We cannot help but value our independence as patients; our individualist culture could know no other way to be sick.

Reflecting that, the political trends of the last three decades have increasingly empowered the individual to decide. We have seen the women's rights movement grow into the patients' rights movement, and go on to spawn rights for the mentally ill, the mentally retarded, those with physical disabilities, and, most recently, those at risk for AIDS. In sickness and in health, as in disability, no longer do we expect people to check their autonomy at the sickroom door, to surrender their freedom of choice precisely when they feel most powerless.

The second reason concerns the stark realities of doctoring. Uncertainty is always the unacknowledged handmaiden of medical advice. Medical practice is not the mere exercise of skills, experience, and wisdom. As much as we pretend otherwise, behind its scientific facade healing is a set of highly educated guesses cloaked in medical jargon and called "differential diagnosis." A simple fever and sore throat may be a common flu, or a more chronic viral infection like Epstein-Barr virus, cytomegalovirus, or the result of deadly leukemia or AIDS. Or it may be just a fever and sore throat.

When medical facts are uncertain, personal values become paramount. Since in many cases there is no one clear answer, our decisions must necessarily depend on the constellation of our own unique personal wishes, tempered by medical judgment and advice. Decisions about care involve a complex calculus of medical, personal, philosophical, emotional, religious, and familial beliefs and convictions.

There is no clearer example of this than breast cancer. Modern medicine offers a woman a wide range of surgical options: a very invasive and debilitating radical mastectomy in which the entire breast and the surrounding muscle tissue are removed; the newer, more accepted modified radical mastectomy (less and less common), where only the breast and nearby lymph nodes are removed, leaving the underlying chest muscle; the surgical middle ground of a partial mastectomy, removing only a portion of the breast and leaving the adjoining nodes; or a more limited lumpectomy, to remove only the tumor itself. The patient may also choose between chemotherapy and, possibly, localized radiation treatments. For many years, we have lacked conclusive medical data about which of these options were surest to increase longevity. In the face of that uncertainty, the best choice for a given woman depended not just on what her doctor could tell her, but on her individual and personal values as well.

For the woman facing such medical uncertainty, a decision must take into account her personal experience and history, her beliefs and opinions, her feelings, fears, and hopes. One woman may value the concept of life over all else, and be uncomfortable with anything less than the most aggressive treatment. In her mind the "most extreme" treatment equals "the best" treatment—although objectively that is not always true. Another might want most of all to keep her breast. She alone understands how she feels about her body, her "femininity," what that means to her self-image and her life, and the most intimate textures of her relationship to a lover or spouse. Whenever there is uncertainty about the effectiveness of treatment, such as in the more experimental treatments, our choices must be resolved by a personal, and not only a medical, calculation. It is important to understand that there is always some degree of uncertainty. Medicine is an art as well as a science because hypotheses and judgment are always part of the diagnosis and therefore always part of the potential treatment plans.

Sometimes personal values affect care decisions in surprising ways. Mr. Hart was in his late sixties, had little education and less money, and had a long history of worsening heart problems. His was a particularly frustrating case for his doctors, because his cardiac problem, while serious, was easily corrected by bypass surgery. It wasn't yet an emergency, however, so for the last six months, his clinic doctor urged Mr. Hart to have surgery, to no avail. Finally, exasperated, and tired of watching Mr. Hart get sicker, the cardiologist requested an ethics consultation.

Ethically, the doctor was torn. Certainly, he could not force Mr. Hart to have surgery against his will. He realized that Mr. Hart had a clear right to refuse this bypass, but the refusal seemed to make no sense. But standing by and doing nothing didn't feel right, either: "Am I supposed to just let my patient die a preventable death?" The worst part, he lamented, was not understanding why. "I could understand if he gave a reason, but he doesn't. He just doesn't seem to want our help. He says he's not afraid, and admits that he wants to feel better. Is it the best thing for him to make that decision—and am I ethically bound to follow a course I know will eventually kill him?"

At the doctor's request, we invited Mr. Hart to join us. As we talked it became clear that he understood he needed surgery, and wanted to be able to walk, talk easily, and perhaps even sing in the church choir again. But he feared that he couldn't pay for it. He realized that Medicare would cover most, but not all, of his costs. He had never applied for Medicaid, which he thought was only for "welfare types," among whom he did not count himself. He was also afraid of the application process, having heard that you needed a birth certificate, among other documents. Born in rural Appalachia, Mr. Hart doubted he had ever had a birth certificate, and certainly he did not possess one now. Nobody had ever sat down with him to explain that he was indeed eligible for Medicaid and that hospital staff would help him fill out the forms and go through the process. It took a while to convince him that all this was true, but when we did, he brightened immediately, then looked troubled. "How long will this take?" he asked.

The doctor explained it would probably require eight days in the hospital, and some six weeks to recover at home. Mr. Hart's face fell. "I can't." He shook his head. He explained that his seven-year-old grandson lived with him. "Since my daughter died, he is my responsibility. If I am not there to take care of him, nobody is. So you see, I cannot leave him . . ." A resigned shrug finished his sentence. Now we had hit bedrock. Mr. Hart thought that getting his own surgery meant nobody would care for the child. As hard as it was, his choice was to take care of the boy first. His initial decision, apparently inexplicable, in fact rested both on misinformation and on his deepest connections— which nobody else could have known. Eventually, we reached a compromise: next summer, the boy could go and live with his aunt. Then Mr. Hart could have surgery without fear of endangering his grandson, and we would see that Medicaid paid for it.

As it was for Mr. Hart, every medical decision is an amalgam of the personal and private concerns of the people involved. His apparent refusal of care was based on reasons that had little to do with the risks and benefits of the medical procedures themselves. Often what may seem to the doctor like straightforward issues are for the patient secondary to family responsibilities and emotional and economic concerns. In our society, where people do not have a right to health care, many people never seek or ultimately refuse medical care because they cannot afford it.

What was true for the woman with breast cancer was true

for Mr. Hart, and is true for all of us. Since medical decisions are often a mix of options and values, the values that count most are those of the patient. No stranger, not even the most eminent medical expert, can balance and weigh these factors with the knowledge the patient has. That is why, although physicians may be more informed medically, each of us has the right to decide what is appropriate medical care for us in any given situation. When it comes to the all-important human dimension of medical care, there is only one informed consent that counts: yours.

As true as that is, the playing field on which you will find yourself making decisions will be shaped by several factors. Respecting autonomy requires doctors and caregivers to work with a patient and help that person to "hear" and consider the important issues at stake, so he himself can factor in the real personal costs and benefits of each option. In doing that, the medical skill of your physician, her philosophical approach to patients, and the culture of the hospital or nursing home, all play a role. Your medical care will be shaped by what you are told, but many things can interfere with your getting the information you need. Some of those things come from you, others come from your doctors.

How much and what you are told will largely be shaped by the philosophy and commitment of your care providers. Some doctors believe in sharing as much information as possible with patients, giving them as many cards as possible to make the decisions about their care and lives. Such doctors are exemplified by Dr. Russell Patterson, former chairman of the American Medical Association's Council on Ethical and Judicial Affairs, who states: "With so many more treatments, choices and options, the physician's role has primarily become to explain the various options of treatment, their pros and cons. We have moved from physician as decision maker to physician as adviser."

Still, too few physicians or hospital staffs act independently to anticipate the patient and family's need for information and discussion. Given the growing sophistication in medicine about the ethical obligations of physicians, and the legal rights and protected autonomy of patients, that is starting to change. As more and more medical students and house staff talk about these issues, and as the medical literature publishes case studies and analyses documenting their importance, greater numbers of medical professionals incorporate these issues into their discussions with families and patients.

I have found it terrifically gratifying to watch the progress of the house staff in the Primary Care Residency Program at Montefiore, where we have taught and conducted scheduled monthly rounds for the last four years. Because the director and faculty of this program are so deeply committed to integrating ethics analysis into the care of patients, it is now commonplace for these young doctors in training to entice patients into these discussions and structure the conversation so that facts, options, and values are presented and discussed—whether or not the patient or family member raises any particular issues or poses the right questions.

But many doctors are not trained and socialized to give information. Some are "benevolent information dictators," who believe their role is to lead patients to the proper outcome, stressing certain options and downplaying or withholding others. Others jealously stand at the gate of all medical information. They may be hostile to the notion of patient choice, seeing that as an infringement on the natural prerogatives of the profession. Because they are ultimately responsible for your care, they want to control what you are told, how, and when. But increasingly, as bioethics comes to be a matter of discussion and concern in medical schools and teaching hospitals, doctors have come to understand that informed consent is a tool both to foster decent and humane medical care and to relieve them of the unfair and taxing responsibility of choosing for others. Some physicians, to be sure, may be doing the right thing for self-interested reasons. Fear of legal liability can make even physicians who are actively hostile to the concept of informed consent share more information with their patients than they once did.

Even with a practitioner who is most comfortable not sharing information, you do have some options:

◆ Set out your expectations directly. Most often, physicians take their cues from the patient. If they feel a patient doesn't want to know, can't emotionally handle knowing, or cannot understand, they may hold back, or talk in euphemisms.

◆ If you feel you need or want more information than you have, the most helpful thing to do may be simply to tell your doctor that you expect to be given all the relevant information pertaining to your case and care. It may help to explain that you find information comforting, and that you prefer identified dangers to scary unknowns.

◆ Your doctor is not the only information source. If you are in a teaching-and-research hospital, you may have much more ongoing contact with the house staff, medical students, and nurses than you do with your attending physician, who may come on rounds once a day or less. Even in a local community hospital, you still meet and deal with many other care providers. Some of them are excellent sources of information.

In general, the more secure one's rank in the medical hierarchy, the more willing and able that person may be to provide you with solid and accurate information. Physician's assistants and nurse practitioners are more willing and able to answer questions than are rotating shift nurses or those hired daily through an agency. In particular, you can ask questions of the specialty nurses in specific units: pulmonary or intensive care, geriatrics, oncology. They are absolutely key players, with a vast depth of experience. Also, they may know you better and have significantly more contact with you than might a physician.

Sometimes, these other members of the care team may feel

strongly that a patient isn't being given all the information necessary to make a fully informed decision. They may even be eager to remedy the situation. Be prepared, however, for the possibility that some of them may duck your inquiries and lob the discussion back into the doctor's court.

Just as this process of informed consent can be hard for patients, it can be equally difficult for physicians, who, in addition to providing information, must probe to help the patient comprehend and choose among her options. By no means are all the barriers to communication on the physician's side. Your lifestyle and personality, ethnic traditions, personal history, level of education, religious commitment, emotional and intellectual style, all make up the context in which you understand and make medical decisions, and each can help or block understanding. We may relate to doctors as we did to our parents, or feel uncomfortable when a doctor is of another gender, race, or class than we are. Some patients may hold theories of folk medicine that distort or interfere with their understanding of what their doctor is telling them about their medical condition. I've often said that if informed consent works at all, it works between two white, middle-class, suburban males. This somewhat tongue-in-cheek overstatement is meant as a shorthand formula for many of the things that can go wrong in the process. Differences of sex, race, religion, or class often make the process more difficult as they bring together people whose assumptions about the world are vastly different. Obviously, informed consent works in other places and between people of different backgrounds, but making it work is a constant struggle for professionals and patients alike.

Emotional issues can also cloud communication. Many people respond poorly when relating to authority figures or people upon whom they are dependent. Others are intimidated by medical information or fear appearing ignorant. Others worry that if they ask too many questions, they will anger or alienate the physician. Still others may be frightened or in emotional denial about their illness and not want—or be able—to hear what the physician might say. And some, especially older people, simply think it is the doctor's job to decide.

Our fear and denial can make all of us less able to hear and absorb information, and to reflect on the medical issues clearly. We may also be physically or intellectually unable to process the information because of injury or incapacity. We may bring our own past personal history—for example, the traumatic death of a parent in surgery—which creates an emotional barrier preventing us from hearing and considering the alternatives. There are practical obstacles as well. One may not understand the medical patois the doctor uses, even if, in principle, doctor and patient both speak the same language—which, in itself, is less and less often the case. Each of these elements can impede the process of informing and choosing the most appropriate care, and none is likely to be known beforehand by the physician. If you recognize yourself here, remember: information is your right as an informed decider. You need it to make the best decisions for yourself and for those you love. For in the alien world that is modern medicine, information and knowledge can mean the difference between life and death—often, quite literally.

4

FACTS, OPTIONS, VALUES, AND THE CIRCLES OF CONSENT

Medical-care decisions can be tremendously difficult. They often involve disturbing subjects and arise when we are emotionally and physically most vulnerable. Almost always, these choices involve new medical information that always feels alien and can seem overwhelming. Given all that, it is hard for any of us to be sure that we are making the best decisions.

Because my law-and-ethics team faces this problem every day, over the years we have devised a pathway of practical steps to follow each time we are called into a case. This framework helps us clarify and resolve the issues so we can help the care team—doctors, nurses, social workers, and administrators—along with the patient and family, to arrive at the best decision possible. You can use this same three-step path. It looks like this:

Facts: Clarify the medical facts of your situation.
Options: Understand the possible options and their consequences.
Values: Identify the value components in each option.

Step One: Facts

Facts are the foundation of any good decision. You must understand the medical reality: what the situation is right now, and what may lie ahead. Medical rounds and bioethics consultations always begin with one of the doctors "presenting," detailing the salient information of the case so everybody knows where things stand. You can follow this model, asking your physician to do the same: "Doctor, can you give us a succinct idea of where we are, and what has happened so far?"

It is crucial that everyone who will be in on the decision is actually in on the discussion. Medical decisions are complicated enough without having to engage in a game of "medical telephone," where facts get misheard, misunderstood, and passed on from one character to the next. When we are called in, right from the start, we make sure that whoever is involved in the decision—nurses, doctors, administrators, risk managers, families—is included. As an ethicist, I respect their perspectives and their knowledge, and know they will think of things I have not. That way, the description of the case can become the basis for discussion, analysis, and choice.

You can use the same method, although your exact cast of characters will differ. Your team won't be solely professional, but rather personal: spouse and family, children, close friends, clergy, family physician, or any combination. For while the ultimate decisions will be yours, it is tremendously difficult to have to make such important choices alone. You are lucky if you have others around who love and care for you and who can help you think through and resolve these complex issues. Whoever you feel can best help and support your decision, you should include in the presentation. If everyone hears the same information, you will all be playing with the same deck of cards.

Questions you can use to shape the discussion include:
♦ What is the name of what I have?

- If you don't know, what are the possibilities?
- Are there tests you need to run to know more?
- What is the purpose of each test?
- Do these tests have risks associated with them?
- What will we do with the information you get? Will it change anything? (If a diagnostic test could only confirm the need for an operation you would never consent to, it may be a useless test for you—although, on the other hand, it might change your mind about the need for the ultimate procedure.)
- Is the information you need worth the risk of the test?
- What is my condition doing to me now?
- How does it explain my symptoms?
- How did I get it, if you know?
- Is it related somehow to my past behaviors?
- Will changing my behavior have an effect on my problem?
- What usually happens with this disease?
- What do you think now will be the likely course or outcome of the disease or condition?
- How severe or advanced is my case?

Step Two: Options

Once you are reasonably confident everyone involved understands what's going on, you move to the second step of the pathway: establishing your options. Ask your doctor to present the whole menu of alternatives—from the most limited to the most aggressive. Bear in mind that doing nothing is always one alternative, and that should be discussed as well, even if you discard it.

Make sure the physician covers the risks and benefits of each option. You may want to ask:

- How will taking this option make me feel?
- What is the statistical experience in terms of success?
- What defines a "success" for this option?
- What will it mean to my quality of life?
- If I am to die, how might it affect the circumstances of my

death? (For example, will it likely necessitate hospitalization instead of home care?)

◆ What are its possible negative side effects?

◆ What is the time line for this decision? Will my condition likely worsen quickly, so I have to decide quickly, or is the usual progression quite long and gradual, so I have ample time to decide?

Finally, ask which option your physician recommends, and why. Is his counsel based on purely medical reasons? Is it based on his own clinical experience? Is it based on what he knows about you, or what he thinks you want?

At this point, you have completed the first two steps. You have a lot of information to absorb, and almost certainly need to go think things over. It is probably a good idea to clarify your understanding, as well as the options you face, with the doctor before she leaves. Then, set a time for a next discussion, and perhaps ask for a recommendation for a second opinion if you've not yet done so.

Step Three: Values

This final step of the path is the one only you can take, although having others to talk to is an invaluable support. It involves understanding how your medical options fit into your own set of personal values. The medical decision you face may touch on your desires for a certain quality of life; on relationships you have with family and care providers. It may be guided by your religious and philosophical commitments and beliefs; your economic means and potential for payment or ruin; your personal ability to withstand pain; or any number of complex factors that are yours and yours alone.

You may have to weigh your chances of getting better with a given treatment, which keeps you in the hospital, against your length of life, which may be shorter if you leave the hospital. Do you value absolute length of life over its quality or intensity? Are you more worried about being sick, dying, or the possibility of being in pain?

Your answer may depend on your faith. Among some Orthodox Jews, for example, terminating or refusing care is a theologically determined issue: the prime value to be respected in any health-care decision is the utter sanctity of life. Some believe that Orthodox medical ethics, discussed at great length in the Talmud, hold that we don't own our bodies to do with what we want. Rather, they belong to God—we are but temporary guardians—and life is to be preserved at all costs. In this community, the refusal of care is not a judgment for humans to make, and patients are ethically and morally bound to accept all possible treatments, just as physicians are to provide them. Similarly, members of the Jehovah's Witness religion, or those who belong to the Christian Science church, may have religious beliefs that lead them to choose one care option over another. The former, by and large, refuse all blood transfusions, while the latter may refuse many standard medical or chemotherapy treatments on religious grounds.

Your own values may not be religious at all. You know your own past experience with illness, doctors, and hospitals, and how that has felt. A friend of mine was admitted to the hospital ten years ago for pneumonia. He was completely terrified, frightened, and depressed. For him, being in the hospital was torturous. Yet for his mother, being a patient is fine: she gets lots of attention from people waiting on her hand and foot, a respite from her life of taking care of others.

Your family relationships also affect the decisions you make. Perhaps, given your relationship to spouse, family, and loved ones, you could not bear to be dependent on them. You may not want them to remember you as a bed-bound patient, in slow decline. Or perhaps you are most worried about feeling like a burden on others' emotions, time, or money.

All such questions about the direction of your care ultimately depend on your basic, personal values. They can be reduced to one simple question: "What do I want?" You may want to seek the help of whoever in your own personal support system you think can best help you make the decision. But ultimately, you know your values better than anyone else, so you will make the best decision for yourself.

Deciding About Debbie

The sequence of facts–options–values looks simple on paper—but if life were that simple, I'd probably be out of a job. When we apply these neat principles to complex human beings things usually become clear, if not right away then eventually.

Debbie was the sort of daughter every mother would be proud of. She was a bright, winning twenty-one-year-old—just one year older than my own daughter, I noted at the time. She had been diagnosed with systemic lupus erythematosus seven years ago. Known as "lupus"—Latin for "wolf"—because the common butterfly rash often results in a wolf-like appearance, this disease is sometimes mild and sometimes severe, but it often allows many years of relatively normal existence, with only occasional flare-ups. Debbie's course varied, and during the last few years she had been seen by a number of different doctors in the hospital's clinics. One episode brought Debbie into the hospital with serious kidney disease.

Worried that she might go into acute kidney failure, her team of doctors recommended the standard treatment, a blood transfusion and dialysis. Debbie refused the transfusion, citing her fear of getting AIDS from contaminated blood despite rigorous blood screening programs now in use. She also consistently refused dialysis, but could not articulate why. As the doctors discussed the situation with Debbie, her mother, and Debbie's twenty-four-year-old boyfriend, Jack, they began to understand that Debbie, a seemingly clear-minded young woman, was in the grip of massive denial about her own illness and overwhelmed by fear of its possibly terminal course.

Despite her mother and Jack's insistence on transfusion and dialysis, Debbie steadfastly refused and threatened to "go AMA"—check herself out of the hospital "against medical advice." This state of affairs resulted in the message I had received that morning: Could I come for an ethics consultation, ASAP?

The caregivers were enormously concerned. Here was a young woman with the potential for many more good years, making a decision that would almost certainly end her life. If she continued to refuse dialysis, she would, at some point, lapse into a coma from uremic poisoning. If her refusal of dialysis was honored, she would likely die.

The care team felt, as did her family, that Debbie's fear and denial were keeping her from rationally considering her options. The choice was so clear to her caregivers and family; they worried she was not capable of making this decision if she could not truly weigh the risks and benefits of treatment versus death. They also felt that the prednisone steroids they had given her to relieve her immediate symptoms, a medication that can cause euphoric side effects, may have made her underestimate the gravity of her medical situation.

The physicians argued that Debbie, while eminently sane and capable in the rest of her life, was simply blocked on the emotionally charged subject of her disease. How, they asked, could we decide that a person so critically unable to consider the issues was capable of making a meaningful decision?

Twenty years ago, doctors had a simple solution: they would have let a patient like Debbie fall into a coma from kidney failure; then, when she could no longer resist, they would have gone ahead and treated her. But modern doctrine of informed consent and our current notions of a patient's right to refuse care are based on the idea that patients have the right to decide what will happen to them. Perhaps, although she didn't put it into words, Debbie had made what for her was a reasonable decision that she could not face what lay ahead, the stresses and anxieties of continued treatment, and the risks and pain of dialysis as she understood them. In that case, she would be well within her rights to refuse care she viewed as burdensome, however much her doctors might disagree. A person's decision, even one that seems idiosyncratic and at odds with what most people would want, may be the proper decision for that person at that time.

As a society, we have also grown more wary of the atrocities of forced treatment or treatment by trickery. To treat Debbie against her will would have meant a gruesome scene in which she would be forcibly restrained, sedated, and tied to a bed to administer her transfusion and dialysis. That would cause enormous stress for everybody—Debbie and her family, the staff of nurses, doctors, and hospital caregivers—and with a determined patient it simply won't work. Yet the idea of letting this beautiful young woman die needlessly was equally unpalatable. A first-year resident summed up our dilemma: "Sure she has a right to decide, but I don't want her rotting with her rights on."

Debbie raised a complex series of ethical and legal conundrums for the care team. Do they best help the Debbies of the world by allowing them to refuse when they may not be able to grasp their situation, or do they impose what they "know" is best? For us to honor a refusal that is not a considered, thoughtful reflection of the risks and benefits may mean abandoning a patient to an untimely, unwanted, and unnecessary death. Yet don't people have the right to refuse, no matter the consequences?

Our discussion, like most discussions of capacity, swung between the poles of autonomy and protection: would we err more by imposing treatment that she had specifically refused, or by respecting her irrational refusal of the care she so clearly needed? An older doctor asked why Debbie alone should decide what was best for her. "She's young, just barely out of adolescence. Don't the wishes of a loving family and boyfriend carry some weight?" A first-year resident answered him: "Don't we endanger all of us if we allow institutions to restrain and treat people against their will?"

Debbie presented a tricky combination of factors: her basic medical picture was complex and her personality problems rendered her a less-than-ideal advocate for her own interests and rights. Lupus affects patients in vastly different ways. It can attack various organ systems in many ways on many different timetables. Going back to the basic decision-making pathway of facts-options-values, this meant that the first step, establishing the medical information about her condition, was very difficult. The second step, establishing options, didn't seem possible for Debbie. She was so overwhelmed by fear and denial she could not even hear the information presented—let alone ask relevant questions. This is exactly the sort of dilemma that I, and the care teams I work with, face every day.

Like Debbie, patients are not always ready to contemplate the alternatives (and their doctors may not have prepared them well to do so). When that happens, many doctors may simply step away from the patient and turn elsewhere for a decision. This might have happened in Debbie's case, as her doctors might have discreetly turned to her mother for the decision to permit the dialysis.

We were not about to do this, however, for several reasons. Legally, Debbie had every right to make the decision. She was twenty-one years old, and no judge had explicitly stripped her of that right. Practically, if we began to deprive Debbie of her rights because we didn't agree with her decision, then when and how could we reinstate her as the appropriate decider? When do you decide to give this young woman back control over her life and its decisions? But the most important reason was a matter of ethics. We all knew in our hearts that, at some point in the future, forgoing dialysis might be the right decision for her. We all knew of cases of young people on dialysis who cannot endure a life tethered to machines. For some, the pain and confinement prove overwhelming; a few actually decide to terminate care. Debbie might turn out to be one such person; we simply didn't know enough yet—nor, we suspected, did she.

For most patients with chronic illness, decisions don't usually have to be made under emergency conditions; we rely on experience over time to provide the basis for deciding whether to live or accept death. Conceivably, there might come a time in the future, if Debbie's lupus progressed and if dialysis proved difficult for her to tolerate, when we could understand, and even support, a decision to forgo care. But the doctor's role is to help the patient navigate through the medical shoals of life until she can reach a real and valid decision. We wanted to support her, to help her analyze her options and values so she could reach a conclusion that made sense in the context of her life. The question we faced was how best to do that.

It was a second-year intern, a young man only six years older than Debbie, who helped break the logjam. "I think we're asking the wrong question," he observed. "Here we have a twenty-one-year-old woman. She's young, sick, and obviously very, very scared." He pointed out that Debbie was a generalized clinic patient with no private doctor. That meant that no one care provider had earned her trust, had connected with her sufficiently to help alleviate her fears. "Maybe the question isn't her competence, but ours." He smiled. "Maybe we haven't provided the right support."

He was right. As so often happens, a refusal of care may reflect poor communication or lack of a trusting relationship rather than a real desire to refuse. To frame this as an issue of capacity—where we would make an on-off decision about Debbie's ability to decide—was precisely the wrong step, the sort of thing that happens in hospitals all the time. These questions could become the first steps in a process of ignoring her wishes and subjugating this strong-willed young woman.

Seeing Debbie only as a case of "impaired" decisional capacity was to create a smoke screen that obscured what was really happening—or more to the point, what wasn't happening: no one had stepped in to create a strong doctor-patient bond. Disempowering Debbie would have been the wrong thing for her and for her doctors. It could easily have broken her will and undercut later attempts to engage her in the fight to conquer her disease. To the young doctors in training, it would have sent precisely the wrong message about caring for patients: that their job was to impose their superior medical knowledge and judgment on the patient. As the discussion moved in this more fruitful direction the nurses and doctors in the room agreed to change their approach.

The first step was to assign her one consistent nurse-and-doctor team with whom she could establish a rapport and meet on her own terms. By taking the time to build a trusting human relationship, we felt, everybody might win. If, after calm and consistent reaching out, Debbie still refused, perhaps we would all be better able to understand her refusal, to divine Debbie's deepest concerns and values and to help her act in accordance with them.

Five weeks later, when I was called back to the unit for our regular teaching rounds, I learned that Debbie did eventually agree to trust her health-care team and begin dialysis. In Debbie's case, getting to know her doctors and nurses made the difference, giving her the support necessary to make that leap of faith into medical care that seemed unknown and terrifying. Helping patients to exercise their right to make decisions is one of the most difficult and time-consuming tasks of the doctors, nurses, and social workers who work with the patient.

It may not happen automatically, for people are not necessarily equipped with the intellectual resources and skills they need to make tough decisions about their own medical care. Some, especially adolescents and postadolescents like Debbie, may lack life experience with confronting hard decisions. They may also be immature, still clinging to thoughts of immortality that pervade the thinking of children and adolescents. Others, some elderly for example, may abdicate the central role in their own decisions to their children and grandchildren.

Many patients, overwhelmed by fear and denial as Debbie was, need help framing questions, absorbing information, and considering consequences. Helping them is as much a part of the job of the modern doctor or nurse as is giving injections and taking blood pressure. More and more, caregivers are willing to engage in the discussions that are a necessary precondition to delivering care.

The three-step pathway of facts-options-values can help both patients and doctors sort these issues out. Over a decade and a half of this work, I have found that most complex medical problems lend themselves to this analysis. These three steps form building blocks all of us can use to exercise our right to make decisions about our own care. More important, they provide the best chance possible to make sure that what we want to have happen, does.

The Four Circles of Decisions

The three-step facts-options-values path concerns the "how" of decisions, but equally important is the "who." Every single medical decision, whether to give an aspirin or to save a life, must be made by somebody. Ideally, as we have noted, it will be made by the person most intimately involved—the one to whom it is happening. It will be made with that patient's fully informed consideration, after supportive discussion with loved ones and friends.

Very often, however, it is made by someone else—spouse, family, physician—or a group of those people, acting on behalf of the patient. Sometimes they act with the patient's prior direction, and sometimes they find themselves struggling to do what is right without explicit authorization. At other times, decisions are made by a guardian or conservator formally appointed by a court, or by a judge directly. Each of these scenarios raises different questions and concerns. Together, they give us an opportunity to discuss what I call the four concentric circles of consent.

The First Circle: The Patient

At the very center, in the innermost circle, is the patient. This circle is ground zero for all medical decisions as established by a landmark legal decision in 1914. In his opinion, New York Judge Benjamin Cardozo wrote: "Every human being of adult years and sound mind shall have the right to determine what should be done with his own body." There is today widespread consensus in law, ethics, and medicine that this is where we ideally want decisions to be made. Reflecting that consensus, the law in every state today recognizes that if a person is capable of making decisions, and if he or she has been provided with information necessary to do so, we need go no further: medically, legally, and ethically, the decision belongs to that individual.

Having that right, of course, doesn't mean you will be forced to make a decision if you truly do not want to. When Mrs. Quayley, who has always depended on her daughter for everything, says "let my daughter decide," she means it and deserves to have that wish respected. I often tell my medical students that you "can't drag someone kicking and screaming into autonomy." Capable people tend to face medical decisions in much the same way they face other major life decisions.

The key word here is "capable," which means different things to different people. In the view of the law, "competence" to decide depends on age. Upon reaching majority (formerly twenty-one years of age, now eighteen), you are presumed by our society to be an adult who can make your own decisions about your life, and our laws reflect that. Having watched one child negotiate majority, I can say confidently that turning eighteen portends no magic vault into wisdom. But this notion of "competence" is simply a useful convention, an artifact of a legal system created by the need to draw an arbitrary line somewhere. It has nothing to do with any one individual's true capacity, judgment, or maturity. Indeed, it can only be changed or removed by a judge after an adversary argument and an examination of the relevant evidence—which rarely happens. As a result, many people who are clearly "not playing with a full deck" have never been judicially declared incompetent.

More and more often state laws let people specifically appoint others to make medical decisions without a judge determining incompetence. In New York, for example, family members and others can now decide about DNR orders when a patient is clearly no longer able to decide. Another New York law—the Health Care Proxy Law—permits a person to designate another to decide for her when she can no longer consider options for care. Both of these statutes to empower surrogates don't require a judge's decision. Rather, they require a physician to determine that the patient is not capable of choosing and then let someone else—either someone appointed by the patient or someone designated by the statute—decide in her stead. These legal tools affect only decisions of limited scope—in no other area of a person's life except the medical decision at hand— and apply only when people are incapable of deciding about their care. In such cases, caregivers must then do the best they can, identifying the next best person to decide. Laws like this are very much the way of the future; if your state doesn't have such a law now, the likelihood is that it soon will.

This is helpful, because in the real world of hospitals decisions about capacity are painted in many shades of gray, reflecting the wide spectrum of capacity that real people exhibit. That is why ethicists distinguish between the legal term "competence"—a term for the legislatures and the courts—and an altogether more subtle notion we term "decisional capacity." It is this capacity that physicians are increasingly called upon to measure.

Decisional capacity looks not at how old you are, but at whether you are, in fact, capable of deciding about a particular question at a particular time. This judgment about capacity is an appropriate medical judgment—that is, a judgment made by those caregivers who know you the best over the longest time—and care providers make it all the time. In a hospital setting, having decisional capacity means that a person can:

1. Understand enough to appreciate the alternatives and options, the risks and benefits of the decision, and to evaluate the medical information that is given her. Her capacities of reason and deliberation must be appropriate to the particular choice about medical care that she faces.

2. Process that information according to a personal framework of values and preferences, such as his quality-of-life wishes, the nature of his closest relationships, familial and religious beliefs—whatever elements mean something to that person.

3. Communicate her decision. A stroke victim may have severe aphasia, leaving her perfectly able to understand, but unable to communicate. Practically, a person is not decisionally capable unless she can express her wishes.

These three elements appear neat and clean on paper, but deciding if a person is decisionally capable is never simple. Remember, "principles are tidy but patients are messy." In many hospitals, if your decisional capacity is questioned—usually when you refuse care—hospital protocols may require a psychiatric consult. Most of these psychiatrists are able and well trained, but any short visit or exam risks isolating a slice of the whole that can be misleading.

The standard twenty-minute "hit and run" psychiatric consultation often makes for bad decisions—in several ways. First, any doctor who visits at 4:00 P.M. may have little idea what you are like at 9:00 A.M., or even at noon. Anyone who has ever had the flu knows that the symptoms of illness wax and wane over the course of a day. You might be decisionally capable in the morning, but later be running a high fever and not seem at all *compos mentis* during the twenty-minute fly-by of the expert psychiatrist in late afternoon.

Instead, decisional capacity is best determined in consultation with those who interact, know, and care for the person over time. This may include nurses and, in teaching hospitals, medical students. Because whether a person falls within the innermost circle of the capable decider is so subtle a decision, and one with such far-reaching consequences, it deserves to be made correctly. If you or someone you love find yourself involved in such a situation, it is important that you make sure those who know the situation are included in the decision process.

Decisions about capacity are some of the most difficult and subtle ones we face on our consulting service. Edna was a delightful, charming eighty-five-year-old woman who had lived in a nearby nursing home for the eleven years since her husband had died. She was alert and oriented, socially appropriate, in fact quite affable. Indeed, she loved nothing more than to reminisce about her long life spent around the world. However, she also suffered from a serious neurological disability where her long-term memory remained intact but she was no longer able to store more recent, short-term memories. The result was that what you saw was definitely not what you got. She was what we call an "articulate but demented" patient: appearing reasonably intact at first glance, but in fact substantially confused and disoriented. Yet for the most part, her condition didn't hinder her much; the staff took care of her well, and she lived her days in a pleasant reverie of yesteryear and in the lively enjoyment of the present.

In her eighty-sixth year, two things changed for Edna: her kidneys started to fail, indicating that regular dialysis would soon be necessary, and she found a wonderful friend in the home, an eighty-nine-year-old resident she termed "my boyfriend" and who returned her affections warmly. Now, in the past month, she had clearly come to the brink of kidney failure, and would soon require dialysis to rid her body of the toxins her kidneys could not. Without dialysis, she could descend into a uremic coma, and die. Unfortunately, this was where things got sticky.

In conversations with her doctor, Edna appeared to understand her medical status perfectly, agreeing to a care plan in a seemingly rational and appropriate way. But within twenty minutes or so, she had forgotten the entire conversation. When the attendants came to transport her to dialysis, she protested vehemently that she didn't want to leave her new boyfriend in the nursing home. This went on for a few days, a steady cycle of consenting, forgetting, then refusing before we could put the plan into effect. As her condition worsened, her doctors were caught, as they saw it, between honoring her consent to save her life and honoring her refusal to save her autonomy.

This charming woman posed a classic capacity dilemma: Was Edna a capable decider? If so, which Edna should we heed? The one who consented or the one who forgot giving that consent? On what basis could we say one Edna was capable of deciding but the other Edna was not?

"Look," said her primary doctor, exasperated, "she's with it during our actual conversation. In those moments, she seems clearly able to weigh the risks and benefits. That means hers is an informed consent, and one we should honor. If you ask me, her decision-making machinery itself is intact—it's her memory machinery that's damaged. Can't we do her remembering for her?" A psychiatric colleague argued that wasn't the only "moment" that counted: "I think that's meaningless. Her memory deficits ensure that whenever we attempt care, in that moment it feels to her coercive, against her wishes to stay put."

The staff grappled with the issue. Was there some way to create an amalgam of the two Ednas? Essentially she was a vital, warm, outgoing individual who loved parties and dancing and her new relationship with her boyfriend. She would not refuse, they felt, if she understood her refusal would compromise her health, or shorten her good life with him. Indeed, they felt that part of what was going on was that she was such a life-affirming person that even a visit for dialysis seemed a waste of time. How could they hope to reconcile the two Ednas?

I pointed out that Edna posed less an ethical dilemma than a practical management problem. When Edna was informed and comprehending, she consistently consented to the dialysis. She was not refusing care, but had merely forgotten the discussion and the reasons for her consent. Could we not somehow prolong her comprehension long enough to treat her?

Her nursing home, a caring and compassionate place, did several things. First, nurses wrote up on a posterboard in her room a brief history of her medical problem and its solution. That way, her decision and condition were always there for her to refer to and help her remember. Second, they scheduled the transfer for dialysis directly following the discussion. Finally, a staff nurse stayed with Edna during the ride to the hospital, the dialysis treatment, and the trip home, to continuously remind Edna of what was happening, and calm her fears. The staff hoped that after a while this pattern would become part of her recoverable memory. If, eventually, her visits grew more frequent, requiring a larger share of precious staff time, they planned to look for a volunteer from a local church group to assist Edna.

Without clear capacity, there can be no informed consent in this first circle of the patient-as–decider. But being a capable decider depends, in part, on the decision itself. Someone may be perfectly capable of deciding whether to have fish or chicken for lunch, yet not be capable of balancing the risks and benefits of hip surgery against those of conservative management of a hip fracture. The capacity necessary to decide varies with the complexity of the decision and the risks attached.

That is why most ethicists tend not to talk about capacity as a global matter, but rather about "decision-specific capacity":

does this patient have enough ability at this time, given these circumstances, to make this decision? Are the risks within her mental, emotional, and psychological capacity to grasp at this point? If the answer is yes, if the patient is indeed capable, then the decision stays where it belongs—in the first circle of patient-as-decider. Framing the question this way lets us give individuals as much freedom and power as possible, while not abandoning them in the face of complex and risky decisions that they could clearly never comprehend or usefully contemplate. My favorite example of decision-specific capacity came from a famous case where an old woman refused treatment to save her gangrenous feet, steadfastly maintaining that "I'll be just fine." Without surgery, the doctors knew her gangrene would likely kill her. A psychiatrist found her perfectly rational about other aspects of her life, seemingly capable of weighing risks and benefits on other issues. But on the subject of her now-black feet, she could hear no argument. She was, in the psychiatrist's words, "psychotic with respect to her feet."

The concept of decision-specific capacity also helps explain why consenting to care is treated differently than refusing care. If the consent entails only minor risks, while the refusal courts great risk or even death, it makes some sense that caregivers weigh them differently. Because, when the stakes are so high, one wants to be really certain that it is actually the patient's values speaking, not some side effect of illness, medication, or incapacity.

Keeping decisions in the first circle is rarely easy, but ideally, that is where all decisions should be made and should stop, for everybody concerned. But often in advanced illness, the patient is incapable of deciding.

In that case, we move to the next widest circle to bring in the next level of decider. If, ideally, the patient has planned ahead of time and has executed what we term an "advance directive," this next circle merely extends the patient's own autonomy and choice beyond the point when he is incapacitated. Moving one step further outward, we come to the second circle.

The Second Circle: Advance Directives

The move from the first to second circle is the move from choosing in the moment to choosing in advance. Sometimes, a patient is simply not capable of deciding when a decision is required. What then? Suppose a person is gravely injured, comatose, or in a permanent or persistent vegetative state, or so severely and irreversibly demented that he can no longer consider and choose among options. Does he then completely forfeit his right to make decisions simply because he cannot participate in them at a particular time? Or is it precisely at such times, when we are totally without personal control, that we most cherish our ability to determine what happens to us? Don't we then have the right to ensure that our care will be managed as we want?

These questions have grown particularly critical with the advent of new technologies like respirators, which can prolong the period when we are alive but incapable of deciding about our care. During the 1970s and '80s more and more people had the experience of watching those they loved die slowly under agonizing conditions, without basic calm and dignity. To help prevent that, a group called Concern for Dying was formed in 1978. Among its goals, it sought to provide legal tools people could use to indicate preferences beyond their own personal ability to do so—what we term "advance directives." Over the last dozen years, they and others like the Society for the Right to Die (now merged with Concern for Dying and called Choice In Dying, Inc.—the national council for the right to die) have helped develop and pioneer two different ways to do that: living wills and health-care decision proxies—also known as "durable powers of attorney (DPA) for health-care decision making," or a "health-care agent." They are the foundation of our second circle.

These documents and the powers they offer extend your autonomy beyond that point when you can exercise your judgment. You execute them when you are capable of making health-care decisions, but they only take effect if and when you become incapacitated. That is why this second circle lies in the shadow of the first, for it is created by your conscious action and explicit behavior. If we have left the first circle where the patient herself decides, the next best way to decide is under her guidance, through a living will or durable power of attorney. When agents in the second circle can simply carry out the directions given by the individual or act as they think the patient would want, it makes everything easier for all involved.

Properly used, these two legal tools are your best messengers to carry your wishes from the first circle to the second. Both of these documents extend your choice in different ways, and both can be helpful to caregivers. But each also has its own advantages and limitations, as we will see in specific detail later on. In combination or separately, a living will and a DPA are the best tools to make sure your wishes are heeded if you cannot speak for yourself.

Chapter 12 gives extensive, concrete information on both living wills and DPA's. In that chapter, I've constructed a unique four-step process designed to help you maintain control of your health-care decisions and state-by-state information on where you can obtain a form specifically tailored to your own needs. There you will also find a values clarification tool to help you think through what you might indeed want in various medical circumstances. Specific examples of a model proxy and living will can be found in the appendix (pages 375 and 378).

For now, the key fact to remember about living wills and durable powers of attorney is that they only take effect if you can no longer decide. If you remain within the first circle of a capable decider, even if you may have appointed someone through a DPA, he has no power over you, and you can easily change, cancel, or revoke your appointment. You don't have to worry about your appointee coming in to challenge you when you are capable of deciding, because legally these documents are triggered only when you can no longer decide for yourself— only, that is, when matters have shifted to the second circle.

If you have thought and acted in advance, if you have made your wishes clear with a living will and empowered a trusted person to decide with a proxy, the second circle can be humane, orderly, and respectful, a setting where your wishes are heard and respected. But sometimes, if people have not prepared, they unavoidably move into the more difficult ground of the third circle.

The Third Circle: When Others Decide for Us

The move from the second to third circles is the move from personal control to surrogate decider. We enter this circle when physicians judge that a patient no longer has the capacity to decide, and when he has left no living will nor appointed a proxy nor assigned anyone to be a health-care agent. This can happen quickly or gradually; ninety-nine out of one hundred people who are decisionally incapable—whom we clearly recognize as "out of it"—won't have been declared legally incompetent by any court. That is not because they shouldn't be, but because their case has not moved through the legal machinery of lawyers, hearings, and judges that determines legal competence.

As I mentioned, it is the trend in many states to give doctors legal authority to make these limited "competency/capacity" decisions. These are decisions of limited scope, and affect only the medical decision at hand. In such cases, caregivers must then do the best they can, identifying the next best person to decide.

Unfortunately, moving to this third circle sometimes has less to do with the patient's actual capacity than with the physician's discomfort: when doctors are struggling to face patients with bad news or a bleak prognosis, they may prefer going to the family to discuss alternatives—even though the patient is capable of deciding. It is not uncommon to find ourselves in this third circle inappropriately or prematurely, when really the decision belongs back in the first circle.

There is a huge difference between the first circle—where others are there to discuss, confer, and advise—the second circle—where others are designated by the patient or can follow the patient's directives—and this one—where someone not chosen by the patient actually decides. Where in the first circle there was one decider—at least in theory—there are now many, all with their own motives, philosophies, feelings, and ethics. Where in the second circle the lines of authority were clear and usually on paper (although some places like New York recognize oral living wills), in this circle various parties may compete with conflicting claims. Phantoms are most likely to descend into this circle, attempting to influence what happens. Now, absent the patient, is when ethicists know we must be most alert to be certain we are proceeding as much as possible as the patient would want us to. It is in this circle, when things work well, that it will fall to spouses, families, and caregivers to make decisions for the patient.

In about half of the states, family members do actually have this explicit legal authority to decide. In the rest—New York state among them—hospitals usually act as if the closest family member has the legal power to decide, even though that is generally a legal fiction. If hospitals had to deal only with legally empowered surrogates, however, they could lock their doors and fire their staffs. Neither ethical theory nor legal practice has caught up to the reality of modern medical care: the vast majority of patients who are debilitated from illness and cannot make their own decisions have no formally identified surrogate. Even in states with family-surrogate laws, informal surrogates are far more common than are clearly appointed and legally empowered deciders. So, although the family's degree of legal authority varies by state, practically, caregivers behave as though spouses, families, and next of kin have that right—at least for purposes of consenting to care.

When we find ourselves forced to decide for others, there are several different standards we can use to guide us. In descending order of preference, they are "substituted judgment," what we believe the patient would want, based on knowing her, her values, and how she lives her life; and "best interest"— what someone thinks is "best" for her, based on what would be deemed best for any person with similar characteristics in her situation.

Substituted Judgment   When a person's wishes are not clearly evident, or the clearly stated wishes of the patient do not cover her current medical circumstance, we have no choice but to move to "substituted judgment." This standard was originally named by the British courts because it required the agent to "don the mental mantle of the incompetent" and do what he would do—a variation of standing in someone else's shoes.

Substituted judgment relies on our knowledge of the particular individual involved. Given all we know about this person, we try to answer the question: "What would she want me to do knowing all I know about her?" Our answer comes from our global sense of who this person is and how she would decide. It begins with an effort to understand the patient's values and anchor our own decision in them. For if she has a value system that could affect this decision, she has the right to have it respected.

We bring to bear our whole knowledge of and history with this individual person. How has she lived her life? What is important to her? How has she behaved? What gives her pleasure? What does she like and not like? Is she a deeply religious person who lived by the dictates of faith?

Sometimes, this standard of substituted judgment requires us to extend what we know, reasoning by analogy. We may not know exactly how Mama would have felt, say, about dialysis, but we do know that she was always fiercely independent, and self-reliance was an important value for her. She was proud of having worked her whole life and helped to support the family, she liked to travel alone, and she was a terrible patient. In addition, when an old friend of hers was on a ventilator, she had adamantly stated, "Don't let that ever happen to me." Because dialysis has certain features in common with a ventilator, and based on what we know about her, we can infer that this is not a course she would want. If, on the other hand, we knew she was a devout Orthodox Jew, that might lead us in a different direction.

Once a surrogate is selected, the hospital must heed her decisions. Usually they cannot, nor should they, pick and choose among the surrogate's decisions according to their standards of care. Just as patients have the right to make wrong decisions, their surrogates—either legally or informally recognized—may make decisions with which the hospital staff disagrees. Only in certain specific instances is the hospital staff obligated to contest such decisions: if they seem blatantly wrong, imperil the life or health of the patient, are ethically unacceptable to the care team, or seem in conflict with the interests of the patient—the niece who wishes to allow her aged uncle to die prematurely so she will inherit his estate, for example.

But what if you are the family member called to act as surrogate and you are in fact concerned, involved, and loving? In that case, how should you go about making the decision? What factors might you want to consider? The most solid foundation for substituted judgment is your knowledge of the patient's likes, dislikes, and patterns of preference. These are the basis for projecting choice.

Best Interest Sometimes, unfortunately, we cannot meet even the standard of substituted judgment. We may know nothing about the person at all. This happens frequently in a hospital, when physicians find themselves making decisions for an unconscious or incapacitated John or Jane Doe—a patient who cannot decide, and is completely unknown to them. The only time this happens in families is when the patient is a newborn or child with no history of making, let alone expressing, an autonomous choice. In such cases, with no history on which to base substituted judgment, indeed with no "judgment" to substitute for, we are left to fall back on the weakest ethical standard, known as "best interest."

The "best interest" standard assumes we know nothing of this particular person, but is based on our knowledge of the particulars of the situation. Here we ask: "What is really in the interest of this patient?" Not what would this patient want, but what would any patient, in the circumstances of this patient, want?

Our decision must ultimately rest in a rational weighing of the benefits and burdens of care itself. This idea of weighing benefits and burdens has its roots in Catholic theology, where moral theologians held that care that has no benefit and imposes burdens of suffering is not morally mandatory. As usual, the hard part is applying these ideas to real life.

Should we consider care a "benefit" only if it relieves suffering or preserves—brings a person back to—a prior level of functioning, or allows the person to experience pleasure or satisfaction? What if it does none of these things—if it imposes restrictions on the patient, causes or increases pain or discomfort with no clear gain? What if the discomfort and suffering are of short duration, which we hope will be followed by pleasure? We might look at this person's care now, and see that she is clearly suffering: although in a coma she moans and kicks each time she gets dialysis. Even knowing nothing of her personal value system, we can objectively see that she is in distress. We could, therefore, judge care to be a burden, not a benefit.

Some would argue that life, however attenuated—even the

mere maintenance of organ function—is the greatest of all possible benefits. To these people, comparison of benefit and burden is irrelevant, for the sanctity of life is absolute. Others feel strongly that it is sentient or cognitive existence, the ability to be aware of one's surroundings and relate to others, that matters. If the person cannot be helped, brought back to a relational state, they argue, there is no need to prolong care.

All of this comes down to our own beliefs. By necessity, if we have come to the point of invoking "best interest" in our decisions, we are relying on some notion of a generic person. We may also be relying on the chimera of what a "reasonable person" would want and our own idiosyncratic sense of right and values, the personal definitions of benefit and burden we ourselves would use. But that is not a juncture to come to lightly, for it means we know nothing of the patient's or family's wishes or worldview. Ethically and legally, we are on the thinnest ice.

But whether we are dealing with substituted judgment, best interest, or some unified combination of them, we are still in the third circle. For all its complexities—for all the doctors and nurses and consultations and principles being argued—what happens here is still largely informal. For all its public nature, for all our careful adherence to the decision-making process of facts leading to options leading to principles, the third circle is largely an informal group of people who come together in the hospital to define the issues, clarify roles and rights, and, ideally, to do the right thing. But sometimes even this third circle is not enough, and the complexity of competing interests moves the decision one step further, into the fourth, and final, circle.

The Fourth Circle: Courts and Bureaucrats

The fourth circle is the arena of last resort, where our society has decreed that we go when the patient may be incapacitated, where there is no clear advance directive, and where it is not clear who should make the decision and on what standard it should be based. In this circle, decisions are no longer made within the health-care system by a coalition of people working informally. Now deciders are formally designated and empowered by legal process in a court of law, far removed from the values and data of the medical system. This formal, legal mechanism may appoint a guardian or a conservator, someone in your family whom you do not like, trust, or want to decide for you, even a complete stranger who has never even met you. In some cases, a judge who has never even spoken with you will take on the responsibility of making decisions about your care, life, and death. These legal players may have only the sketchiest understanding of the medical issues involved, may have never seen what the patient is suffering, and may base their decisions on a brief legal hearing.

Sometimes cases find their way to court when family deciders disagree, and the hospital is forced to choose among them. Hospital administrators know that rejected surrogates are likely to be a constant irritant to the care team and to take things to court if things do not proceed to their liking. They also know a judge's ruling protects them from the anger of the loser.

Unfortunately, judges bring differing degrees of skill to the enterprise. Yet once a specific judgment on someone's competence is made by a court, the patient can lose a wide range of rights to control his care, his life, and his property. This is why the fourth circle can be the worst of all possible worlds, in which the full power of the legal system to enforce its wishes is brought to bear at the greatest distance from the wishes of the person in the bed.

When that happens, as it did to Herbert Buriel, it can be a nightmare. Herbert was an eighty-eight-year-old man, slightly confused, forgetful, and disoriented. He had been in a nursing home for three years, placed there when he became too difficult for his family to manage at home. From all reports, he was a nasty, disagreeable sort at the best of times, and had not improved with age. For a year or so, he had been receiving kidney dialysis in various outpatient centers, but had grown increasingly fractious and disruptive. Finally, all of the outpatient units refused to treat him and he was brought into the hospital. He was facing imminent uremic coma and was in urgent need of dialysis to save his life.

But at this juncture, he dug in his heels, categorically refusing to be dialyzed. Although his verbal communications were less than clear, his actions spoke loudly: he regularly fought off his nurses and doctors, ripping out his dialysis and intravenous tubes, and generally did his best to thwart care. The week before, he had torn out an intravenous needle and almost bled to death.

The options were stark: objectively, he was not doing well on dialysis and was experiencing enormous pain and discomfort. If the dialysis team didn't dialyze him, he would slip into a coma and die of uremic poisoning in a matter of weeks. But to do so would require the nurses to "snow and snug" him—sedating, then bodily restraining him for twice-weekly dialysis treatments. As grim a prospect as that would be for Herbert, it would be devastating for his care team. They were tremendously conflicted about feeling like medical thugs, tying down and drugging this patient as he struggled and kicked—all to save a life he didn't seem to want saved.

Stymied, the care team called in risk management, who called the Law and Ethics Consultation team. That afternoon, about a dozen of us met on the dialysis unit: several of the unit's specialist nurses, two physicians who were caring for Herbert, and various members of the hospital's administration staff, including an attorney.

We began, as usual, with the facts about his condition and his prognosis. Seeking to anchor the discussion in his life pattern of wishes and behavior, I asked who else could help us know more about Mr. Buriel. Unfortunately, the primary physician who had treated him for several years was out of town. Mr. Buriel's own family was both uninvolved and divided. In short, nobody in this discussion had a track record with Herbert or his family over time. Clearly, we lacked some important tools.

Given the family's absence and division, risk management was understandably concerned. If the hospital doesn't treat a treatable condition, it, and the responsible physicians, could be sued for negligence. The risk of suit, everyone knew, is especially acute when there is family conflict. Herbert might not want dialysis, but not treating was riskier for the hospital—and the job of the hospital administration, after all, is to avoid that risk. They recommended we go to court for an order to compel care. That way, at least, they knew someone else with proper legal authority would make the hard decision. Other staff members argued that it was wrong not to treat him when treatment would prolong his life and when it was not crystal clear that he was capable of making decisions. Nor did everyone agree that his disagreeable behavior amounted to a clear refusal.

I argued that he should have the right to determine his care—if he was of sound mind. While Herbert was cantankerous and somewhat confused, disoriented, and forgetful, his wishes seemed clear and consistent. He was not telling us in the "appropriate" formal way what he wanted, although he always said, "No, no more." But this feisty old gentleman was speaking with his fists, fighting off doctors and nurses at every turn. When we asked what he was doing, he would occasionally say, "I'm ready to die—I don't want this." In Herbert's own way, as refractory as he was, with whatever capacities he possessed, he knew what he did—and didn't—want. Moreover, he was letting us know it in no uncertain terms, as the many scratches on the nurses' arms could attest. So while his may not have been a rationally expressed decision in the ways we usually hope for, I felt that he was clearly fighting for what he wanted and that his consistency could help us overcome our concerns about his capacity. Sometimes in cases like this the patient is reacting to the discomfort and inconvenience of the treatment. But with

Herbert, the nurses at least were convinced that it was a real refusal of care and an earnest acceptance of death. I argued that we owed it to him to do no less than what he said he wanted.

Besides, our only other option was worse. Was the care team, I asked, prepared to battle him, overpowering and physically restraining him twice a week for the rest of his life? Was that humanely or ethically better? On balance, I argued, it seemed eminently more appropriate to respect what I thought was clear refusal of care.

If we were uncomfortable with that, perhaps there was a middle ground. Since the doctor who knew him for many years would be back soon, we would have more information—maybe even specific information on Herbert's wishes about medical care, which he had expressed before his disabilities worsened. Perhaps we could stall for time to keep the decision within the hospital. If we kept Herbert stable with dialysis until his doctor returned, perhaps we could learn something from his relationship with Herbert and his family.

It was not to be so easy. In this case, risk management prevailed, insisting that, no matter what, this case had to go to court. They argued that there was too much uncertainty—a reasonable argument. We all suspected what the outcome would be. In such dilemmas, it is always more comfortable for a judge to extend rather than curtail life—especially if the person's wishes are subject to interpretation. A judge honors the concept of life and protects the state's interest in life by ordering treatment continued. Like Herbert, those ordered to live are usually powerless to complain. It is hard for any of us to permit death, even more so for a judge. Still, Herbert's nonverbal communications seemed so clear and consistent to me.

That afternoon, at 2:30 P.M., a judge of the state supreme court heard Herbert's case. He ordered the dialysis to continue.

When decisions make it to this fourth circle, out among strangers, you learn never to ask a question unless you are willing to live with any answer you might get; I would have preferred not to live with this answer. Sadly, it is not I, but Herbert, who now has to live with it. Twice a week, he is transferred, under duress, sedation, and restraint, to receive a treatment that I'm quite certain he does not want.

Like most medical ethicists, I believe that the courts are not, by and large, the place for medical-care dilemmas to be settled. They are public arenas, always expensive and often exploitative. They are impersonal and far removed from patients' and families' private values. With so many eyes watching, they may respond to personal and political interests other than the patients'. They are not geared to deal with the issues of medical care, procedure, and prognosis, the subtleties of how life actually works in a hospital. For all of these reasons, courts are not places to entrust your most important health-care decisions if you can possibly avoid it.

Of course, in real life, things never break down easily into clear-cut circles and steps. With flesh-and-blood people in real situations, it is rarely perfectly clear whether someone is capable in general or for this specific decision. It may also be unclear who are the best surrogate deciders, and the basis on which they are deciding. The "case of the imprisoned patient" shows just how complex things get when we try to put principles into practice.

It began as many of my cases do, with a chance meeting in the hospital corridor. On this particular day, it was David Dayton, the nursing supervisor on the floor, who pulled me aside. "We've got a problem, Nancy. Have you heard anything about Mr. Piot?" His concern was evident in his eyes, and I agreed to meet the care team as soon as possible. On returning to my office I found a message from a social worker: "Consultation request re: Mr. Piot." For whatever reason, Mr. Piot had a number of people worried.

Josiah Piot was an eighty-four-year-old retired plumber who had suffered from worsening Alzheimer's disease for a dozen years. His wife, Nette, herself eighty, had devoted her life to caring for her husband since his diagnosis. In the past years she had seen him grow ever more confused, disoriented, and incontinent. As Alzheimer plaques grew in his brain, they interfered with thinking, disrupted his logic, and slowly stripped him of his ability to function socially. The Piots had no children; they had been part of a very large extended family, but all of their close relatives were now dead. For the last three years, Mrs. Piot had lovingly cared for her husband at home, in a more and more lonely existence. She had done it virtually single-handedly, only rarely calling on neighbors for help.

While out walking the previous week, Mr. Piot had doubled over, clutching his chest in pain. Frightened, his wife helped him home and gave him his nitroglycerine pills. He didn't recover—indeed, appeared to worsen—so she called a cab to take them to our emergency room. Not having a regular doctor at our hospital, Mr. Piot was seen by an emergency attending physician, Dr. Ruevens. Tests showed that Mr. Piot's chest pain was a relatively minor event, leaving no long-term heart damage.

But in the two days it took to be sure, hospital personnel had begun to focus on this elderly couple. Dr. Ruevens noted in the medical chart that Mrs. Piot "seemed unsure of the medications her husband was taking," and another time, that she "seemed confused and couldn't always answer my questions." A nurse observed that on Mrs. Piot's daily visits her clothes were neat and clean, but she had not changed them in four days. Might this apparently devoted wife be forgetful or failing? A second-floor nurse observed that she wore sandals, conspicuous in the cool of a New York autumn, and had a dirty-looking bandage on her foot.

The caregivers were concerned that perhaps Mrs. Piot could no longer care for her husband properly. There was clearly nothing acutely wrong with him, and on his second day in the hospital some staff began wondering aloud if he could be better cared for in a nursing home. The mere suggestion made his wife panic: "We have been married for sixty-four years. I have taken care of him full-time for the last five; I know him much better than you do," she argued. On the verge of hysteria, she at one point lashed out: "If you make him go to a nursing home, I will kill myself and him."

After several daily visits and talks with the staff, they reached a compromise: Mr. Piot could go home if she would sign a statement agreeing to get home care. The agreement was written in his chart. Mrs. Piot signed it on Monday and was told to come the next morning to take him home. On Tuesday, she came promptly at eleven o'clock, her new home care attendant in tow, but the social worker could find no discharge order in the chart from the doctor in charge of the case, and nobody on the floor had been informed that Mr. Piot was to leave. Without that order, the staff felt they could not legally release her husband, despite the fact that the chart note stated quite clearly that this was the plan. At this point, Mrs. Piot became completely distraught.

That same afternoon, there was an emergency meeting with the care team: the nursing supervisor, social worker, three floor nurses, a patient representative, and a series of administrators. The social worker spoke first: "I worry she's not up to caring for him; she looks fine but she has a lot of deficits. She's socially appropriate, can relate to other people seeming normal, and she's able to recall things she has done for a long time. But if you try to explain new things—the medications he needs and the schedule—she can't grasp that. Even if you write it down and give it to her in a chart, she gives him too much of his nitroglycerine. She has very compromised short-term memory. I hate to say it, I know she is trying as hard as she can, but I worry that she can't handle the burden of his needs. This man needs a nursing home." The nurses, I noticed, were silent. As to Mr. Piot's wishes, he seemed unable to grasp or discuss what was at stake. He would only say, "Let my wife decide."

I could see why the case troubled the team. Mr. and Mrs. Piot present the mix of incapacity and inability that so often characterizes the reality of hospital care. The team clearly wanted care that would support and extend the life of their failing patient, who could neither speak nor decide for himself. Ethically, we all wanted to do what was best for the patient.

The problem was how to determine just what *was* in his "best interest." Was it better to discharge Mr. Piot to his home, under the care of a loving wife who could perhaps not take care of him adequately, or to discharge him to a nursing home offering care that would be medically more correct but far less loving? In the first case, he might come to physical harm; in the second he would certainly suffer extraordinary loss caused by separation from a loved one who had been part of his life for sixty-four years. Would losing his wife overwhelm whatever good more formal care could provide? Would loneliness and disorientation, which inevitably follow transfer to a nursing home, counterbalance the technical improvement in his medical care?

The nurses and social workers who had talked with Mrs. Piot over the days felt strongly that she was much more confused and debilitated than she appeared. It was not surprising, they said, that she could remember the phone number of the cab company she had called—she had been calling it for years. But when confronted with new information about her husband's care, she became confused and disoriented. As much as it clearly pained the nurses, they felt he should not be released to her care.

Legally, the staff knew they could not discharge Mr. Piot to someplace he didn't want over the objection of his family—at least not without a court order. Nor could they hold him over her objections without a court order—and no court would likely issue such an order given Mrs. Piot's fervent conviction. One nurse halfheartedly suggested we let him go home, then petition the court to get an impartial and objective conservator appointed in preparation for his next admission, which everybody assumed would be merely a matter of time. That wouldn't work, I pointed out: it would require the court to deal in "maybes," and judges do not like hypothetical situations. They must concern themselves with the present. To a judge what matters is whether Mr. and Mrs. Piot together had some sort of joint ability or not.

The social worker had his own concerns. As the caregiver primarily responsible for creating the discharge plan, he is required by state law to ensure that any such plan is "safe." But he also knew that "safety" is relative. A classic study showed that if you take a matched cohort of elderly patients with similar disability, and discharge half back to an abusive home environment and half to a nursing home, those at home live longer than those in nursing homes. Did that make it "safer" in the eyes of the regulators who monitor the law? How safe was it if his wife could not understand or manage his heart problems and worsening Alzheimer's disease?

For Mr. Piot, what was the best plan? Who decides what "best" means? Who, when staff and family disagreed, would determine Mr. Piot's best interest, and the course of his care? When a person of uncertain mental capacity is faced with a choice about care plans and cannot assess the risks of the various options, and if each plan has clear and significant risk, how is the dilemma to be resolved?

In most cases, the first and most important step is always to ask what the patient wants. But what if, as in Mr. Piot's case, it is not clear that he possesses enough thinking ability and judgment to assess the risks involved? Mr. Piot's "spoken choice"—what he said he wanted—was to stay with his wife. But what if that might shorten, or even end, his life. What then?

The ethical dilemma was clear: how could we respect a person's long-held preferences yet not permit him to unknowingly bring harm upon himself? If Mr. Piot could tell us, did we think that he would opt for five years in the sterile safety of a nursing home or for only six months under the loving, if probably inadequate, care of his beloved wife? Some might argue the length of his life should be paramount; others would argue that it is the quality and joy of that time that count. If he could consider that question and give us an answer, there would be no dilemma. Unfortunately, he could not, which left us, strangers all, in the position of making that decision for him. Or maybe it was not our decision at all—maybe it was solely for his wife to decide.

The discussion focused on the ethical issues at stake: Mr. Piot's own capacity to choose his care, and whether his decision was really "autonomous" or "authentic"—considered and consistent with his history. We debated whether we could substitute his wife's judgment or ours, and whether that would be in Mr. Piot's best interest. We discussed his right to make the wrong decision—something most of us do more or less frequently—and whether this right survived his incapacity. Some ethicists, among them my colleague John Arras, argue that the right to be wrong requires a clearly functioning intellect. Once a person's thinking closes down, someone else's judgment should be substituted, or caregivers should be led by a sober and sound assessment of what is in the patient's best interest.

The next question facing us concerned Mrs. Piot: What happens if the obvious next decider has problems that cast doubt on her capacity to decide for someone else? By what right could we allow her to assume these responsibilities? In New York State, no law automatically identifies· and appoints a specific family member as a surrogate decider, without some prior legal document. Here, as in most states without such laws, things are done informally.

In this case, we had no choice among surrogates. Mrs. Piot was the only applicant for the job. Still, we faced questions: was his wife the proper surrogate? What sorts of guidelines or standards of review should we apply to her decisions? Could we both recognize Mrs. Piot as a surrogate yet assure appropriate review of her decisions?

We were now in the third circle, where a surrogate decider acts in the hospital. To reject her outright would have forced the case into the fourth circle where we would seek a formal, court-appointed decision maker. This case exemplified how easily the third circle can shade into the fourth, as the hospital realizes that it cannot discharge its obligations to the patient while following the directions of the informal surrogate.

But the fourth circle, I argued, would not help the Piots. In essence, both husband and wife would be on trial. They would be thrown on the mercy of distant deciders. First, a judge would have to determine that Mr. Piot was incapable. Then, a related judgment would have to be made that his wife was also incapable of managing his care. Only then could the judge appoint a stranger to shape and supervise the case. In New York that might take six months or more.

Having gotten as far as we could, I suggested we invite Mrs. Piot to join us. The nurse ushered in a neatly dressed, white-haired woman, slightly bent over and a bit arthritic.

She began to describe the care she had observed on the floor. "When he soiled himself, nobody cleaned him for twenty minutes. He was uncomfortable and in pain." Her eyes flashed. "At home, I would never make him wait like that. Here you hand him a pill—he can't take a pill by himself." She described the loving care she took with his medications, emptying each capsule into a spoonful of his favorite applesauce, carefully mixing them to hide the taste, feeding it to him a spoonful at a time. She went on to describe the limitations of the hospital: the lack of privacy, the food he couldn't eat, the strangers, the confusing constant rotation of new caregivers.

Her eyes teared as she described how frightened she had been the day Mr. Piot fell sick, described in detail how she got him here, gave the date and the names of the two cab companies she had called. The picture that seemed to emerge was not of a failing woman but of a person overwhelmed by a sudden emergency—as any of us might be—and truly terrified. She told us how excited she had been yesterday when the doctor promised her husband would come home today, how she had put in fresh flowers and the food he liked, and spent all afternoon arranging the home attendant for this morning at eleven o'clock. "Now it is Tuesday." Her voice held a desperate edge: "You say come tomorrow, but you said that yesterday. Tomorrow, people leave for Thanksgiving. Josiah will not be properly tended to until next week." Her words rang with a lifetime of the love they shared. "None of you were born when I married Josiah." She looked around the room. "To you, he is a patient. To me, he is my husband, my heart, and my life. I will never leave him to strangers."

As she finished, we sat silent. It was clear that this extraordinarily brave and eloquent woman was in a desperate fight to save the man she loved. Terrified, eighty years old, completely alone in an unfamiliar place, her last five days had been a blur of physicians in white coats, social workers with their pads and clipboards, a conspiracy of strangers with their rules and their good intentions, all telling her she could not take her husband home. Without any help in the world, she was fighting as hard as she could against this intimidating place. She finally started to sob: "How can you do this? How can you keep him imprisoned like this?"

I heard in her the voice of my own mother-in-law, who had cared for my father-in-law with Alzheimer's totally on her own for years. Like Mrs. Piot, she proudly rejected her children's attempts to hire a home attendant. She spent her days preparing special meals for her husband and then coaxing him to eat. The rhythm of her days was built around meeting his every need. Of course, she was a little foggy sometimes, especially when she was distraught. The one time we had to take my father-in-law to the doctor she came in a torn housedress with old sneakers; the reason, she explained, was that she didn't care how she looked, only that her husband receive the care he needed as soon as possible. I knew that my own mother-in-law was the world's expert on caring for her husband—but if he had ever been hospitalized, I knew just as well, she might have appeared as a frantic and disoriented old lady to the care team. That comparison was sobering, and it lodged in my thoughts as we discussed Mrs. Piot.

Her words helped make our decision easier: Mr. Piot would go home that day, as had been agreed. We could not again subject this courageous woman to broken promises and missed communications without completely violating her trust. Within the hour, the head nurse reached Mr. Piot's physician in his private office, who authorized the floor resident to write a discharge order. Mr. Piot was discharged at 6:00 P.M., seven hours later than his wife had anticipated that morning. But they would spend their Thanksgiving together, as they had for sixty-four years.

This story was not to have a happy ending. Soon after going home, Mrs. Piot fired the home attendant and barred the visiting nurse who managed Mr. Piot's medications. Despite a weekly pill planner setting out the day's medications for a week's span, Mrs. Piot mixed them up, forgetting that the visiting nurse had filled the slots, and rearranging the pills according to her own private scheme. Mr. Piot's case soon came to the attention of a city agency that protects the welfare of dependent elderly people. Within the month, he had another, more serious episode of heart problems due to inadequate medication, and returned to the hospital.

At that point, the care team faced the same dilemma. After much discussion, one of the geriatricians, a physician with thirty years of practice in such matters, gave us his cardinal rule: "It's like baseball. Every patient gets three strikes, then they're out. This lady's had two." The team felt that, while Mrs. Piot remained adamant about taking her husband home, she had clearly been frightened by this second bout. Perhaps, they hoped, this second experience had sufficiently sobered her, so she would recognize her limitations and allow others to assist her in the future. If not, if she failed this time, her husband's welfare meant she would not be given another chance. So it was that the Piots went home; but nobody on the floor thought they had seen the last of them, and the next time a judge would decide.

The three steps and the four circles discussed in this chapter are simply ways to impose some order on the chaos that is medical decision making. As a clinical ethicist, I use these steps and standards as touchstones in every case. These very real decisions always come down to a complex interaction between who decides—the four concentric circles—and how they decide, following the three-step process of facts, options, and values. Together, they can help you to take control.

5

REINVENTING
DEATH

Throughout history, death has been the one universal, and utterly involuntary, human experience. Since one prehistoric man cradled another's shaggy head to ease its final breaths, our species has shared a common quest to stall death as long as possible. To that end, we have employed hope and prayer, incantation and medication—hopeful stratagems to keep the darkness at bay. Yet only in the last fifty years have we actually exerted any measurable effect on the particulars of our passing. Now, armed with electric defibrillators and powerful drugs, commanding resuscitation and respirators, we have taken unprecedented dominion over the timing and technicalities of our own demise.

That power has brought paradox. Having at last gained ground in our age-old campaign to postpone our passing, we have been forced to reexamine the wisdom of that goal. We have learned that sometimes, the only thing worse than dying is living too long. The last two decades has shown us that the very interventions that afford us our final days can pose a burden as well as a benefit, bring as much horror as hope. For millennia, the most natural human impulse in the face of mortality has been to contest and conquer. Within one generation we have found ourselves cooperating with—at times even courting—death.

As a society, we are only now beginning to grasp the enormity of that transformation. In our quest to devise deaths with dignity and comfort, we test our deepest ideals of compassion and mercy. We struggle to know when it is most compassionate and humane simply to let people die. We strive to develop a vocabulary for the task, so unused are we to contemplating, much less discussing, the details of our passing. Most of all, we are just getting used to the idea that we can choose for ourselves—at least some things at some times. It is an idea unprecedented in human history: Whether you strive to grasp every last possible moment of life's span or want your final days and hours to be dignified and painless, you have the right to control your care.

As the enormous popular success of the book *Final Exit* shows, our society is struggling with our understanding of death. More and more, we are coming to accept what other traditions have long known: that death is an integral component of the art of caring for people. This is still not an easy concept for much of Western medicine.

In my work, like that of doctors and nurses, one comes to accept death as a fact of life. At some time in life, all of us stop living—a certainty not to be feared, and sometimes, indeed, to be welcomed. I have seen many patients and families, especially older ones, make their peace with this fact. Facing death—our own or that of a beloved person—is never easy, and is always sad. But taking it in hand, knowing its contours, is an important part of taking control of our final time.

Because we will all meet mortality one day—our parents', our spouse's, our friends', our own—we should appreciate what changes have occurred in medicine's perspective on death and what they mean. We do well to understand the changed face of death, and what decisions it entails. Only then can we be sure that our final days and hours will pass as we want them to.

The Good Death

All of us—no matter our age, faith, or beliefs—harbor a personal vision of our own "good death." If we let ourselves envision the event at all, we may imagine the familiar cinematic conventions of the Good American Death. The scene may occur at home or in a decorous hospital setting. It includes the patient: lucid, composed, hungering for blissful release—and the family, gathered in grief to mourn the passing of a beloved life. The murmurs of sad good-byes, the cadence of quiet tears shroud the scene in dignity.

Cut to real life. In the harsh realities of the modern medical center, such scenes are becoming less and less likely to happen to you, or to those you cherish. According to the American Hospital Association, more than two in three Americans will have a negotiated demise—where patient, family, and physicians must actively decide to stop or limit treatment to allow death to occur. Such decisions are made every minute someplace in an American hospital. Given the odds, if you want an appropriate passing, your own good death, you can't leave it to chance. You must make decisions, not solely about death and dying, but about controlling your life and most intimate options at every stage.

Each of us has our own version of the "good death," but they might include some common themes. You may hope that your final moments will be humane, compassionate, and dignified, your death not prolonged unnecessarily, and your final waking moments be spent with loved ones and consoling caretakers. You may ask that death be quick, merciful, and painless. Many of us hope we will have lived long enough, but not too long. We may hope to reach what the ancient scriptures counted as the fullness of life, numbered in Genesis as 120 years, the time when death comes, not as something terrible, but as the rightful end to life's passage. Some people need most of all to make peace with those people to whom they have to say good-bye. Others prefer death to be sudden, so they have neither to confront nor participate in their own passing. It is my goal, for example, at some appropriately venerable age, to die in my sleep, quickly, without pain or panic. (A friend of mine has his own variation on the theme: he wants to go after age eighty-five, while walking outdoors on a beautiful day, hit on the head by an errant asteroid.)

My husband's father recently died, at his own home and in his own bed, of Alzheimer's disease. In visiting with his mother three days before his father's death, my husband raised the issue of a good death. My mother-in-law had her own definition: "It's a good death when you've done all you can to make the person comfortable, free of pain, and know they're loved. When there is no guilt, that's the good death."

By many of those conventional standards, Joseph could not be said to have had a good death. He was an immensely learned man. A very observant Jew with a Ph.D. in mathematics, he had taught all over the world, and was now a professor at a prestigious university in the Midwest. When he was not thinking about mathematics, he was studying the Talmud, the compendium of Jewish law. In the spring of 1989, at age forty-five, his scholarship had earned him the respect of colleagues around the world. Equally important to Joseph, he and his wife, Sarah, had just borne their second child: their five-year-old, David, now had a baby sister, Nancy. Nancy was not yet six months old when her father became concerned about his persistent cough and weight loss. He went to his doctor, who began a two-week whirlwind of tests that confirmed that Joseph had a virulent form of cancer called adenosarcoma.

Tests showed it had spread widely. Often, in such cases, cancer specialists discourage treatment, for about only one-third of patients get better, while one-third get worse, and a third experience no change whatsoever. Joseph's physicians were straightforward: even with the most aggressive treatment, he would have but a very small chance to survive to see his forty-sixth birthday.

Joseph took charge of his illness from the outset. He plunged into the medical literature to read scores of journal articles on adenosarcoma. When a specialist offered recommendations, he requested the research articles supporting the suggestion, read them himself, and filed them in the laptop computer that traveled everywhere with him. From the first day, he carefully documented his complete history—symptoms and feelings, discussions with doctors, treatment options. With each new consultation, his caregivers received an up-to-that-day printout of his history and research; afterward, Joseph duly recorded their discussion, his options, risks, the newest findings.

He focused the same fervor on his scholarship. In doctors' offices, waiting rooms, at transfusion appointments, even when he was admitted to the hospital, he could be found, furiously tapping on his machine, racing to finish lecture notes, editing a colleague's work, readying yet another learned article for publication. Several months into his illness, he called together a group of scholars and friends to study Jewish law. In doing so he was following traditional Jewish custom, using study of the ancient texts as a form of intellectual and spiritual devotion.

Joseph had his own vision of a good death in mind. He was determined to squeeze every possible moment of living from the time he had. To friends and family, he was unwavering: "Whatever measure of time God allows me, I will live it as fully as I can." Spiritually, Joseph committed himself to living his life as fully and as long as possible, no matter what suffering it might entail. He interpreted Jewish law to say that life is sacred and may only be taken by God, and felt a personal obligation to take whatever measures were available to sustain life as long as possible.

Medically, he wanted everything—absolutely everything—his doctors could provide. Access to treatment was all-important. If he read of a new experimental treatment, he was on the phone asking a specialist about it. If some new, hopeful research protocol might promise to beat back his spreading cancer for even a week, he fought to receive it. His behavior was not desperation, but an utter resolve to fight for anything that could provide even an extra few minutes of the life he held so dear. His battle would continue until three days before he died, when he took one last experimental drug. At this stage, he knew, it would not stop the cancer, but might promise a few drops of increased strength.

As his body deteriorated, he left explicit instructions in a living will as to the extent of care he wanted. Most people think of living wills as a way to limit care, but they can also be used as Joseph did, to state a strong preference for care. The document itself is what ethicists term "value-neutral," and can be used in whatever way the patient wants. For Joseph, that meant, above all, aggressive resuscitation.

On a Thursday in late April, Joseph's heart stopped, and he was given cardiopulmonary resuscitation. Awake afterward, the ventilator tube in his throat preventing speech, he was mentally acute. In a note to his beloved Sarah, he scrawled one word: *Hope.* That one day of alertness after he was resuscitated was vitally important to Joseph and to his family. Although his body was wasted, he was mentally active until the end—just as he had wanted it. That evening, he suffered another arrest, and never regained consciousness before finally dying two weeks later.

Most doctors and hospitals might argue that such an aggressive course was inappropriate for a person at the edge of death. I disagree. An immensely intelligent, deeply religious man, Joseph calculated his odds and took them. His goal was to get as much time as he could—even minutes mattered—and he steadfastly stuck to that decision. Above all else, he wanted to do all he thought required, theologically and personally, to see his life through to its end. Ethically, despite the feelings and judgments of some physicians that it was futile to buy Joseph one more day of dying, they were bound to support those wishes. Until the very moment he lost consciousness, Joseph did not shrink from his deep faith. Sure in his values and deep religious commitment, he administered his own good death, asking only that his physicians and care team give him the most blessed parting gift possible: to let him die his way.

Joseph's case raises the question of whether a patient has the right to demand a certain type of care or intervention that his physicians deem futile. In general, the answer to this question is no—we do not let patients dictate care; rather, we let them choose from an array of options that doctors propose. Usually, a doctor knows what she thinks is the most appropriate treatment, and will state it if asked. But informed consent requires doctors to explain if there are other options, with differing risks, benefits, and degrees of invasiveness, discomfort, or intrusion. But nobody requires a physician to present options she believes are futile or useless.

So why should Joseph have had the option to choose resuscitation in the face of imminent death, when it was clear to all of his doctors that he had only the slimmest chances of surviving for any substantial time? In offering him that option, weren't his physicians compromising their most basic ethical mandate to "do no harm"? In a patient so clearly near death as Joseph was, a "successful" resuscitation would provide at the most days or hours of extended life; such aggressive intervention would also almost certainly prolong his suffering for a most marginal gain.

But Joseph's physician took the notion of patient autonomy very seriously, ultimately respecting that Joseph's values must direct the path of care. The doctors recognized that, for Joseph, the possibility of even one more hour to relate to his family was tremendously meaningful. This is informed consent at its toughest, calling on caregivers to respect the variety and range of individual values in patients. Hard cases like Joseph's demand immense respect for the broadest spectrum of personal choice.

Not all of us would make Joseph's choices; we have different ways of dying, as of living. One who did not was Gina Pallone. Gina first noticed her muscle weakness one weekend afternoon eight years before, during a game of tennis. Soon thereafter she was diagnosed with amyotrophic lateral sclerosis (ALS, Lou Gehrig's disease), and had to close the business she had built doing fine carpentry and cabinetwork in some of Manhattan's most elegant buildings.

For eight years she was in steady decline as the disease relentlessly progressed and her muscle strength and coordination failed. Now, at age forty-two, her creeping paralysis had spread through her whole body, leaving this once-active young woman inert on a bed in the back ward of a chronic-care unit in a large public hospital. Her chest muscles frozen, she could breathe only with a ventilator. Unable to chew or swallow, she was nourished through a gastrostomy tube directly into her stomach. The only vestige of voluntary muscle control left to her was in her eyelids. Yet in the living hell that is this disease, her mind remained utterly intact within her immobile body.

This was her condition in late February when a third-year medical student rotated onto her floor in his first placement in the hospital. Having extra time on his hands, he set up a letter board and worked out a complex series of blink codes with Gina. The first message she blinked out was "Thank you." The second was: "I want to die."

Those four words began a five-month ordeal. The medical student called her attending physician, who called the family. At first her parents and siblings were distraught and divided. Her mother, particularly, could not accept her daughter's decision to die so young. For several weeks they "talked" using the letter board in a tearful series of visits to Gina's bedside. As they did, Gina's mother came to accept that her daughter's helpless locked-in life had become unredeemed torture. Having nothing to look forward to, knowing it could only get worse, she wanted out, and the family sadly agreed.

At this point, two psychiatrists were called in. Using the laborious letter code, they determined that Gina was neither demented nor clinically depressed. It was now mid-April; the original medical student had rotated to another floor of the hospital. During the past six weeks, whenever anyone took the time to communicate with Gina, her wishes had been consistent: she simply did not want to continue life as it was. By legal, ethical, and psychiatric standards, she was perfectly capable of deciding about her medical care. But what that meant in practice was something else. For Gina could do nothing but blink; she needed someone's help to carry out her last wish. People seemed highly uncomfortable with what that might mean.

Gina's case was referred to the hospital administrators, as any complex case might be where a patient or family member wants to choose death—but, in this case, it was an administration within a bureaucracy. The next step was the office of risk management. After review, they bumped it to the legal office, which sat on it for months. Finally, one of the neurologists involved brought Gina's dilemma to the hospital's ethics committee for discussion and analysis. This ethics committee, like most, has three goals: to educate hospital staff, to consult in difficult cases, and to help develop policies to guide caregivers in similar cases. We were not there to make a decision, which properly belongs to patients and families with their physicians, but rather to consider, clarify, analyze, and comment. With Gina, we faced a difficult dilemma: we did not want to facilitate her death if she wasn't certain that she wanted to die. But we wanted above all to help her think through the issues and to respect her clear wishes. It was, we concluded, unethical to subject a patient to the suffering that this sort of continued life presents when her wishes were so clear and consistently opposed to that course.

Despite the commitments of doctors and nurses to support and protect life, Gina presented the conflict between the good of extending life and the good of individual choice. After talking at length with Gina and her family, the ethics committee was unanimous. Gina was capable and hers a considered, albeit hard, decision. The decision to permit her to die was supported by case law and statute, and was ethically principled, as it permitted an autonomous patient to exercise her values in determining care. Four months and one week had passed, and Gina had not wavered in her stated wish to die.

Now the care team faced its own ethical conundrum. Somebody had to act. But who? And how? Emotions ran high; after months of watching her valiant struggle, many members of the care team were now devoted to their brave charge. Some felt very strongly they wanted to be with her when she died; others felt equally strongly they didn't even want to be on the floor. Long discussion ensued about what medications to give her, how to sedate her sufficiently that she would not feel pain as she suffocated. One physician objected that giving her sufficient morphine would have the side effect of depressing her breathing and could hasten her death. Legally, he worried, could he be sued, or charged with murder? Morally, did that violate his professional oath to "do no harm"? Finally her private physician agreed that he would be the one to disconnect the machine. He had resolved that, for him, the goal of heeding her wishes and preventing any more suffering took precedence; once the ventilator was disconnected her illness would take its toll. The family gave their blessing, but finally chose not to be in attendance.

Late one Tuesday afternoon, five months after Gina Pallone had desperately blinked "I want to die," the medical staff who did not want to be present left the floor. She had been moved into a private room that morning where her physician, several nurses, and the medical student now gathered. They had increased her IV morphine to make sure she was comfortable.

As she slept, her doctor gently reduced the pressure of the ventilator. Together, they stood by her bed, holding her hand and singing softly to her as she drifted away. After a few minutes, Gina died peacefully.

Ethically, legally, and medically, we had done our best to heed this helpless woman's wishes. It had taken five months to sort through the concerns and perspectives of all whose philosophies, feelings, and ethics were involved. That, in itself, might seem a travesty. Why did it have to take so long? Why did she have to suffer, immobile and helpless, staring death in the face for almost half a year?

The answer has three parts. First, we want decisions about death to be hard-fought. Before permitting or facilitating a death, all those involved—patient, spouse, family members and loved ones, physicians and nurses—must be absolutely certain why they are doing it. The care team has a professional and ethical obligation to know that this patient's choice is informed, voluntary, and is not a product of a reversible mental illness such as clinical depression. We owed Gina no less than to carefully explore her wishes and history, her reasoning and mood, to understand as fully as we could her request. For how much worse an alternative it would have been if we had to look back and feel we had made a mistake.

Even given that appropriate caution, five months seems much too long a time—and it is. In a very real way, Gina was the victim of a spiral compounded of defensive medicine, the huge rise in malpractice lawsuits, and our nation's fundamental lack of a coherent national health-care policy. To see why, we need to stand back one step.

Even in the best of all possible medical worlds, with no negligence and optimum care, it is an inescapable fact of medical practice that some things simply don't work. Others, even the most seemingly appropriate, unavoidably cause harm. In a more humane system, those facts would be recognized and their victims compensated, so that they would not have to worry about paying for their ongoing care. However, America does not guarantee adequate basic care, so those people who are harmed by medical treatment have no recourse but to turn to the courts to seek monetary damages to mend their shattered bodies and lives. They are, in turn, aided and abetted by law-yers—who argue that it would be foolish for injured patients not to attempt to secure money damages for their injury—and whose own incomes depend on contingency fees won from malpractice awards. Together, this has created a specter of mal-practice that has grossly distorted the practice of good medi-cine. Because of that specter, it took five months of everybody checking and double-checking, passing along and postponing decisions, and consulting their lawyers, to grant Gina's blinked-out request.

The third element prolonging Gina's agony involved the increasing politicization of medical decisions. Gina's case—in-volving a hopelessly handicapped patient, a stated wish to die, the turning off of a ventilator—was precisely the sort of case where doctors must be constantly vigilant to the presence of a Roving Stranger. Like every hospital, this one wanted to avoid a sensational headline that read: "DOCS KILL HELPLESS WOMAN." So the usual standards of cautious discussion and clear documentation become even higher in this case, not only to protect Gina from incorrect or untimely decisions, but to shield the institution from damage to its reputation. That, too, helped create the web of caution and concern in which Gina was snagged for five long months. In the end, we accomplished for this brave young woman what she could not do for herself. No, she never should have had to wait five months; but nobody ever said it was easy to deliver a brave soul by committee.

Gina and Joseph both chose their own version of a good death. The options they faced did not exist fifteen years ago; what options any of us will face fifteen years hence can hardly be imagined. Those developments make it all the more impor-tant that you have a voice in what happens to you. While you might not make the same decisions they did, all of us want to come as close to our personal ideal as possible.

That includes the right, if you are ill and disabled, to choose to die at the point and in the way you want. Whether you wish to be alone or with others, to have everything done or nothing, to be at home, in the hospital, or in a hospice—each of us deserves the chance for our own good death. If you care about these decisions, there are steps to take, and things to know, now.

The New Mortality

Ours will go down as the era that reinvented death. Up until twenty years ago, we all knew death when we saw it: that moment when a person's vital heartbeat and breathing ceased. But the fledgling technology of transplants required us to rethink death. In cases involving massive brain damage, the human being known and loved by family and friends is irretrievable, but organ systems like heart and kidneys can be maintained relatively intact for days or weeks on life-support systems. As the body winds down without the brain's delicate regulation of organ systems and chemistry, these organs will deteriorate until eventually, the heart ceases beating. But by then the eyes, kidneys, liver, bone marrow, and other organs have degenerated and become useless for transplants. So if we were to salvage organs to help other people, we had to rethink what death really meant.

Through the 1960s, groups of physicians, biologists, ethicists, and theologians around the world had begun searching for a solution both philosophically sound and medically practical. Their job was not to *define* death: that was a task of theology, and lay beyond human understanding. Rather, their task was to *determine* its onset. In 1968, new criteria for the determination of death were published by a team of researchers at Harvard Medical School; in that same year, the Twenty-second Congress of the World Medical Assembly adopted a document called the "Declaration of Sydney," dealing with the same issue. These tandem efforts were nothing less than a renegotiation of humanity's age-old compact with mortality.

Since our species emerged, the moment when heartbeat and breathing ceased had forever demarcated the end of life. It was a moment all could recognize and understand; anyone who has seen it knows that it possesses an utter, preternatural finality. Now, recognizing that artificial respirators and other life-sustaining technologies made these classical standards obsolete, both the Harvard team and the Declaration of Sydney moved us away from our intuitive reliance on this clear-cut marker. "No single technical criterion," they wrote, "is entirely satisfactory in the present state of medicine, nor can any one technological procedure be substituted for the overall judgment of the physician." Instead, scientists in both Cambridge and Sydney agreed that the physician's "clinical judgment," supplemented by EEG readings of brain activity, would determine mortality's new perimeter.

Since then, the rules of modern medicine acknowledge that irreversible cessation of all brain function adequately determines death. Recognizing the brain's integration of the body's organ systems, medical science has agreed that when all brain activity in the upper and lower brain stem ceases to be detectable, there is no possibility, short of a miracle, that the person will ever reemerge as a sentient being able to interact with its environment. (Wisely, they were properly reluctant to base public policy on the incidence or prevalence of miracles.) Medically, if two electrocardiograph (EEG) readings twenty-four hours apart show no brain activity, if the person's pupils are fixed, dilated, and unresponsive to light, and there is no corneal reflex or response to sound, then neurologists can attest that it would be unprecedented and biologically impossible for the person to recover.

That, of course, is not what we have traditionally called death. But given the miraculous ability of machines to keep pieces of us functioning, and given our new ability to transplant organs, the mere beating heart or breathing lungs—with mechanical help—no longer suffice to clearly demarcate life. These new rules for determining death, this new compact with mortality, allows the wizardry of transplantation. We are redefining death in the service of greater life, to permit us to take functioning organs from a body. By recognizing a body on life supports as dead we may therefore comfortably remove its organs without fear that we have "killed" the person. We have given hope and life to others, without effacing the line between right and wrong.

It is, of course, much easier to change protocols and statutes than it is to change the feelings of the human heart, so while the medical and clinical questions have been answered, the spiritual and emotional ones remain. We may believe that it makes little sense to keep the heart and lungs pumping artificially when there is no ability to relate to others or experience pleasure, and no prospect that the situation will change. At the point when we are in death's antechamber it is ethically appropriate to discontinue care, at least theoretically. But it is never so easy in real life.

Last month I was called to the cardiac care unit about the care of a woman named Rosalina. Barely twenty-four years old, the daughter of a recently immigrated Italian family, she had been in a devastating car accident the night before. Suspended in a web of life support, she was diagnosed as "brain dead." Medically, that meant that although her body was being suffused with oxygen and blood, her upper and lower brain had ceased to function. Without the support of machines her body would have been still. The requisite two EEG readings showed no brain activity at all over twenty-four hours. There was, quite simply, no Rosalina who could come back. Until recently, without our artificial interventions, she would have been deceased. Now, in such cases, the law in every state recognizes the fact of brain death.

The cruelest part of brain death is that the patients often look intact: they are breathing and rosy-cheeked—yet utterly, permanently, gone. It feels obscenely counterintuitive to call such a person dead. But that was exactly what we were asking this unsophisticated, uncomprehending family to accept: that their beloved daughter was dead, while in the next bed, someone else's daughter, looking outwardly the same, her chest rising and falling like Rosalina's, was uncontestably alive.

Then the senior surgeon arrived to explain Rosalina's status to the family. Rather than simply stating that the patient was dead, he sought permission to disconnect the machines. "Your daughter is dead, but she's being kept alive on machines." I cringed as I heard the words. Dead but alive? What could these poor people be expected to make of that? How does a patient like Rosalina "die" when she is already "dead"? If doctors can't keep it straight, how can families? The doctor's approach to the family was likely determined by his own discomfort with the concept of brain death and by his earlier discussion with the transplant team. He knew that the team would soon ask the family for permission to "harvest" Rosalina's organs. Brain death is also immensely hard for the caregivers who care for the inert body. They must continue to minister to it, checking temperature, taking blood, adjusting various medications, monitoring infections. They do so, not for this patient's sake, but for the next. If there is any possibility whatsoever they will be able to "harvest" organs for another person, death must be exquisitely stage-managed. So the nurses care for the corpse until the last possible moment. When the warm, "breathing" body is disconnected from machines in the ICU, on the way to the operating room, or in it, it is officially pronounced dead by a physician. Only then, when it is certain nobody has "killed" the person, is it wheeled into surgery for the removal of its organs. Of such fine hairs are some deaths now made, and it can create terrible intellectual, physical, and emotional dissonance for all involved. For all of us, the reinvention of death remains an unfinished task.

Brain death is but one of the new, and enormously difficult, concepts we as a society are straining to absorb. We are
only starting to grasp the new and complex issues around death.
And no wonder. Having put our energies into extending and
continuing care, we are far less adept at knowing when to stop
it. We have become the first human generation forced to choose
between confronting death and colluding with it.

From Home to Hospital: Death Among Strangers

The next largest change in death has been its venue. Fifty years
ago, most Americans died at home; today, you have an eighty-
five percent chance of taking your last breath in a hospital—and
the odds are rising. No longer can we count on bidding our
farewells among family, where our nearest and dearest gather
and our familiar values and codes govern. Our partings are far
more likely to occur among strangers with their own priorities
and needs, in situations where institutional, legal, and bureaucratic rules control.

Hospitals clearly provide the most professional and intensive levels of acute medical care. What is less clear is whether
they are necessarily the best place to spend your final days.
They can be the best place to defeat illness, but unfortunately
they may not be the best place to prevent suffering. That is
why, when you check into a hospital, you need to know about
the important trade-offs that occur when you become a patient.

To start with, hospitals are not, by and large, consensual
places. At best, they are benevolent dictatorships, run primarily
for the benefit of their bed-bound subjects (and secondarily for
profit, for teaching, or research). In principle, of course, as a patient you have the right to consent to or refuse care. In practice,
you often won't be asked—you'll be done to. The nurse who
enters your room doesn't ask if you want your temperature
taken; she just pops a thermometer into your mouth. You won't

be asked if you want to be the subject of medical rounds, to receive an IV drip, or a bath—you'll just get them, unless you clearly, consistently, articulately, and loudly refuse, and sometimes even then. Your very presence in that bed, your coming under their authority in the first place, carries with it the assumption of "implied consent"—that you grant the doctors and nurses the right to diagnose and treat you as they see fit, whether this reflects your wishes or not. This is true, despite the fact that the concept of implied consent has no support in ethical theory or law.

Medicine could work no other way. If the staff had to stop and discuss every single act with every single patient, our already overburdened and understaffed hospitals would grind to a halt in about ten minutes. Besides, hospital patients are often simply too sick to enter into prolonged conversations; that is why they are there. We cannot expect them to listen, understand, and make informed judgments about every aspect of their care. (Where this is clearest, in emergency rooms, the law specifically allows doctors to presume consent for whatever procedure they perform when your life or health are in immediate danger.) For those on both sides of the scalpel, most of the time, this arrangement makes sense. Trouble arises, however, when someone—either the patient or a family member—doesn't want the tests, procedures, and treatments being offered. Nine times out of ten, that happens around the end of life.

The second fact is that entering the hospital can change the basic relationship of doctor and patient. When most of us were growing up, and certainly in our parents' day, we were treated by a family doctor who belonged to the community he practiced in. In my home town of Bayport, Long Island, our pediatrician knew us as patients and as people. He would stop by if he saw the house lights on late at night, just to make sure we were all right. (Despite my somewhat ample middle-aged appearance, I was a skinny, allergic, and frequently sick child.)

Our doctor might chat a while over coffee, then head home. In those days, when medical interventions were more limited, the primary-care family physician knew you and your family, knew your values, and most likely shared them.

Today, in many large university teaching-and-research hospitals (termed "tertiary care" hospitals—"primary" being the doctor's office and "secondary" the community hospital) you may not even be able to identify the doctor responsible for you. You will be seen and treated by many physicians; the one who admits you is almost certainly not the same one who takes primary charge of your case. Many of the house staff physicians treating you shift from month to month as rotations change; while there is an overall attending physician on the floor, you may never even meet this person, or you may be unaware of his or her role. To enter the modern hospital is to enter the realm of the specialists, doctors who come see you by the dozens, bringing their expertise in livers or hearts or cancer. Unlike our primary-care doctors who know us when we are well and see our illness in the sweep of our larger life, these experts are strangers, whose focus is a particular pathology. They are not expected to have any connection to the patients, their families, or values; to them, coming in for a fly-by five-minute consultation, the person you think of as Dad is "the esophageal carcinoma in room 4010." So it is that in the modern teaching hospital, where strangers treat strangers, we find ourselves making our most intimate and painful decisions with people whose names we may not know, whom we will likely never see again.

The pace of our hospitals, particularly large tertiary medical centers, guarantees that even when you can determine who your doctor is, he or she may not be easily available to discuss these matters with you or your family. When they come to the hospital is not necessarily when you do. Your meetings may be brief, rushed, and sporadic. You may find yourself debating and discussing matters of life and death on the telephone or in the hallway. You may also simply feel overwhelmed by this place with its white coats, alien procedures, and constant stream of new faces. The atmosphere of the modern hospital can be a remarkably inhuman setting for your most human dramas.

The final important fact about hospitals is that they have a bias to treat you. Whether you are in a "secondary care" local hospital or a tertiary care medical center, the hospital's practitioners have been systematically trained to use, not withhold, their skills. Such is their clear social mandate: ours is not a society that passively puts our oldest, sickest, and feeblest out to drift on ice floes. Our medical culture, like our broader culture, is one of verbs: we act, treat, intervene, do something, make better. If there is even a chance that someone can be made better we expect our designated agents, the ones in the white coats, to intervene at all costs. If doctors are to err in any direction, our society prefers them to err on the side of life.

This interventionist ethos pervades our medical system. Medical education spends years inculcating the view that illness and trauma can be cured. Medical practitioners have historically been paid for what they've done, what procedures they've performed, what interventions they've mastered. Medical technologists invent pacemakers, respirators, and transplant technologies to reverse illness and defy death. Together, we have fashioned a series of systematic, thorough, and powerful incentives to *do something*. We can hardly then be surprised that medical care develops its own momentum toward more and more intervention.

But there comes a time when more is not necessarily better. At some point at the end of every human life we stop living and begin the process of dying. Then, it no longer makes sense to race full-throttle toward ever more massive medical interventions. Rather, wisdom and humanity decree that we reverse the medical juggernaut of greater and greater treatment, to allow something more elemental to occur. Unfortunately, it can be hard to turn around the ship of treatment, to accomplish what my philosopher colleague John Arras terms "stepping off the escalator of care." It is doubly hard in the hospital, because it goes against the institution's very core values. It is this conflict—the hospital's inability to restrain the impulse to intervene—that has given birth to hospices, a place where people go for comfort care without aggressive interventions.

To Treat or Not to Treat?

I die by the help of too many physicians.
—Alexander the Great, 323 B.C.

It is not just our new technologies themselves, but their inappropriate use, that can make modern death so anguished. Each medical advance—ventilators, resuscitation, antibiotics, artificial feeding—can be applied appropriately to save lives, or used mechanically to support a care plan that no longer makes sense. When the natural progress of illness has made the hope of cure obsolete, many people want the hospital to stop functioning as a curative institution and instead direct its efforts solely to care and comfort during the dying process. Data demonstrate that is what most of us would choose.

The hard part, the central ethical issue in dying, is the same one we have confronted before: who makes that decision, based on what standards, in accordance with whose values? It is ethically wrong to withhold or remove life-sustaining interventions when they can be of some help and when the person wants them. Yet we don't want to impose life-sustaining processes when they are not of help and the person doesn't want them. It becomes instantly more complicated when the person can't decide and it falls to others to figure out what he would or might have wanted, or what is best. We cannot allow our machinery and interventions to get the upper hand, making us unnecessarily prolong the indignity, pain, and suffering of the terminal stage.

Recent political horrors have put each of these dangers in

stark relief. In the post-Nazi age, our experience has made us acutely sensitive to the specter of socially condoned euthanasia. We know the morally horrifying and reprehensible consequences for a society that loses its reverence for life. The idea of willfully killing people whose lives are not valued—the infirm, retarded, or old, or any deemed by others to have inferior social worth—is the horror lurking beneath every discussion of these issues. We are properly reluctant to enter that inhuman terrain, so caregivers properly shy away from making any judgments based on the "worth" of a life. That same reluctance is often the engine that powers the spiral of more and more medical care. Nobody wants to withhold care because of a judgment—explicit or implicit—that this life is not valuable, so it is easier to treat, even when such treatment may only prolong suffering. It is a fine but real distinction between the worth of a life—an ethically unacceptable notion—and the quality of that person's life—whether the person is suffering—that we must always take into account.

Balanced against that is an equally horrific specter. Most of us dread ending our days as a futureless corpse kept alive in a web of intravenous tubes and machines. We do not want to share the fate of Nancy Cruzan, curled into a fetal position, permanently vegetative, reduced to a sack of organs on a bed. Such a macabre scene feels to many of us like the grossest violation of our privacy, our dignity and human sanctity. We struggle against its horror for ourselves and for those we love. In such circumstances, many agree the humane thing to do— what many have requested—is to deliver the patient from her bodily prison.

These twin images swirl around our discussions of the end of life. But between those two extremes lies another idea, which turns the question around to reflect what the ancient Greeks meant by euthanasia—originally, "good death." It involves a judgment, not on the abstract notion of the worth of a person's life, but on its subjective quality to that person. It is a decision made by him, not by another. Law cases and commentaries have unanimously agreed that removing care that prevents the underlying illness from causing death is neither assisted suicide nor killing. For a decisionally capable patient it is honoring the patient's refusal of care. For an incapacitated patient it may respect a prior advance directive or end suffering.

Refusals of care must be distinguished from euthanasia and from assisted suicide. Euthanasia is generally used to describe a purposeful act by a doctor to end someone's life. In an assisted suicide, the doctor helps to plan, and the patient acts alone. Some argue that if the major action is carried out by any other party, not the person dying, it should be called euthanasia. The term is used by bioethicists, generally, to discuss the plight of people with an underlying, chronic, or terminal condition who are suffering and whose condition will not on its own end the life. Most argue that euthanasia should not be motivated by transient or treatable depression, nor reflect a transitory whim. It should be a thoughtful, considered taking of control by a person afflicted with grave, usually life-threatening, medical problems accompanied by uncontrollable physical or psychological suffering that needs the help of others to reach its goal. Even then euthanasia is illegal in all states; assisted suicide is illegal in almost all states. In November 1991, the state of Washington rejected a referendum that would make euthanasia legal under certain circumstances.

Despite this vote, surveys demonstrate that when a patient is beyond all hope of recovery and nothing can be of benefit, many people think that it is most humane and appropriate that the person be able to choose to discontinue care and end life—especially when that care is burdensome or painful and the person is suffering—even if discontinuing requires the help of others. The discussion about euthanasia is often confused with discussions about terminating care when the decision can no longer be made by the patient and must be made by others. Most now agree that if the patient is suffering, or if care can no longer help the patient by making him better and permitting him to relate to others, then terminating care should be a readily available option.

But not everybody agrees. The Roving Strangers, for example, remind us that this view is by no means universally shared. But they represent a small, and shrinking, minority. Only 8 percent of Americans categorically oppose laws that would let patients decide about being kept alive through medical treatment. A strong 80 percent of the public frankly approves such laws.

In 1991 the Roper Organization of New York City conducted a poll in California, Oregon, and Washington that was commissioned by the Hemlock Society. Sixty percent of those polled thought that the law should be changed to allow doctors to assist a suffering person to die; 32 percent believed the law should stay as it is; and 8 percent did not know. Yet in Washington the electorate voted no—one more indication of ambivalence.

Clearly, we as a society are undergoing a profound evolution in our attitudes and perspectives about death and dying. Fifteen years ago, a majority (53 percent) of Americans believed that a person with an incurable disease never had the moral right to take her own life. Today, only 41 percent of Americans say that, and a significantly larger percentage, 48 percent, believe we do have that moral right. In cases where a person is suffering great pain and has no hope for improvement, fully 55 percent of us would grant them the right to choose to end their lives.

Such discussions are not directly relevant to medical caregivers, implying as they do the independent action of the individual without help or assistance from a doctor. For many Americans are no longer willing to leave the details of their death to luck or to a deity. For many that prospect is too uncontrolled, terrifying, and personally dangerous.

As our population has aged, polls have documented a clear and consistent shift to allow people the right to take control for themselves. Six in ten people surveyed believe that if they had a terminal disease and were suffering a great deal of pain, they would tell their doctor to stop treatment and permit them to die, and another 13 percent feel such a decision would depend on circumstances.

Behind the numbers is a growing public consensus: that we should have the right to take control of our lives and make our own decisions around the termination of medical care. Such an approach has been tried in the Netherlands, the only country to have extensive experience with euthanasia. The Dutch embarked over a decade ago on a great national experiment, codified not by statute or law, but respected in common custom and the actions of prosecutors, to permit active euthanasia. They take great pains to distinguish euthanasia from homicide by the preexistence of an underlying medical condition or problem, and to make it available only to such people. The Dutch have accepted a rigorous set of circumstances under which euthanasia may be performed:

◆ The patient must repeatedly, explicitly express the desire to die.

◆ The patient's decision must be "well informed, free, and enduring."

◆ The patient must be suffering from "unbearable pain"— mental or physical—with no prospect for relief.

◆ The patient must have refused or exhausted all other options for treatment and care.

◆ At least two physicians must agree that the patient's request is reasonable.

Then, and only then, may a qualified, licensed physician carry out euthanasia. The courts have not, interestingly, required that the patient's condition be terminal. But even more interesting, some commentators report that almost twenty percent of the instances of euthanasia involve incompetent patients who could not possibly qualify under the protocol. It seems that these rules, unique in the world, have created the first open, freely discussed, often-used, and perhaps abused process. Other countries are watching the Dutch experiment closely.

The issue exploded in American headlines in 1990, when Dr. Jack Kervorkian, a retired pathologist from Michigan, used his famed "suicide machine," a device that delivers a lethal but painless dose of intravenous medication in response to a switch thrown by a patient. The patient who did so, Janet Adkins, was a woman in her mid-fifties, still healthy and functioning but reported to be at the very early stages of Alzheimer's disease, who wanted to be spared the indignities and suffering she feared her disease would bring on herself and her family.

I know of no physician willing to justify the use of medicine to terminate a life still so vibrant and productive. But the general public has been much more forgiving: polls at the time showed that 53 percent of Americans at that time supported Dr. Kervorkian's actions, and Janet Adkins's right to avail herself of his lethal machine. Such large numbers attest to deep and understandable fear: if we are suffering or are too confused to manage, we fear becoming unable to control or end care that has become torture for us. From that dreaded specter, Dr. Kervorkian's solution seems to offer a way out.

Ethically, however, it raises a raft of troubling issues. The basic obligation of health-care providers is to save lives, not to take them; that is how we train our healers, and that is what our society wants them to do. Clearly, that is not always possible, and certainly, there are extraordinary circumstances when someone is truly suffering, when she and her doctor know they stand at the edge of life and a physician may be moved by the person's suffering to help her die. It is the rarest of physicians who, when being candid and in confidential conversations, will not admit, sometime along the way, having done just that.

Dr. Timothy Quill, of Rochester, New York, caused a stir when he wrote publicly in the *New England Journal of Medicine* about just such a case, when he provided barbiturates to a woman suffering from terminal, acute leukemia. The case has been described as a medical milestone. The woman was well known to him, and had been his patient for eight years. She was clear, smart, and honest, and seemed to understand her prognosis, the medical options, and their likely outcomes, perfectly. In her view, the 25 percent survival odds medical science could offer her were not worth the months of pain, suffering, the loss of dignity and independence such treatment would necessarily bring. After deep and searching consultation with her husband and teenage son, multiple conversations with her physician and a meeting of her family and physician, she decided to forgo medical treatment for her condition. It was her wish—fervently held, clearly and consistently expressed—that she spend what time she had with her beloved family and friends, and then take control of her dying process when the time came that she could see no quality time, no time without pain, suffering, and indignity, ahead. Dr. Quill's article details how he provided the prescription for barbituates and explained a lethal dose. It is eloquent testimony to the complexities—moral, legal, medical, and spiritual—physicians confront as they try to support their patients' wishes to choose a dignified death from a terminal illness.

The Quill case is being widely seen as an important test of patients' rights to medical help in ending their own lives, a landmark test of the bounds of professional responsibility, compassion, and ethics. Equally important, it brings into public scrutiny and discourse a practice that occurs often and widely, yet has been surrounded by secrecy.

The complexities of such a case are entirely appropriate, for we as a society want this to be an enormously hard decision. Causing death should never become banal. It should be a decision made only in specific circumstances when the patient understands the medical facts or diagnosis and prognosis, and clearly and consistently requests it, in response to that person's overwhelming pain and suffering, when doctors are powerless to alleviate the suffering. Those were indeed the circumstances of Dr. Quill's case, but they were not at all the case with Janet Adkins. For that reason, virtually all physicians—all ethicists—are loath to condone Dr. Kervorkian's lethal actions.

We cannot lose sight of the fact that permitting death in a society like ours raises deep ethical concerns. If we as a society acquiesce in the commonplace termination of life, we have taken a profound moral step away from the sanctity of life. It is no accident that the only place to have indulged in the social experiment of assisted euthanasia is a society like Holland—a racially and economically homogeneous country, where socialized medicine gives everybody access to basic care.

But America is not Holland. We are a pluralistic nation of haves and have-nots, profoundly stratified by class and color, where thirty-seven million people have no health insurance, and tens of millions more go without proper care. So long as we have no universal access to health care, so long as people have to pay for it, so long as we have a fee-for-service system, some people will refuse care for economic reasons and not as a matter of broader personal values. It may seem unnecessary to add that the people who will refuse care will probably be the poor, and the poor are disproportionately women and minorities.

In this society, allowing physicians to help people end their lives has a real danger. To permit active euthanasia under our health-care system would be to make physicians the "executioners" or "enforcers" of our society's inequitable distribution of resources and unfair health-care policy. When people must confront a choice between staying alive and driving their whole family into poverty and homelessness; where, already, people routinely don't seek care or refuse it because of economics; where we view health care as a privilege and not a right, and ration it depending on class and skin color; and where we historically have done so poorly in protecting our most vulnerable citizens: in such a nation, euthanasia becomes a particularly horrific, and inappropriate, prospect. Until we have health care for all, we cannot ethically or humanely seek a policy of assisted euthanasia for some.

Were we to do so, what could become a help to the privileged could be a horror to the poor. Might some people forgo care, not because they don't want to live, but because they worry they will bankrupt their families? Would death become a "cost-effective" option to shirk the more fundamental issues of fairness? If a patient were poor, would caregivers struggle so hard to control disease and pain if they had the option to neatly end it all? In a society like ours, such policies raise as many questions as they answer.

To be sure, many in our society have grappled with these issues by taking matters into their own desperate hands. Around the country, a score of "mercy killing" cases have made headlines: the eighty-five-year-old Florida man who shot his long-suffering and dying wife to put her out of her misery; the distraught young father in Chicago who held nurses at bay at gunpoint as he disconnected his six-month-old, hopelessly vegetative son from a respirator because the hospital would not let the infant die; the Brooklyn family who forcibly disconnected their beloved father from a respirator after a stroke made him a vegetable, knowing that he had a horror of living that way; the two young men dying of AIDS in California who executed a suicide pact rather than face what seemed to them inevitable pain and suffering.

All of us can sympathize with the human drama in such cases. Survey after survey finds that they tap into a motherlode of popular sentiment. Polls show that well over half—63 percent—believe it is always justified for a person to kill a loved one when that person suffers from terrible pain with a terminal illness. Fully 70 percent find it "sometimes or always" justified. Six people in ten say that they could imagine taking such an action if someone they loved was suffering terribly from a terminal illness. Only one American in five believes it is "always wrong" to kill a suffering loved one in such situations.

But no matter how justified we believe these people to be, the underlying truth is that each such tragic case reflects the failure of our health-care system. In each of these cases, the families and caregivers might better have reached timely and comfortable decisions that take into account patients' and families' human values and dignity while not needlessly prolonging mere organ function. We can all expect that our newspapers and news shows will bring us more stories of concerned relatives acting from love to deliver a beloved person in pain, or living against their will as a vegetable. In such rare cases, we can hope our justice system will deal with them compassionately. Indeed, it is the essence of our humanity that there are times when people must take action at real risk to themselves to end the clear suffering of another person.

But for the moment, until we better sort out these questions, these must remain the most personal sorts of decisions between individuals and their consciences. Our nation cannot afford a public policy condoning the taking of a life, even a suffering life. If those behaviors are to exist, they must do so in the inner reaches of the human heart, lest we corrupt our shared ethical consensus.

Physicians sometimes face questions of assisting death, albeit less dramatically, in a hospital, nursing home, or hospice. Most often it arises around the administration of pain-killers, specifically morphine. Because morphine both relieves pain and depresses breathing, physicians express concerns about prescribing it. They are reluctant because giving any drug that could hasten death raises the specter of active euthanasia—voluntarily ending the life of a patient. However, there is a subtle, but quite clear, moral distinction, which should reassure the physician and family alike. It rests on two pillars of argument.

The first pillar depends on the answer to the question, can we provide this medicine? It is the somewhat discredited doctrine of double effect, which moral philosophers and Catholic theologians have recognized since the late Middle Ages. This argues that there are situations where we are morally justified to court harm in our pursuit of good. It allows, for example, a physician to inflict the discomfort of surgery in order to save a life. It is also applied at the end of life. Clearly, the steps we take to ease suffering and pain—such as the administration of morphine—can have the "double effect" of hastening slightly the moment of death. But nobody argues, not even the most ardent vitalist, that a morality that reveres life requires doctors to cause suffering or even allow it to continue. When a person is suffering, then care providers—whether medical staff in a hospital or even family members at home—have an obligation to do what they can to alleviate that suffering. So if medication is provided in a sincere effort to reduce suffering, and not to hasten death, that has traditionally been viewed as a legitimate, appropriate, indeed humane, course.

The second pillar responds to the question about withholding care and concerns the overall goal of care. At the point when nothing remains that can help the patient recover, providing more care simply prolongs the process of a painful and lingering death. If a medical judgment is made that intervention will only prolong suffering and the patient's process of dying, and when there is truly nothing one can do to reverse or ameliorate the underlying illness, then it may be appropriate not to treat. If it is morally appropriate not to treat, then it must be clearly permissible to treat in the way that most promotes comfort.

Conscience tells us that we must not make mortal judgments lightly or erroneously. We require that the decision to comfort instead of treat cannot reflect a doctor or institution's bias or prejudice, nor be made on the basis of age, race, class, or on any other inapplicable or inappropriate standard. We have set up ethics committees and review mechanisms to make sure such decisions are made in public, explained, defended, and explored before a jury of peers.

But when we now command powerful life-sustaining treatments, we must be equally vigilant to ask the larger questions:

◆ What is the goal of care?

◆ Does the original care plan—for recovery, cure, release from the hospital—still make sense?

◆ Has new information changed the situation since this person's care plan was established?

◆ If so, who has the authority to redefine the goals?

Clearly, the new faces of death pose more questions than we have ever had to confront before. Making decisions about death is, and should be, hard. As we cast about for solutions we keep coming around to one fundamental truth: the best answers lie with the person in the bed.

DNR: Three Letters that Spell Death

As our society has gradually accepted the idea that patients have the right to decide, we have faced new questions. One of those concerns resuscitation. In TV and films, cardiopulmonary resuscitation (CPR) is portrayed as a high-drama, high-tech process used heroically to beat back encroaching death. In the hospital, it is a good deal more complex. For all of us, when someone we love is dying, there is a natural tendency to want doctors to "do everything possible" to save them. But with so powerful a technique as CPR, we owe it to the patient—and to ourselves—to know what "everything" really means, so that our decision is based on hard fact, not hopeful fiction. Resuscitation is often included in "everything."

Once invented on the battlefields of World War II, to remedy trauma, this medical genie came out of the bottle with a vengeance. CPR began to be used in ways that were never intended, on very different kinds of patients. First, it was moved into the local hospital. Rather than being used selectively in trauma cases, it became routine to resuscitate everyone whose heart or breathing stopped—regardless of the reason why. There were some remarkable successes, as when the city of Seattle demonstrated that training enough citizens in CPR reduced the incidence of death from sudden cardiac arrest. But it also grew clear that most uses of CPR merely complicated the business of dying.

This was most true when CPR was applied as an end-of-life intervention for wasted or frail patients, those dying inevitably from systemic disease. For these people death is imminent, and may even be a welcome relief. For patients dying of a terminal disease, resuscitation may be at best a stopgap, at worst a horror. For them, it is not a doorway to extended life, but the entrance to a tunnel of prolonged dying.

Were resuscitation not a medical procedure, it would look to outsiders like a most brutal torture. In this case, however, appearances are deceptive: the person is, at least at the start, beyond pain. What most people do not realize is that resuscitation occurs only when the patient has *already died a natural death*. When in such cases resuscitation "succeeds," it means bringing back the dead; occasionally it is a great friend, yielding years of healthy and productive life. Sometimes, it merely prolongs the function of some of the organ systems like heart and lungs but only with mechanical support. Sometimes—indeed, all too often—it leaves nothing recognizable as a functioning, integrated human being, able to relate to its world.

The trauma of resuscitation has a very different outcome in a healthy, fit twenty-three-year-old soldier of 165 pounds—for whom it was invented—than it does in a frail woman of eighty-seven, weighing 91 pounds and suffering from widely disseminated metastatic cancer. For people with a terminal disease, dying after a "successful" resuscitation is usually much worse than dying before. The process virtually ensures a slower, harder, more painful death, often on a respirator, condemned to the bizarre netherworld of the ICU, where there is neither day nor night but always light, noise, movement, and suffering.

To the caregivers on the front lines wrestling with their new technology, blindly imposing resuscitation on every patient felt like medical technology run amok. Many physicians and nurses felt it violated their Hippocratic oath to "do no harm" each time they subjected a dying person to a traumatic resuscitation that would not significantly prolong life but would only assure a worse death. Caregivers grew increasingly uncomfortable being asked to use this technique routinely in futile cases when people were about to die.

For these reasons, delicate questions of life and death were left vague, depending on the discretion of the attending physician or house staff doctors, based on their own medical judgment and values. In the 1970s and 1980s, that was seen as the best way to slow the steamroller of routine resuscitation and make room, in the high-tech hustle of the modern hospital, for an old-fashioned notion: mercy.

Mercy, in this case, was spelled "DNR"—for a Do Not Resuscitate order. With a DNR order in place, a patient could be spared the brutal ministrations of the "code" team. Resuscitation gave us the capacity to drag people back into life (at least halfway); DNR's gave us the means to stand back and let nature take its course when that seemed best.

If making such decisions was hard to begin with, making them work was even harder. Since patients could be cared for by a score of people over the course of a day, hospitals needed some way to let care teams—the nurses, the house staff, and the attending physicians—know which patients were to be resuscitated and which were not. Throughout the 1970s and 1980s, most hospitals across the country developed their own systems under which DNR orders were written.

But in New York events took a bizarre twist, a classic case of how outside interests can distort care decisions. Here, where there are more medical malpractice lawyers per square foot than in any other place in the world, DNR's became a medical hot potato. Some malpractice lawyers, driven by the usual motives, argued that the letters "DNR" on a chart spelled "murder"—or could in the eyes of a jury. They argued it was legally mandatory to resuscitate every patient; doctors began worrying that writing a DNR order could be seen as tantamount to conspiracy to commit murder. In short order, a cloak of secrecy was drawn across the practice. While hospitals in other places were writing policies, doctors and lawyers in New York City were creating a climate in which it seemed illicit, illegal, or shameful to let someone die as humans used to—unimpeded.

As DNR became a three-letter dirty word, New York hospitals devised their own systems to avoid writing down the dreaded "DNR," yet still discreetly indicating those patients marked for a merciful, uncontested death. The systems were as varied as human ingenuity: some hospitals had inscrutable red or blue adhesive dots stuck on the outside of the medical chart; some kept card files with different-colored cards; other hospitals had blackboards at nursing stations with all the patients' names on them and easily erased stars placed next to the DNR patients.

One common solution in places like New York, where DNR's had historically been controversial, or when families and doctors disagreed about a DNR—was a subterfuge called a "slow code." This meant that everybody on the code team arrived on the floor and was given a signal to slow down, to do their tasks deliberately, without haste, so they would exceed the eighteen-minute goal for successful resuscitation. This allowed the person to die an uninterrupted, peaceful death. Then, when it was a medical impossibility to bring the patient back, they could commence modest efforts on the lifeless body. Another variant, the "show code," was merely the semblance of resuscitation—doctors and nurses assembled, equipment was wheeled in and sometimes even attached, but nothing that qualified as medical resuscitation was ever really done, and eventually someone would pronounce the patient dead. It was theater, staged for the benefit of family, with the ostensible goal to "do everything." But behind closed doors, as onlookers thought all efforts were being made to save their loved one, the bustle masked inaction. Such sham codes are one of the secrets of the medical system, a humane, if confused, effort to do right within a shifting and uncertain moral and legal climate. One of the goals of medical ethics in recent years has been to help avoid such dishonest codes, to foster open discussion among doctors, patients, and families, so everybody can discuss, understand, and agree on what should happen.

When medicine is driven by fears of malpractice and prosecution, systems of bogus codes seriously compromise care. Practically, for the nurses and doctors, it was monumentally unsettling, a waste of time, and a dangerous misuse of the scarce resource of physician expertise and the hospital's crash cart. Most confusing of all, each hospital used its own different secret system. To add to the confusion, different staff members made very different judgments about resuscitating the same patient. This could lead to a "shift war," where Mrs. Benson might be recognized as DNR on the 4:00-P.M.-to-midnight shift, not labeled DNR between midnight and 8:00 A.M., and who knows what by the next morning. That meant her treatment would depend more on accidents of timing than on any rationally determined plan of care reflecting her, her family's, or her doctor's wishes.

It was also ethically unacceptable. Life and death were being decided in back rooms, out of public view, and nobody was clear just how or why. Because the process lacked any participation of patient or family, these "star chamber" decisions opened the door to terrible abuses. One of those almost happened in the case of Beverly Jackson, one of the first cases on which I ever consulted, in the mid-1970s. Beverly was a forty-five-year-old black woman, a severe alcoholic with a long series of health problems who had recently broken her hip after a drunken fall. In addition, she had advanced Korsakoff's syndrome, which results from alcohol abuse and irreversibly damages the brain, and diabetes. She was the most unpleasant sort of patient: disagreeable and hostile, acting out her alcoholic rage with the staff. Her husband had also been abusive and threatening to the doctors.

I was called to meet with the care team, which was uncomfortable with the management of this patient. They felt conflicted about their responsibility to the patient and hostile toward her husband. We met in a small room behind the nurses' station as one of the physicians presented the medical facts.

Then Mrs. Jackson was brought in. She was clearly disoriented and confused. One resident suggested some of her problem was due to a diagnosed hearing problem, for which a hearing aid had not yet arrived. As we spoke, I noticed the blackboard at the end of the room: next to Mrs. Jackson's name was a DNR star. Why, I wondered. In itself, a broken hip did not justify a DNR order. Even her long list of problems seemed more chronic than imminently life-threatening. Was there some other medical fact, some terminal disease, I didn't know about? After Mrs. Jackson left, I asked if she or her family had requested a DNR order. And if she hadn't, why was it there? Who had ordered this, and why?

I felt the confusion as my questions hung in the air of the small room for what seemed forever. Finally one resident, a particularly arrogant young man, broke the silence. You could hear the contempt and frustration in his voice: "She got a DNR order because society has spent enough on this lady." I was stunned. We like to think that decisions are made in the patients' best interests. In Mrs. Jackson's case, it was based on completely inappropriate grounds: the physician's prejudice, perhaps the anger and resentment of a few staff people, cloaked in a disingenuous argument about costs. There are times, to be sure, when cost may appropriately be used to set public policy, but costs should never govern care decisions at the bedside. The doctor's job is to be an advocate and provide the best care for all of his patients. For Mrs. Jackson, two intertwining factors had gone awry. As there were no clear rules governing DNR orders, one person's racial prejudice and economic values had meshed to deny a patient access to possibly beneficial care. Had nobody questioned it, Mrs. Jackson's DNR order could have slipped through the cracks, taking her with it.

We have come a long way since those days, and such an inappropriate decision could not be made in our hospital today. But it gave all of us a sobering lesson in what happens when we allow fear of lawyers to drive important decisions underground. There, in the closet and out of scrutiny, we set the stage for decisions to be made for all the wrong reasons. Clearly, we needed a better way to deal with DNR's.

Then, in 1982, a landmark case at a New York City hospital changed everything. A woman in her late seventies was admitted with terminal cancer and given a DNR order, apparently without anyone having consulted her or her family. A few days later her grandson, a medical student, was visiting at her bedside when the woman had a coronary arrest. As she was slipping away, he frantically sought help, only to be told that his grandmother was not to be resuscitated—the first he or his family had heard of it. She died, and the outraged family pressed charges, which led to a grand jury investigation.

The jury said what most of us in hospitals had argued for years: we needed to bring these decisions out in the open and into public view. Such life-and-death decisions, they said, should be arrived at openly, with family and patient involved, with a clear and consistent system to communicate the order to staff.

In an attempt to remedy this traditional situation, where doctors could decide informally, without any scrutiny or patient consent, New York State passed a law, the only one of its kind in the country. In New York today, if you are a capable decider, not impaired by age, infirmity, illness, or medication, you have the legal right to decide about DNR. If you are not, then the decision may fall to spouse, family member, or a significant other. There is a growing movement around the country to involve patients and families directly in these decisions, and all states now recognize your right to make these decisions.

The New York experience is helpful for all of us, no matter where we live, because it sheds light on the many questions surrounding DNR's. No other state has the statute New York now does. In most places, DNR orders are handled as they always have been: informally, discreetly, as part of the medical subculture. Most hospitals, however, both community and teaching, have evolved their own DNR policies—happily, without the absurd machinations New York experienced. But you should know, if you or a family member are ill, that the hospital has some DNR policy that will affect you. In nursing homes, which are rarely equipped to do full-scale resuscitation, the analogous question usually concerns a "DNT"—Do Not Transfer—order. These prevent emergency transfers to a hospital where resuscitation can occur. But DNR orders may also be necessary to prevent a call to 911, triggering the arrival of the emergency medical squad.

In most places, most of the time, the great majority of families and patients don't discuss DNR at all; of the few who do, almost none have any idea what resuscitation really means. Two researchers at Harvard, in cooperation with Boston's Beth Israel Hospital, studied all of the resuscitations at Beth Israel Hospital over one year, and found that the patient and doctor had actually discussed the patient's wishes concerning resuscitation less than 20 percent of the time. Even among doctors who believe patients *should* participate in decisions about resuscitation, only 10 percent actually have discussed it with patients beforehand. Barely twice as many—a mere 21 percent—had even brought it up with the patient's family. That leaves four out of five doctors who had not, who were left with making that decision on their own.

Unfortunately, the same research study shows that doctors and patients do not always agree about what should happen with a DNR. The Beth Israel researchers asked the patients, their attending doctors, and the house-staff physicians their views on resuscitation. Ninety-three percent of the physicians thought the patients favored resuscitation; but 30 percent of those patients who survived the procedure "stated unequivocally that they had not wanted resuscitation and did not wish to be resuscitated in the future." That research has led one of my colleagues, the eminent public health physician Victor Sidel, to argue that we should change the basic presumption. Rather than assume everybody would want resuscitation, as we do now, and requiring them to refuse it, we should assume everybody would refuse resuscitation, and require them to specifically consent to it.

Such an approach would have helped an elderly Chinese woman whose case I saw several years ago. In her mid-seventies, she had been admitted in the end stages of inoperable, untreatable heart disease. Her disease was clearly progressing to its inevitable conclusion, for within the first twenty-four hours of admission, she had six separate cardiac arrests. Each time a code was called, the crash team came running, and she was brought back. By the time I was called to the floor, it had become clear that this repetitive process was simply not doing any good.

It was also clear that nobody had ascertained her wishes. When she was stable for a brief period, we asked her son to come in to interpret for her. Her response was clear: she did not want to be resuscitated again, but wanted to be allowed to "go join my ancestors in peace." The attending physician wrote a DNR order. That same evening, after her son and a daughter had left, she had her seventh arrest. This time, because of the DNR, we were able to respect her final wish. There was no ethical dilemma once we had established her preference, as we were ethically and morally bound to honor her stated wishes. But the hours before, when she was subjected six times to a resuscitation she didn't want, were morally problematic.

There is one place where DNR policy is more complicated: in the operating room. There, heart or breathing arrests can result from surgical or anesthetic stress, and are not necessarily a step in the natural dying process. In most cases, the surgeons presume that if you were well enough to go to surgery, you're well enough to come out, and aggressive measures should be taken to see that you do. If the person entering the operating room has a DNR order, however, the doctor should discuss with the patient beforehand whether he or she wants to be resuscitated, should an arrest occur in the specific circumstance of the operating room.

Resuscitation within the OR is quite different from that outside, whether on the hospital floor or outside the hospital. The arrest is detected immediately, the team is right there, the best equipment and expertise are present and in motion seconds after the arrest occurs—in many cases the patient is already intubated. For all these reasons, resuscitation in the OR is often successful—indeed, many people who require it would never have had an arrest but for the stresses of the surgery itself. There are many thousands of people walking around today whose lives would have ended prematurely on the operating table but for the medical miracle of resuscitation. For these reasons some patients choose to change their DNR status while in surgery.

Outside the operating room, there remains something of a conspiracy of silence surrounding DNR's. It is extremely unlikely your doctor will bring the subject of DNR's up with you, even in New York State where, by law, she must. One of our doctors, an immensely caring man, recently admitted to me that "I would rather shoot myself in the foot than talk about DNR with a patient." In my experience, most of his colleagues feel the same, although they may not say so.

Their reasons are complex. Often, they don't want to upset, worry, or discourage you unnecessarily, or lead you to think you are sicker than you are. In the Boston study, physicians termed these discussions "too threatening," or feared they might in fact "bring on an arrest itself." Also, for almost all caregivers, the subject of death in general, and DNR's in particular, feels like the ultimate defeat, an admission that they are losing. They, like all of us, don't like to talk about losing. Add to that the fact that even the most thoughtful doctors are simply unused to talking about these matters with patients at all, just as we are unused to talking about it with them. Finally, a few physicians still regard these discussions as a gross intrusion into their traditional professional turf. To them, this is a purely medical judgment, and they are the best qualified to make it. This is a holdover from the paternalistic medical tradition of the past, when it was the doctor's perception and values, not the patient's, that mattered.

Beyond these reasons, there is a profound and legitimate ethical reason why your doctor isn't likely to raise the subject. She may have decided that resuscitation is simply medically futile for you, due to age or illness—that it will not prolong your life for any substantial period of time. She may then reason that it is not an appropriate option in your case. Doctors worry that if the law makes them broach the subject with each patient it will unwittingly open the door to greater suffering. Most physicians feel that a person who is dying can only be harmed by resuscitation. Since this is the case, it is neither compassionate nor wise, they think, to offer them false hope of what may be a misguided and ultimately terribly painful option. In such cases, some doctors feel it is even unethical to present an option they feel can only hurt you. That is especially true when patients don't know what that choice may really entail—although at this point in the history of the doctor-patient relationship, that should never be the case.

Others argue that patients should always be permitted the

choice of whether or not to be resuscitated. How we die is the last significant fact of our existence over which we have any control. If you are going to die, they say, shouldn't you be able to choose whether you want to do it with resuscitation or peacefully?

If you have strong feelings about this issue—if you, like Joseph, desperately want to be resuscitated or are equally sure that you do not want that sort of violent behavior to surround your death—it requires a bit of foresight and initiative. These are hard issues for doctors and patients both, but there are some ways we can make these discussions easier for all of us.

First, bring it up with your primary doctor. If you are in a local or community hospital, your family doctor probably admitted you and is likely to remain your primary doctor, responsible for coordinating your care. In a tertiary-care hospital, it may be hard to even recognize "your" doctor. You may have to actually ask, "Are you my main doctor?" or, "Which physician is primarily responsible for my care?" Once you know who identifies himself as your doctor, raise the issue. You may ask: "Are you the one who would write a DNR order?" Most important of all, ask for a clear description of what happens in a resuscitation. Think carefully about whether you really want that for you.

Next, bring the discussion around to the specifics of your own case: "What are the chances that my specific condition might lead to cardiac or pulmonary arrest?" For many serious illnesses, the chances are high. For yours it may not be.

"Given those odds, what do you think are my chances of surviving that arrest?" If your doctor doesn't know, she can find out—there is now a medical literature demonstrating, for specific medical problems, the approximate chances for successful resuscitation.

"If I am resuscitated, what shape will I likely be in? Will I be conscious? Will I be able to talk, or communicate in any way?"

Beware the pitfalls of euphemism here. Your doctor may say, for example, that chances are "very slim" you will regain the ability to relate to others. Ask her to be specific: does she mean 25 percent, 5 percent, or less than 1 percent? Doctors like to be hopeful and encouraging, but you deserve the best factual answers possible, to make the best informed decision you can.

Make sure to discuss those specifics important to you: "What might I expect to be my quality of life? Will I be able to leave the hospital and go home? Is it likely I will be in pain?" If, after consideration, you don't want to be resuscitated, ask what the hospital policy and procedure is. Make sure your family, spouse, or care partners understand your wishes.

Raising any issue around death and dying can be immensely hard for all of us, patient and physician alike. People tend to wait to let their doctor bring it up. If he doesn't, we may avoid it, fearing all sorts of possible repercussions: that our doctor will be angry with us, will subtly punish us for going against his will, that he may even abandon our care.

These issues are also very uncomfortable for your doctor, and he may greet this discussion with some equivalent of "Don't worry, that won't happen to you." That may well be, and if he is right, so much the better. But you should not be put off. If the subject of DNR is important to you, you deserve to have a full and frank discussion. You are well within your rights to say: "Of course, Doctor, we both hope that is true, but just for my own comfort, I will feel better if we have discussed it."

Remember, your goal is to make sure discussions happen while you can still decide. If you care about this, you don't want to leave it to chance because in most places, without a written DNR order it is assumed that you consented to the procedure. That doesn't mean you will necessarily be resuscitated, but it does mean that the decision has been taken out of your hands and put into the doctor's.

It is also crucial to involve spouse, family members, or friends—whoever are your designated care partners—as much as possible in these discussions with doctors. Often they are the ones who will be asked to make the final DNR decision if you no longer can. They should know what you want and know, too, what "do everything" really means in terms of consequences for you, the person it is done to.

Bear in mind that in most places, a DNR order only applies if you have an abrupt cessation of heart or lung function. It does not apply in cases of a slow decline in function, or respiratory or cardiac distress. Nor does a DNR order permit caregivers to abandon you, withdraw pain medication, stop treating infections, leave you alone, or ignore other treatable medical problems. In any given case, it may be appropriate not to treat, not because there is a DNR, but because of other clinical considerations—when, for example, treatment would be futile and only prolong suffering. But then, you have other tools to control those decisions, as we will examine in detail in the final chapter.

Most important of all, the simple fact of placing a DNR order does not necessarily have to mean that you will die alone, neglected, or abandoned. It simply conveys your wishes regarding one specific end-of-life intervention: no more and no less. In all candor, it is true that in some places, placing a DNR order may create an informal, largely unconscious process, where doctors "disinvest" from DNR patients. Especially in a busy teaching hospital, where house staff are always tired and overworked, DNR patients may fall down on the doctor's list for evaluation, care, and treatment. In contrast, the nursing staff often understands only too well that DNR patients, for whom comfort and dignity is the prime concern, may require higher levels of nursing care and attention. But the fact remains: DNR orders refer to one specific procedure, and one only. They do not give anyone license to abandon or neglect a patient—ever. If you or someone you love think that may be happening, you should talk with your doctor and remedy this neglect.

For all of us, patients and practitioners alike, DNR's are new and uncharted territory, and we are all feeling our way. They are far from a perfect solution. If they are overused, then some people who do want to be resuscitated won't be. If DNR's are not used enough, as is often the case today, then too many people who could be permitted calm and painless deaths will instead have assaultive and prolonged deaths. That is why, ultimately, you must be the one making this decision.

As we define our public policy, it seems wiser to put in place systems that bring this discussion into the open and compel us all to have it, because if we don't require that these discussions occur, they probably won't. Of course, nobody wants to put well-intentioned physicians in a position where they must violate their ethical principles to protect patients from harm. But as a society, we do better to ask doctors to resuscitate a person they might not otherwise choose to resuscitate than to allow them to routinely override patients' wishes. Any formal DNR policy is a compromise, but if somebody must be uncomfortable, better it be our professionals than our patients and families. Best of all, of course, is getting used to the idea of having these discussions together, openly and honestly, so that the decisions we make are the right ones for all concerned.

For all of us, the new death is not yet fully defined. The tools we have developed are yet imperfect and using them always courts some danger. If our society agrees to honor DNR orders and advance directives like living wills and durable powers of attorney, we will certainly terminate care for some individuals who might, if they could choose at that point, change their minds and wish to receive it. Yet without these instruments, we would just as certainly prolong the agony of many more people by means they would refuse if they could.

They are but the crude tools our society has forged in our quest to balance the values of autonomy and compassion at life's end. They are the human hopes we stack against our mortal dilemmas, our fumbling recognition that all of us deserve nothing less than the chance to be the actor in our most irrevocable human act.

6

SENIORS AND
THE RIGHT
TO TAKE RISKS

It came a few days before Christmas, the call dreaded by every child of every aging parent. About 1:15 P.M. on a Friday, I was attending adolescent rounds when word came that I was wanted on the phone. I picked it up to hear my aunt's voice on the line, taut with worry. My aunt Rose speaks to my mother, Bessie, every day by phone. This particular Friday morning, she had tried three times, and gotten no answer. She was worried, she explained, because she knew my seventy-seven-year-old mother was in bed recovering from pneumonia, and could hardly have gone out. She had called the office in a panic and they had transferred her call to me. As I hurriedly excused myself from rounds, two doctor colleagues of mine offered to accompany me to my mother's apartment, "just in case"; I refused and they came anyway.

We arrived at my mother's at 2:05 P.M. to find her collapsed in a heap on the floor. Kneeling at her side, one doctor determined that she was unconscious, but alive. They checked her vital signs and threw on some blankets as I sat holding her hand. They also called a private ambulance to take her to Montefiore rather than to the nearest emergency room in a city hospital at the center of New York's collapsing public health system. They estimated that she had lain alone and unconscious since about eleven o'clock the night before—fifteen hours. Although they succeeded in rousing her to a groggy state, she had little idea where she was, and less of what had happened. She did, however, know her doctor's phone number, her Medicare number, and the location of all the objects she wanted to bring with her. My stomach twisted in a hard knot as the ambulance screamed into the Montefiore emergency room.

Two hours of tests and exams, including a CAT scan, showed that my mother had a large layered blood clot under her skull. Termed a "subdural hematoma," it was pressing on her brain so much that the brain was compacted into one side of the skull; the doctor worried it could threaten her life. Unchecked, it might soon interfere with her heart and lung function. That night, a small hole was drilled into my mother's skull to drain the hematoma; the next day, after she suffered some seizures, her doctors concluded surgery was required to remove the blood clot; they took her into the operating room, opened a two-inch round incision in her skull, and surgically removed the clot.

My fifteen years on hospital units have taught me that neurological events, especially in the elderly, can create extraordinarily peculiar manifestations. Often, I have heard cases of people who may look and sound 100 percent normal, but whose ability to comprehend and process information is gravely damaged. But never before had I faced this set of symptoms without the protective distance that my professional role provides. Dealing with my mother, not surprisingly, felt wholly different than elaborating abstract arguments.

My first clue to how disabled she was came as I returned to the hospital the next day after a one-hour absence, and found her tied to a chair. The nurses told me she could not really grasp the fact that she was connected to various IV tubes and monitoring wires, and had a catheter—although they were quite clearly visible. She stubbornly kept attempting to get up and walk, which would rip out her tubes, IV needles, and wires. If she were to fall, she risked reinjuring her bleeding brain. For her own safety, they'd had to tie her down using a restraining vest—called a "Posey," after the company that makes it—that is commonly used with seniors.

My mother begged me to remove the ties, saying: "How can you tie me up like this?" I did, and immediately regretted it. I had to beg her not to get up, then physically restrain her in the bed, because she was simply incapable of understanding she could not move around. Although apparently lucid, she could not understand this basic fact of self-preservation. She required twenty-four-hour special-duty nurses to keep her safe from herself.

Ten days later, my mother was home. Physically, she had made a remarkable recovery, but she was still quite disoriented. She was also totally unaware of problems with her balance that made it impossible to move out of bed on her own without falling. Nor could she understand that the risk to her brain was still very real, so she still required twenty-four-hour home care. She adamantly refused to use a commode by her bed, and insisted upon going to the bathroom. Not accepting that she could not walk on her own, she got up and fell again, and was rushed back to the emergency room for another brain scan. This time, fortunately, there was no further injury, so the neurologist sent her home with a restraint vest and her solemn promise that she would wear the vest as a reminder that she could not get up on her own.

Things were not to be so easy. My mother is a fiercely independent and fastidious woman, the unchallenged queen of her own home, utterly adamant about doing things exactly her own way. I was hardly surprised when the home care worker called to say that she refused to wear the vest. Only after much wheedling, cajoling, and threatening did she grumpily agree to it. But later that day, as her nurse took a three-minute break to go to the bathroom, my mother grabbed scissors out of her night-table drawer and triumphantly cut her restraint vest into tatters. She was halfway out of bed when the nurse returned; had it been one minute later, her next fall might have been her last. But no matter, my mother had made her point, loud and clear. For me, her gesture was curiously, exhilaratingly, liberating. She had made her choice, not based on real understanding, but based on the consistent principles of personal behavior she had always used to guide her life. She would get better, or continue her decline, on her own terms. The cost of living her life on my terms was too high for what was left of my mother's self-esteem. My job was to make peace with it.

My mother's case is a veritable textbook of issues that can arise with many older people. At its heart lies the central question we confront in caring for an aging loved one: Does a person's autonomy—her personality, the sense of who she is, and her right of self-determination—survive the mental deficits and physical disabilities that illness, injury, or age can bring? If not, how do we decide when to take over? What if they are so adamant that imposing our notion of what is right means tying them down? Do some values that should be respected and supported survive mental decline? Can old people always be trusted to know what is right for them? What are our rights and responsibilities when we find ourselves playing parent to our parents?

We must always remember that old people are old only incidentally, but are people fundamentally, people whose rights, protections, and responsibilities do not wither at age sixty-five. First among those rights is the prerogative to chart the course of their own lives. Like all of us—we are, after all, only old people in training—they have the right to make their own mistakes. As a former litigator I have real sympathy for seniors; in general they need more of the kind of advocacy for autonomy that clinical ethicists, or at least my variety of the beast, can provide.

Often, as in my mother's case, their personality and wishes may challenge our impulses to do for them and to them. We may then find ourselves in the tremendously hard position of standing by and watching those whom we most love—our parents, aging relatives, even friends—make decisions that we feel may hurt them. Then what? If their decisions do not reflect adequate consideration of the issues at stake, then doesn't our honoring such a decision truly abandon them? How ought we to treat a decision made by one who clearly lacks the mental resources of a capable decider? What if their decisions embody the clear and consistent preferences of their past known decisions—does that change our assessment?

This is the ethical tightrope we walk when caring for our elders. How do we best empower and not abandon? How do we helpfully support an elderly person without imposing our own narrow vision of her safety and well-being? We do not want to force them to be someone they are not, yet we still want to protect them from unknowingly injuring themselves or suffering needlessly.

This is such delicate ground precisely because we can find ourselves playing the very roles we most adamantly resist in other circumstances: "knowing better" for the patient than the patient does. Sometimes we do know better; sometimes we don't. Often, our elderly patients know best for themselves and our job is simply to support and respect their wishes. The better part of wisdom, of course, comes in knowing which case is which.

Doctors, nurses, and social workers face these anguished decisions every day. Take the case of Sam Barrone. An eighty-one-year-old man, Mr. Barrone had a long history of diabetes. Until recently, he had been managing his regimen of insulin on his own, with occasional check-in calls from a visiting nurse.

But the nurse was worried. He lived at home with his granddaughter and great-grandchildren, but things had recently been going very badly. Several small strokes had left him severely confused and disoriented, and his diabetes left him almost completely blind. Sam was increasingly confused and lethargic and his memory was growing much worse. It was evident that he was starting to have real trouble managing his medications. With his sugar way out of control, his diabetes had led to an infection in his leg, great pain, and fever. At that point, he was brought into the hospital to stabilize his diabetes and for a lifesaving amputation of the infected leg below the knee.

Great efforts were made before the surgery to involve Mr. Barrone in the process of deciding. Once his fever and pain were controlled by medication, Sam could discuss his options. He mobilized all of his emotional and intellectual resources to focus on the issue of his potential surgery. In those talks, he was very clear and consistent: he consented to the surgery; he did not want to die.

In the hospital, after the surgery and with his medications controlled, he improved dramatically. But it felt like only half a victory to his care team, for they were very reluctant to let him go home. During his stay it had become clear that, in addition to his serious loss of vision, he had serious memory and judgment problems. Left alone, the nurse worried, Mr. Barrone might easily misjudge when to take his insulin, forget to eat on schedule, and thereby slip into a life-threatening diabetic coma. Sam, however, did not recognize his mental impairments, and insisted that he wanted to return home immediately. Vociferously, he claimed that he could manage "as well as always" with his family and only four hours of home care a day. The thing he enjoyed most was being home with his grandchildren and being out on the stoop so he could talk with his neighborhood cronies. He explained that he would navigate his ambulator trolley out to the stoop of his building, where he could sit and visit the days away with his circle of buddies. Besides, he hoped, the family would help out. His statements left no doubt: he wanted to go home.

A social worker from the home care agency saw it differently. She pointed out that although his granddaughter had offered to help in the past, she had shown herself to be completely unreliable and even seemed somewhat mentally unstable. The home care agency reported that she had, in fact, actually been competing with the ailing old man for the attentions of the home care worker, and generally disrupting care. In the social worker's judgment, Sam required an aide for at least twelve hours each day. Unfortunately, Sam was not eligible for Medicaid-funded home care because he had too many assets, despite the fact that he was really in quite a precarious financial situation. He also did not want to go to a nursing home, which would have quickly consumed the meager assets he had, eventually making him so poor that he would be clearly eligible for Medicaid. Nor was he willing to pay out of his pocket for the care the team thought he needed, as he preferred to save what little money he had so he "wouldn't live out my days as a pauper."

A consulting psychiatrist, called into the case, noted that Sam's was a subtle set of impairments. Although his judgment and memory were weak, he presented his wishes in a lucid, rational discussion; he was not babbling or incoherent, disorganized or inconsistent. The doctor believed that the same mental problems that prevented Mr. Barrone from maintaining his medications adequately also clouded his understanding of just how impaired he was. The team agreed that letting him return home alone would be courting medical disaster.

All told, the caregivers felt wedged between two unpleasant options. They could let Sam go as he was insisting, to respect his autonomy. But was this truly respecting autonomy, or abandoning Sam? They could force him to accept care that he neither wanted nor felt he needed and that he would have to pay for. But this solution of care imposed on him could happen only with a court order; even if he was somewhat compromised, he was clear and consistent in his refusal. There was an interim step, that of trying to cajole or badger him into accepting the care plan. This works sometimes, with some patients, but it seemed highly unlikely to succeed in Sam's case. The team's collective experience told us that even if Sam agreed to the plan, understanding it was his only chance of leaving the hospital quickly and quietly, he would probably fire the home care person as soon as he was out of the clutches of the care team.

To go to court is a drastic step, difficult for the hospital and patient alike, and is never taken lightly. But for Mr. Barrone, might it not be humane, assuring him the care he needed to function, indeed perhaps to stay alive? It would also be legally and administratively prudent, so the hospital could not be sued by a relative who might appear, or cited by state regulators for discharging a patient without a safe care plan. Yet what would going to court mean for Sam? Who were they to deprive him of all that was important in his life by sending him to a nursing home he didn't want to go to?

Caught between their duty to protect him from medical harm, their concern that he was not entirely capable of deciding for himself, and their desire to honor his wishes to return home, the care team sent up a call for help. One of the nurses, Derek Chin, cornered me in the hallway outside the geriatrics office. The next morning, I found myself sitting down to discuss Sam Barrone with our multidisciplinary geriatric team.

Such groups gather on a regular basis to bring their collective expertise to a particular case. This particular round collects an extraordinary range of skills: geriatricians, nurses, social workers, physicians, dieticians, pharmacists, neurologists, psychiatrists, physiatrists (physical rehabilitation experts), speech therapists, lawyers, and philosophers. Many members of this large cast are accompanied by students or interns doing rotations in various departments under their supervision. Mr. Barrone's case was on the agenda because his attending physician was baffled, and hoped to get some new ideas on what to do next for his recalcitrant patient.

We started by applying the three-step decision-making process: First, understand the medical and social *facts* of Mr. Barrone's case, and second, know the *options* available. So far, these were exactly the same steps you or any patient would take to help clarify such a decision for yourself. But where, for an individual, the pathway would normally next move to one's own values, we could not clearly ascertain Sam Barrone's values. He loved being with his cronies, but he also wanted to live. The next issue to resolve was which circle did this case fall into? Was it the first? As the fundamental question of whether Mr. Barrone was capable remained unresolved, different answers emerged depending on how rigorous a standard was applied. If we were to use a weak standard of capacity—"able to make a choice"—then Mr. Barrone would be home free, and his decision one we must respect. But if our standard required the "ability to understand," it became harder to say if he was indeed capable. And if we required "actual understanding" of the risks and benefits of the choices at hand, many would rule Mr. Barrone out of the game.

So our next step—the step we always use when decisions are made by someone other than the capable patient—was to examine the relevant *ethical principles.* The first of those was "autonomy"—Sam's right to determine what happens to him according to his own preferences and values. We knew Sam was not really up to the task of considering the risks and benefits of the proposed plan of care; was his what could be properly termed an informed choice? His refusal seemed to be based on a mental or psychological inability to understand and face his life-threatening condition. But it also was clearly based on his consistent choices, made over a lifetime, to do things his way, and do them alone.

The next principle we considered was that of beneficence, the principle of "do no harm," the basic axiom of medical care since Hippocrates. If we were to honor his refusal of help and discharge him to his home, would we not be colluding in his overoptimistic assessment of his ability, and so subject him to the risk of diabetic coma and death? Many of the team believed this violated their professional mandate to "do no harm."

It is a powerful irony of the medical system that, had Mr. Barrone accepted his doctors' recommendations, nobody would have questioned his capacity. We rarely ask questions when people say yes, but when they say no, capacity questions are often raised. Indeed, the fact that somebody is considered "capable" may simply mean that they have not made a decision at odds with caregivers, giving nobody any reason to challenge them. Simply agreeing with caregivers speeds the process of care. But when the patient is not critically examining his options, it may mean that nobody is bringing a skeptical eye to the care plan. Without that, it means the doctor's judgments are given tremendous importance and the patient's own values and preferences are diminished—a trade-off that few patients would willingly make. A "decision" by a patient incapable of making health-care decisions, which simply agrees with the doctor's suggestion, has in effect ceded the power to decide to the person in the white coat.

With Mr. Barrone, we all agreed that we had left the circle where the clearly capable patient has the right to determine his care. But where that left us was not altogether clear. We were struggling as third parties to decide if we should challenge his refusal in court. But what standards were we using to determine this? Whether or not a judge would find him legally incompetent, his explicit wishes were clearly and consistently opposed to his care team's views.

Throughout his discussions, Mr. Barrone had consistently repeated, "I am going home." That statement of desire—what my colleague, attorney-ethicist Connie Zuckerman, terms his "spoken choice"—had to be taken very seriously. He might be confused, but his position was clear and consistent.

Had he been unable to participate in the decision, we might have used a test of "substituted judgment" to try to reach the decision that Mr. Barrone himself would have made if he were capable. This is often a difficult test to use, especially if we lack evidence of what the person would have wanted. But with Mr. Barrone, we thought we knew exactly what his prior "capable" self would have wanted—two things: to go home and to stay alive.

We talked, then, about the principle of "authenticity," that Mr. Barrone's decision seemed to fit the strong and consistent pattern of his life. Those patterns make up what I have called a "sedimented life preference": the consistent bedrock of personality laid down and solidified over time. This man had lived alone for nineteen years, taking care of himself, traveling on his own. He was a person who valued his independence above all. His decision to refuse care fit in with those values.

Balanced against those was another principle, his objective best interest. The medical professionals had little doubt that forcing him to accept help was in his medical interest. The geriatrics team was properly concerned that his wrong decision would open him to risk of grave harm. I pointed out that we faced another question: If our concern was to prevent harm, was there not also harm in taking his independence away from him?

There is no harder idea for people trained to help others to accept than the fact that patients have the right to make the wrong decisions—even when they are old and somewhat compromised, even when the stakes are so high. I argued that older people, like the rest of us, have the right to order their lives as they see fit, and we have very little right to stand in their way. Yes, it can be hard—for families and caregivers both—to see elders take risks in support of their lifestyle. I knew this all too well, having been through it with my mother. But the surest way of respecting seniors as people is to let them decide for themselves. Our human independence is a notion at once so mighty and so fragile that it deserves our full respect, even when it makes us uncomfortable. We must remember that it is only the vagary of fate that puts people into our hands where we can impose our will.

Practically, we could not override Mr. Barrone's spoken choice except by legal means. But his wishes were so clear, and fit so well with his prior patterns of preference, that we were reluctant to do so. Given our previous experience with the courts, we were pretty sure that they would side with the caution of the care team against the clear position of this man. But what would be gained by setting up this tremendous imbalance of power and forcing this man to fight for his independence? Ultimately, we felt, the job of caregivers is to care, not to direct people's lives or force them to bend to our perception of their good. I argued that unless we could be certain that letting him return home posed the likelihood of "direct and immediate harm," we should let him go. The care team felt it was clear he would have a slow decline, and he would eventually be back, but his choice was also overwhelmingly clear. We could have coerced him, put him in a situation where his insulin was managed medically more tightly, but that would have separated him from his family, friends, and beloved pastimes. Our role was to give care—his was to choose his fate and determine how his life would be lived. Yes, we worried he would be harmed but, who knows, maybe he could manage after all. Finally, one of the geriatricians offered his "three strikes and you're out" rule: if Sam went home and came in twice more in life-threatening condition, the third time we could no longer continue to be a part of the process of putting him at risk. But until then, that still gave him two good tries at doing things his own way.

Mr. Barrone was so difficult precisely because he sat squarely at the confluence of many key ethical issues: uncertainty, autonomy, self-determination, the care team's duty to avoid harm, and their will to do good. He inhabited that messy middle ground we often find as we contemplate deciding for our elders, and taught us again that there is something fundamentally important about letting others make their own "wrong" decisions.

The Differences when Seniors Are Sick

We always try to work from the cornerstone principle that older people have the same rights to autonomy and self-determination as all of us do. In reality, however, when seniors are sick, certain things happen differently, and these can affect how decisions are made by, for, and about them.

To start with, by simple virtue of their age, seniors are more likely than others to become sick in the first place, to be confronted with issues of care in general, and life-sustaining care in particular. True, every human, at any age, can face disability, diminished or fluctuating capacity, even the eventual withdrawing or withholding of life-sustaining care. But for the oldest among us, such problems are both more acute and relatively more common. It is not that all seniors have all these problems, of course, but as a group, they are statistically more likely to encounter them. This statistic says nothing, however, about who is an appropriate candidate for aggressive medical treatment. As the case of my mother, Bessie, reminds us, elderly patients can as easily benefit from aggressive care as the younger. Age says nothing about what is the best medical plan.

In purely medical terms, there are things we need to know when the person in the bed is older. By the time that seniors come under a doctor's care or enter the hospital, they are far more likely to be significantly debilitated. Often, they have suffered for years from chronic conditions like arthritis, diabetes, and heart or kidney problems, which have taken a significant toll. They are also more likely to manifest what are termed "toxic metabolic reactions" to illness. For when older people get sick, they look, feel, and act very sick, very quickly. A teenager with a temperature of 102 degrees may barely be affected, and a thirty-five-year-old with the same fever might feel significantly sick but remain functional; but a 75-year-old with a 102-degree fever may be in a confused delirium, severely dehydrated, her vital functions unstable, and she may be dangerously incapacitated, both mentally and physically.

These reactions influence and shape what happens to old people in important ways. The fact that seniors can get so severely ill so quickly means that they often cannot effectively advocate for their own care—as one must in a hospital. Their voices are weaker—literally and figuratively—so they may not be readily heard or heeded in the din of the modern medical center.

This, in turn, subtly skews how doctors and nurses treat them. As strangers, these professionals have no way of knowing what the older patient's baseline functioning was recently, nor how vital, healthy, and strong a life they could lead when well. These patients can look so severely ill when they come into the hospital that caregivers assume they are dying or are severely and chronically compromised. Simply being old, by itself, is never a reason to withhold, delay, or, for that matter, impose care. But consciously or unconsciously, doctors, especially those in training, may put older patients lower on the list for attention and treat them less aggressively. A senior patient may be disdained, explicitly or implicitly, despite the admonitions of senior physicians, as a "GOMER"—"Get Out of My Emergency Room"—that class of demanding or difficult, unpleasant, unrewarding, or hopeless patients. GOMER's are the first to be shunted aside, medical pariahs in the whirl of the busy hospital. Even my own mother, I learned after she had been admitted to the hospital, was what the house staff referred to as a "LOLFOF"—a Little Old Lady, Found on Floor.

It must be admitted, as well, that doctors, nurses, and administrators, like all of us, are not immune to the insidious pressures of prejudice. The rampant ageism of our larger culture becomes a particular danger in medicine. Care providers may write off the older patient as disabled, confused, or "senile"; they may believe that chronological age necessarily determines a person's ability to function. In fact, these are useless, unsupported generalizations, medical myths. In reality, a given senior's individual abilities and the rate of psychological and physical aging are unique, and they can vary widely from person to person. Ethically and medically, we are required to assess each individual's function fully as the foundation of her personal care plan. And, for the elderly even more so than for younger persons, an assessment must include knowledge of the person's level of function *before* the event or illness that brought the person to the hospital.

A former colleague on the Montefiore ethics team, attorney Connie Zuckerman, now at the Bioethics Center of the State University of New York Medical School in Brooklyn (Downstate), witnessed this firsthand with her grandfather. Connie had long been the nearest family member to her aging grandparents, deeply devoted to them and a mainstay in their lives. One day, her eighty-six-year-old grandfather suddenly fell sick with pneumonia and was taken to one of New York's leading teaching hospitals. Connie arrived at the hospital later that day to find that the young resident treating her grandfather wasn't caring for him very aggressively. Having no idea what this very sick old man had been like only yesterday, the doctor had prematurely judged that her grandfather was too far gone to benefit from aggressive care. The doctor had presumed that this quite old, very sick man was on the way out.

But Connie knew otherwise. After all, her grandfather had been, up until two days before, mentally acute and physically vital, walking about five miles each day for exercise. Knowing this, Connie waded in to advocate on his behalf in no uncertain terms. As she is short and tends to be very calm, we were all amused by her ferocity as she recounted events to us. It must have been rather impressive, for she described how the whole atmosphere of care for her grandfather changed markedly. Her actions, and the information she as a concerned advocate could provide, put this patient's case in a new light for the doctors. They stabilized his condition; three days later, her grandfather went home and was soon again taking his long strolls around Queens. Yet without the aggressive support and advocacy of a family member, Connie wondered whether her grandfather would be alive.

Even when they are not so severely ill, many older people are more likely to have a degree of cognitive compromise that can get them dealt out of decisions about their care. One in four people over the age of sixty has a significant loss of hearing in one or both ears. This may mean trouble hearing or distinguishing different doctors' voices. Three-fourths of all older women and about half of senior men have moderate or severe vision problems, and may not be able to read the small print of forms or instructions they are shown.

Other elders may have short-term or long-term memory problems, forgetting facts, explanations, or medications. Some are slower to process and absorb information, both printed and verbal, and can require doctors and nurses to talk slower, louder, and explain more clearly than they otherwise might. And, according to a recent review of the literature, about 10 percent of people over the age of sixty-five are likely to have Alzheimer's disease or some other illness that significantly diminishes their mental capacity.

Unfortunately, those particular problems are precisely the worst sorts of disabilities to have when you're in a hospital. The very pace of the institution—especially the impersonal, rushed setting of a major teaching-and-research hospital—conspires against the older patient. Events move quickly. Faces, players, and plans change hourly. Scores of new individuals rotate through every day. Comforting habits and routines are shattered.

Add to this the fact that, in the maelstrom that is the modern medical center, many doctors have never even met their patients before. So, precisely when they need to take extra time to discover a patient's preferences and foibles, their personality and values, the system allows them less time to do so. And some caregivers may simply not be willing to put in the time and effort required for communicating with the elderly. For the older patient, the modern medical center can be a frustrating and dangerous place. No wonder so many elderly patients slip through the cracks.

All of these elements combine to remove decisions from the hands of seniors. Families and doctors both begin talking around them and deciding without them. Older people, if they are not strong, determined, and forceful, get bypassed in decision making all the time. It is standard procedure for doctors to turn to loving and involved relatives to make decisions for the older person, even when that person is perfectly capable of deciding for herself.

For doctors and care staff it is often simply easier to deal with family members of the elderly person than to deal directly with the patient. The particular communication skills needed for elderly patients all take extra time and effort, not to mention that it is increasingly likely English may not be the patient's native language, necessitating an interpreter. In addition, older patients may hold different assumptions about treatment or how the hospital works, and may be less familiar with technologies, treatments, and procedures than younger patients.

With seniors, it is often tricky to get a clear view of capacity. In my experience, diagnoses of capacity or incapacity made on the basis of a single evaluation are as likely to be wrong as right. The margin of error grows when the elderly person is traumatized: in a new setting, recently injured, or in the throes of an acute illness. Caregivers and family should ask: when was the patient assessed, by whom, and over how long a time?

If a patient seems incapacitated at the particular moment, other questions arise: Is the incapacity likely to be temporary or permanent, and, if temporary, will there be moments or windows of lucidity when we can clearly communicate with the person to understand her true values and preferences?

We must also factor out the effects of what the American Bar Association Commission on the Legal Problems of the Elderly terms the "Four D's": diet, drugs, depression, and disorientation. All of these can and do masquerade as dementia or mental illness in the elderly and many can be reversed with the right care.

Finally, we should ask if the tests done to assess a person's capacity make sense for that individual. People are complex beings, and when physicians and caregivers are strangers to those beings, they can easily misinterpret personal idiosyncrasy as incapacity. When my mother, Bessie, was being examined by a neurologist, he kept asking her to whistle, seemingly attaching importance to the fact that she couldn't. It was only when she began to improve and become reoriented to her surroundings that she upbraided him: "I've never been able to whistle." You see this happen every day in a hospital: the eighty-five-year-old illiterate laborer who never went to school, being asked to count backward by sevens; aged immigrants being given competency tests in a language they may not even speak.

Another element often at play with older patients is a recognized medical phenomenon termed "sundowning," where patients grow more confused, forgetful, and disoriented as the day wears on. It is not uncommon for an aging patient to seem perfectly spry and alert in the morning, but seem completely "out of it" late in the afternoon. This is further complicated by the behavior that we have labeled "the demented but articulate patient."

I first witnessed this bizarre neurological phenomenon shortly after John Arras joined the consultation service. We were called to consult on the case of Mr. McGregor, an eighty-two-year-old patient who was refusing diagnostic tests for blood in his stool, the likely symptom of bowel cancer. The

PGY-1 treating Mr. McGregor called to say that the patient was refusing care and the consulting psychiatric fellow had said that he was not capable of providing informed consent. Did that opinion mean, the PGY-1 wanted to know, that it was ethical to go ahead and do the tests that were "medically necessary"? "Hold everything," we cautioned, "we're on our way."

We arrived to find Mr. McGregor amiably visiting with his daughter. We had a charming conversation about his long and happy life, and about the fact that he knew he never wanted surgery. His daughter related that over the years, he had checked out of a series of hospitals when tests were recommended to determine the necessity for surgery. Since he was never going to undergo surgery, he apparently figured that he didn't need the tests—a bit of logic that certainly sounded right to me.

Upon returning to the office, we called the director of the Division of Liaison Psychiatry—the branch of psychiatry that consults about problems in the hospital—to announce that one of his fellows may have missed the boat. He himself offered to reinterview the patient, and called less than an hour later to report that the patient was utterly confused and so were we. The patient had no idea where he was, what day it was, or what was supposedly wrong with him. Mr. McGregor presented a classic example of some geriatric patients who are charming, socially appropriate, amiable, articulate—and quite confused.

The doctors faced a conundrum: Should Mr. McGregor make this decision himself? Would it truly be fair to him, the best way to respect his autonomy, to leave the decision to him? Or would it be merely abandoning an enfeebled patient to the maelstrom of medical chance?

Unfortunately, in Mr. McGregor's case, the issue became moot. His doctors felt that he was simply too fragile for the risks of surgery, his chance of surviving both the tests and the surgery were too slim. Moreover, the death he would suffer after such a surgery would be much more painful and drawn out than the death he would suffer without it. His daughter added that her father hated being in the hospital, had always been terrified of surgery. He sensed, she felt, that the end of his life was drawing near, and did not find it frightening, but merely somewhat sad. We could offer Mr. McGregor nothing more; he was discharged to his daughter's loving care and, two months later, he died.

With certain elderly people, it can be very hard for doctors and nurses to distinguish between mental impairments and personality. In my mother's case, the doctors wondered, was she uncooperative, cantankerous, and obstinate because her memory and mental function were impaired, or was she a woman who had spent a long lifetime being uncooperative, cantankerous, and obstinate? As her daughter, I could help them sort it out; she had always been obstinate, but being uncooperative and cantankerous were new characteristics, more than likely associated with her injury. But what if no family member had been there? How could the care team know when it was her disability, and when her personality, that was speaking?

When my father-in-law was in the hospital with pneumonia, one of the residents told my husband: "We had hoped that he was getting better, but your dad is very confused. He doesn't know what year he was born in." My husband patiently explained to the doctor the realities of first-generation immigrants: "Of course he doesn't—he never has. He came to this country by himself, an orphan after the chaos of the Russian Revolution. And believe me, even if he knew, he's not about to tell you, some young stranger he's never met. Dad just doesn't work that way." In many places, and perhaps here if we hadn't been there to run interference, Dad would have been labeled incapable and his decisions not respected because of that—simply because he didn't fit into the cultural assumptions of his doctors.

Too often, the next step is that decisions are simply taken out of the patient's hands. That almost happened with Alice

Morgan. Alice had lived a wonderfully colorful life. Born to a wealthy, proper Baltimore family in 1914, she had left home as a teenager, striking out on her own as a dancer, appearing in saloons and cabarets on the West Coast. For four decades, Alice danced in minor clubs in Denver, San Francisco, Los Angeles—and finally in New York. She had scrimped and saved to buy a small house in the Bronx, and even amassed a tidy nest egg for retirement.

Recently she had also acquired a sexy young companion, Raimondo, an Italian man about thirty years her junior who worked as a clerk. Their relationship was very unclear; it seemed they might be or had been lovers, and Raimondo had clearly lived in Alice's house for several years. Now, he took care of her, leaving food out for her meals when he left for the day. They also shared a love of theater and dancing. Each week, Raimondo would call a limousine and take Alice out for an evening of musical theater, and dancing until the early-morning hours. This erstwhile chorine obviously loved her evenings out on the arm of her willing squire.

Although at seventy-three Alice remained physically vital, her mental faculties were failing—the diagnosis was early Alzheimer's disease—leaving her increasingly confused, forgetful, and disoriented. In the last few months, she had become so disabled that she no longer remembered when it was time to eat the food Raimondo left. Recently, Alice's niece in Oregon had grown worried. On her last visit, she had met Raimondo, and noticed that several valuable family heirlooms were apparently missing, among them an expensive rug and an antique vase. Alice, confused, seemed not to have noticed, and Raimondo's answers seemed vague and evasive. The niece worried that this companion was preying on Alice, living in her house, using her money, and selling her possessions.

Alice was an outpatient in our geriatric clinic, and her caregivers were worried: she was losing weight, and they feared she was being neglected. Yet Raimondo was very opposed to paying for help in the house. When Alice's case came up on our regularly scheduled geriatric rounds, several of the doctors and nurses were very distressed. Some felt Raimondo was a gigolo preying on her infirmity; others, that he was in effect her companion/husband but woefully unaware of the gravity of her failing condition. Was this a case of an older woman being taken advantage of? Was theirs a relationship of medical neglect? If so, we had a legal and moral obligation to intervene, to bring the matter to court or report it to protective services for adults. The object of outside intervention would be either to protect her assets or to force Alice to accept the home care she seemed to need. The courts could also have a guardian appointed for her, who might decide to move her to a nursing home where her medical and nutritional needs would be taken care of. But, we feared, at a very high cost.

The caregivers faced a stark dilemma: should they invoke their power to interrupt this relationship, when neither Alice nor Raimondo was complaining? Did they know better what was good for Alice than she herself did? They worried that, by leaving her alone, they were breaching their professional and legal obligation to prevent neglect and abuse. But were they abandoning a helpless old woman to an abusive situation or simply minding their own business?

Such abuse is always on the minds of a geriatric care team. Victimization of the elderly, often labeled abuse or neglect, includes mental and physical abuse, yelling, tormenting and beating, as well as the inadequate provision of food and medical care. The United States House of Representatives Select Committee on Aging found that 5 to 10 percent of the elderly may be victims of moderate to severe abuse. Yet research suggests this abuse is far less likely to be reported than child abuse. Ruth Luckasson, a professor at the University of New Mexico and an expert on problems of aged and disabled people, has found that the elderly and those with disabilities are unlikely to complain about abuse, neglect, or victimization. They often fear they will

lose whatever support, even abusive support, they have, that
their complaints will trigger reprisals or get them sent to an
institution.

In Alice's case, there was no clear evidence of abuse. Her
case was made more complex by the fact that Raimondo seemed
to genuinely care for Alice. They both came to speak to the
weekly geriatric conference, where he seemed quite solicitous
and loving. That he was unable to care for her as well as a
medical staff was hardly unique. Yes, theirs was a nontraditional relationship—but it was consistent with her whole life,
which had been decidedly nontraditional. It was also clear that
she dearly loved their soirees: she bubbled to the staff about
going to the theater and dancing and, although she could not
recall what they had seen even a few days before, she was
clearly very happy. The final element in the stew was that the
niece seemed particularly upset by what she perceived as the
disappearance of Alice's possessions and property, including
several heirloom items from her family. Her keen interest in
these valuable items, it was noted by one nurse, was perhaps
not altogether selfless, for the niece was the likely beneficiary of
her failing aunt's estate.

After much discussion, we decided—with fear and trem-
bling—that we should not interfere. Involving the legal authorities could only interrupt a life that was giving two people
enormous pleasure. Yes, we might be able to improve Alice's
nutritional and health status, but we risked robbing her of something much more important: her independence and her source
of joy. For a lifetime she had taken risks, choosing to pursue her
personal pleasures often against the dictates of society. Because
there did not seem certain and immediate harm to letting her
dance her nights away with Raimondo, I argued that our task
was to respect her choices—at least for the moment. I pointed
out that in our society in general, and in the medical profession
in particular, there are a number of ways we endanger the autonomy of seniors. Sometimes we do so by excluding them

from decisions, or by encouraging dependency, or when we focus on the length and not the overall quality of their lives. People who are idiosyncratic or noncompliant usually are the first to have their capacity to make decisions challenged. If Alice chose to exit this life dancing, we should honor that wish. We could not, and should not, protect her from herself.

One other element that can lead us to disempower seniors is the specter of malpractice. In reality, it is extremely rare that malpractice cases involve older patients. That is true not because seniors aren't often victims, but for the more mercenary reason that our courts assign value to a life by its potential for lost earnings. This devalues seniors, whose prime earning years are behind them. Consequently, knowing that cases involving seniors are unlikely to bring large settlements, which generate fat contingency fees, lawyers are far less likely to take them on.

While the threat of malpractice is more apparent than real, it still exerts a tremendous force in the hospital. Physicians and administrators understand that when it comes to making difficult decisions for dying patients, dead patients don't sue. Unhappy family members do. Far too often, hospitals are led to practicing medicine defensively, shifting the discussions and decisions from the older patient to that person's family.

For their part, family members often collude in that process, unwittingly or not. They can bring any of a hundred reasons of their own to want to avoid involving aging loved ones in such conversations: their own fear and denial, long-standing family rivalries, or even self-interested concern for property or inheritance. Most often, of course, they act with the best motives, insisting that, "You'd just kill Mama if you talked about that." In fact, if Mama is dying, she probably already knows. When most old people are gravely ill, experience shows they think they are dying, even when they are not. Often, they are willing, even eager, to discuss their options and what lies ahead. It may, in fact, be the family members who are less ready to hear it.

Not long ago, during a lecture at a local elders' center, we were discussing the importance of discussing health-care issues with their families and, if they felt strongly about it, executing living wills or durable powers of attorney. A tiny, sprightly eighty-seven-year-old raised her hand at the end of my speech: "You don't understand. I want to talk about these things, but my children say: 'Don't worry, Mom, you'll live forever.' But I know that I am eighty-seven years old, and I won't live forever. That's what I want to talk about, but it is they, not I, who can't face up to the facts."

No matter who practices it, whether family or physician, excluding the elderly patient from discussions and decisions is both very common and ethically unacceptable. The golden rule calls for us to do to the one in the bed as we would want done to us were we in that position. That means our first impulse must always be to include, not exclude, the patient, to leave these decisions as long as possible in the center of the first circle. That makes it even more important to "talk to Mama," to involve her in discussions and make sure she is the one making the decisions about her care.

Once having made the decision to do that, you may find yourself having to stand up for that principle. If, for example, you are concerned that a member of the care team is trying to put you in the role of decider, you may want to clearly set him straight by saying: "Have you talked about this with Mom? This is something we should all discuss together." Nor should you let yourself be placed in the role of carrying information or discussion to your ailing relative if it makes you uncomfortable—that is part of the physician's responsibility, and should fall on his shoulders, not yours.

One of the most interesting lessons I have learned in almost two decades of working in such situations with elderly people is that if we are open, their communications are often easily understood. Seniors—even those with profound mental, physical, or emotional deficits—make known in a myriad of ways who they are and what they want. The hard part is remembering that even when they are in a somewhat compromised state, even when their decisions might not be reached by faultless logic, if the wishes of the person in the bed can be understood, we should respect and honor them as best we can. Being old, after all, is no reason to be deprived of the ability to control your life.

7

DIFFERENT PLACES, DIFFERENT RULES

Throughout this book we have focused on what happens when people are sick in the hospital. But for many seniors, hospitals play only a small role in their latter years. In our society, we are as likely to spend some or all of our later years in other circumstances: under the long-term care of a nursing home; living at home with family members or with an attendant for "home care"; even, in what is clearly the end stage of life, in a hospice.

All of us are more likely than our parents or grandparents to face such alternatives, and that likelihood increases with each passing year. The reason is simple: never before have so many of us been so old. Between 1950 and 1989, the number of U.S. citizens older than sixty-five grew by more than 270 percent, from 11.3 million to 31 million, and that group now represents about 1 in 8 Americans. Demographics suggest that this trend will only continue. By 2030, there will be two and a half times as many people over sixty-five as there are today—some 66 million Americans. The group of older Americans is, itself, aging: there are twenty-four times as many people eighty-five and over today as there were at the turn of the century. In the next forty years, the number of people over eighty-five—what demographers term the "old old"—will grow 25 percent each decade, while the overall population will grow very little.

With that demographic trend comes new challenges. For the first time, tens of millions of Americans will not be acutely ill, but will be old and unable to manage completely on their own. They will either need help in their own home or will need to be placed somewhere—in long-term-care institutions or in someone's home. Each of these poses its own distinctive challenges, ethical and practical.

Outside of a hospital, the ethical landscape changes markedly. How we should act—our responsibilities and rights, what we can expect as families, loved ones, or patients—will vary tremendously depending on where we are, and who is there with us. As we have seen in the acute-care hospital, the patient is the central character and has the right to make decisions if he can. In the parlance of ethics, we would say he or she is the decisive "moral agent," with the authority to decide; hence "autonomy" has been our watchword. This principle remains clear whatever the setting, but outside the hospital, whether at home or in an institution, the picture grows more complex.

Outside the hospital there are other people whose rights and interests are directly affected by the plans and choices the patient makes. Now, the patient's needs, rights, and interests must be balanced against the very real stakes and rights of others. For decisions that are strictly medical, the patient always remains at the center; but in the far larger arena of decisions about lifestyle and day-to-day living, that person must share center stage with others. At that point, the ethical principle of "autonomy" gives way to "accommodation."

In a family situation, for example, what is happening to the elderly person is also affecting the lives of a number of others. Statistics suggest that trend will only grow with our aging population, shrinking insurance coverage, and diminishing national incomes. A study by Dr. Francis G. Caro, at the Gerontology Institute of the University of Massachusetts, looked at seniors living outside of institutions and found that one in five needed some help with cooking, feeding, washing, shopping, basic housekeeping, or personal hygiene. For those over eighty-five, more than 50 percent required help. Many of those people don't want to go into an institution, so living at home—their own or a family member's—is the best solution. More than five million disabled elderly Americans now live at home.

What we term "home care" actually takes many forms. Perhaps eighty-four-year-old Grandpa still lives in his own home, and depends on his forty-eight-year-old daughter, Barbara, to come over daily to check on him, bring in shopping and groceries, and generally look after him. Or, if Grandpa can't manage on his own, he may actually move into Barbara's home, where the task of caring for him will fall to her, family members, and friends. In the most recent year sampled, more than seven million spouses, adult children, other relatives, friends, and neighbors provided unpaid assistance to disabled elderly.

If the family can afford it, there is a middle ground, which may include paying for someone to come into the senior's home. That person may be called a home health aide, a home attendant, or a personal care attendant; this person's job is to come in to do for, take care of, or even live with the senior. But even when you can hire home care help, family members almost always are required to play a huge role. So in reality, "home care" might more properly be termed "family care." When someone goes into a home instead of into an institution, it is usually assumed that a family member will be primarily responsible for the person, or will serve as secondary support to a paid care provider. Statistically, the great likelihood is that person will be female, and, equally likely, will receive no compensation for what can be virtually a full-time job. As all who have done it know, this work can require an extraordinary commitment of time and energy. Eighty percent of these unpaid caregivers devote an average of four hours each and every day, seven days a week, to caring for their elderly charges.

Often, family care involves someone who is chronically ill, who may be physically debilitated, mentally impaired, incontinent, incoherent, or even profoundly handicapped. When the child becomes parent and the parent child, it can raise powerful emotions. There is a vast emotional gulf between diapering your son and diapering your father, as anyone who has done it knows. As adults, having passed through the Freudian phases of separation and individuation that have distanced us from our parents, these adult relationships can be much more emotionally fraught. We carry the emotional detritus of decades of child-parent history, and we may feel anger, frustration, and resentment, all of which may interfere with the caring for a parent in ways it would never in caring for a child. Infants are cute and appealing, nature's way to ensure that this long dependency period will be respected. But old people confront us with our own mortality, often presenting pictures of decay and decrepitude; they may be smelly, even, to some, offensive. As autonomous adults, they may be resistant, unruly, and uncooperative. In sum, our parents are not our infants and we respond very differently to them when they become dependent.

As a result, in home and family situations, the ethical ideals of autonomy, self-determination, and patient preference are not the sole yardsticks for our discussions. It is not enough just to do what the patient wants and says. Now, family members in general, and the primary caretaker in particular, have the right to be considered and included in decisions. They have strong practical and ethical claims here, for their lives and families, their time and home, are affected.

Like it or not, the older person must accommodate the ability and willingness of other family members to meet those needs with time and money. Unless that happens, the older person is in the position not of making an ethically defensible choice, but of being self-centered and selfish.

Not surprisingly, conflicts are virtually inevitable. Often, ethical dilemmas in home care concern issues of control and power. These are the "oatmeal or cornflakes" decisions, those myriad struggles over who gets to make little decisions about daily life. In a shared living situation, these are the areas where flexibility must often temper autonomy. It can be hard to fit a new person—particularly an ailing elderly relative—into the routines and systems of the household, and hard, as well, for that older person to make the changes that are required.

Often, these interpersonal stresses grow acute in situations with a paid home attendant. When a stranger comes into someone else's home to do for them, they step into a lifetime of set patterns and routines, as well as the physical space of that person. By a simple act—say, moving a vase from the piano to the cocktail table—the aide may, in the eyes of the older person, upset familiarity and balance, the very essence of the household. Often, the aide has been invited by someone else, particularly when the person can no longer do for herself, so the elderly person may harbor strong resentment. When it is difficult for older clients, they often take it out on the health aide, becoming difficult, even abusive. When my mother, Bessie, was still quite shaky on her feet and could walk only with a walker, she became enraged when her home care attendant attempted to move a piece of furniture that clearly presented a danger to my mother. That night at dinner, she retaliated: when she put up dinner to warm, Bessie insisted that the food was enough to feed two, when it was barely enough to feed one, quite disabled, seventy-seven-year-old. Her message was clear: she would exert control simply by starving her home care helpmate. It was, I had to explain to her, an unacceptable response.

The financial arrangements for home attendants can build in resentment as well. Because virtually no insurance plans reimburse long-term home care, these aides are usually paid for out of the senior's, or the family's, own pocket, which can create its own stresses. Often, these strains pop out around the most commonplace issues: mealtimes, which television shows will be watched, who stays too long in the bathroom or on the phone. Ethically, the challenge becomes to balance the real rights and interests of many different participants, to temper one person's personal freedom to be, act, and do things her own way with the practicalities of social coexistence.

Nor is it just the family whose needs count here. In home care, the senior's needs must also be balanced against the larger community of lives affected by this person's staying at home, like neighbors. The classic example, known to every local family doctor or community-based geriatrician, is the Alzheimer's patient who wanders around, disoriented and confused, ringing neighbors' doorbells at 3:00 A.M. Clearly, we cannot permit elders' behaviors to intrude so seriously on others' lives.

Often, the community shapes what we can do for those we care for. In the small rural Long Island town in which I grew up, there was an eight-year-old girl with Down's syndrome who was sent out at 3:00 P.M. every weekday to do errands for her mother. All the townspeople knew her, and looked out for her, helping her cross streets and intersections. The grocer, who knew her family, helped her shop, carefully counting out the right change from the family purse. The child could do this independent errand for her family because the whole community was deeply involved in caring for her.

Not so long ago, such community involvement was often the rule, especially in small towns. Today, in this country, we most often find such steadfast community support in two distinct settings: those who belong to a tightly knit church, especially in smaller towns, with their traditions of people bringing food, helping with household chores, and helping each other in times of trial; and those in the nation's urban gay communities, where the devastating AIDS epidemic has brought an overwhelming outpouring of friends and volunteers, devotedly caring for each other. In both cases, the caring of the community itself allows those who are ill to stay at home, and out of institutions, long beyond what would otherwise be possible. Because others' lives are so intimately interwoven with the life of the patient, they have a right to be counted into the calculus of what happens, at home and beyond.

Getting Along with Strangers

For all of us, the notion of being "home" remains a magic and precious one. Yet many of us will not have that option. We may spend months or years of our lives in something called a "nursing" or "retirement," "board-and-care," or "long-term-care" "home." These terms, of course, are highly euphemistic: these are not true homes, but institutions. And they are growing ever more common. A recent study in the *New England Journal of Medicine* showed that almost half—43 percent—of people who turn sixty-five this year will spend some time in long-term care. Today, as you read this, nearly two million Americans are living in nursing homes, and it is projected that seven million of those alive today will end up in some form of institutionalized long-term care. If current trends continue, this figure will rise to fourteen million in forty years, so that by 2030 the number of elderly people requiring nursing home care will more than triple.

"Long-term care" means any place you go when you are not sick enough to be in a hospital, but cannot manage on your own. Often people are quite ill when they go to long-term care—if they weren't, they would probably still be at home. Some have just come out of the hospital, staying briefly while a hip mends; for others, it is a chronic way station on the path to death. Some are there because they are too feeble, frail, or compromised to live without the support of skilled professionals around the clock. Others are physically healthy, but mentally failing. Approximately 80 percent of people in long-term care have some significant cognitive disability such as memory loss or confusion; about one-half of all nursing home residents suffer from Alzheimer's disease. Some are propelled into nursing homes simply because of their sex: because women outlive men, and often don't have economic means, they make up nearly two-thirds of the residents in nursing homes.

In fact, an increasing number of people find themselves driven into a nursing home not because of physical or mental fitness, but because of economics. In almost every state, Medicaid and Medicare benefits cover virtually no home care and the great majority of insurance plans don't either. (In some few cases, Medicare may cover a short period of home care, which may then open up options for you to receive Medicare-enhancing private insurance, so called "Medigap" coverage. You should check this in your own state if you think it might apply to you or a family member.) Far more commonly, coverage is available if you go into an institution, but not available to pay the bills for the help you might need in your own home (which, ironically, may be much less expensive). Unfortunately, our nation's health policies make the far more rational and humane option of home care the exception to the rule, available only to the few who can afford it or who have selfless relatives to provide it. We have designed a cruelly efficient engine to drive people into expensive alternatives they would not otherwise choose. Even those who might be much better off at home with part-time assistance, and the many who would choose to stay at home, can rarely do so.

This economic structure makes more acute the ethical dilemmas the older person faces: When the time comes to leave the hospital, should she go home where the situation is risky and there is no way to finance the services she needs? Or should she go to long-term care where funds are available—providing that she has fallen into poverty—but where she must give up her privacy, independence, and a lifetime of comforting patterns and surroundings? For although the best of our institutions try to minimize that fact, ultimately, the comfort, security, privacy, and dignity that come from living at home simply cannot be duplicated in an institution. (On the other hand, for some people institutions provide welcome relief from the isolation, loneliness, and physical dangers that living alone can entail, and there are elders who enter a nursing home under great duress, only to find themselves thriving in that environment.)

Almost everybody in long-term care struggles with at least some of the same fundamental issues. One of those is grief, for it is virtually impossible to go into a nursing home willingly without deep ambivalence and even grief. Commonly, a period of grieving surrounds one's entrance into an institution: grieving for the independent person that you were, the objects you loved and left behind, the familiar pattern of managing your own days. That life change brings with it a significant alteration in the ethical contours of our decision making, as well.

No longer are you permitted to be the sole and autonomous center of your decisions. Now there are others to take into account. In the nursing home we must live by institutional policies and systems, schedules for meals and bedtime, the sensibilities of other residents. Where the ethical matters in acute-care hospitals often center on life-and-death decisions, in long-term care they involve the meshing of one's individuality to the other individuals in a larger community. One study from the University of Minnesota showed that what mattered most to people in nursing homes were not weighty issues of mortality, but their ability to use the telephone when they wanted to. Such issues comprise what bioethicist Arthur Caplan and gerontologist Rosalie Kane of the University of Minnesota term "the ethics of the mundane."

In nursing homes, problems often revolve around the antisocial or disruptive behavior of one of the residents. Both ethically and practically, that presents trying times for everybody. In my early years as a clinical ethicist, I was called to a nursing home consultation which involved the delicate "case of the public masturbator," a fellow of sixty-eight years who was perfectly friendly, disoriented, and confused. He continuously masturbated in the hall, in full public view, to the great dismay and consternation of staff and other patients. His roommate also objected. The ethical challenge was to work with this resident to keep his private behavior private, allowing others their right to go about their days without his unwelcome intrusions. It was solved when he was given one of the institution's very rare private rooms. The only other alternative would have been to tie him up—physically restrain him—or "snow him out" on an antipsychotic drug like Haldol—to chemically restrain him (both practices now illegal under federal regulations).

Similar ethical issues arise in different forms: the case of the secret smoker, or the reluctant bather so neglectful of his personal hygiene that he is offensive to other residents. To take the latter case—some variation of which comes up every few months in the long-term homes where we consult—the options are usually unappealing. Nurses and aides can cajole and whee-dle the reluctant bather into the desired shower—often a completely futile exercise; he can be calmed with drugs and cleaned; he can forcibly be tied into a chair for a shower when his odor grows intolerable.

In the case of the odoriferous Mr. Levinsky, a friendly but completely confused seventy-six-year-old man, the most ingenious and humane solution was found by one of the nurse's aides. Danny, a genial bear of a man who stands six feet four, used Mr. Levinsky's own beliefs to help him. When Mr. Levinsky had grown intolerably smelly, he follows his nose to his oblivious charge: "Mr. Levinsky," Danny says with a smile, "it's nearly time for *shabbas*. You want to be clean for *shabbas*." In fact, it may be days before the start of the Jewish sabbath at sundown on Friday evening, but Mr. Levinsky knows he should be clean for the sabbath celebration that has been so important throughout his life. His mind in a reverie of *shabbas*, he smilingly shuffles off to the showers in Danny's care. Ultimately, he will be clean for the Friday-night *shabbas* that week, and life for the staff and other residents is immeasurably better in the meantime.

Despite the arguments of some ethicists that lying is always wrong, in this case it strikes me as a benign strategy for success where everybody benefits. In cases like Mr. Levinsky's, where the degree of the deception is minor, and when it is clearly the most humane course among the available options, we are once again reminded how our black-and-white absolutes shade into gray when the idiosyncrasies of real people are involved. As nursing homes devise strategies to streamline and operate more efficiently, their systems may cut corners off the desires, values, and needs of residents. They can create a syndrome that psychologists call "learned helplessness," "infantilization," or "institutionalization," where people gradually become less able to choose and determine for themselves. Then the demands the institution has introduced into people's lives make it an affirmatively dangerous instrument, draining them of their very humanity. Soon, their lives are circumscribed in ever-smaller spaces, their autonomy all but extinguished. From an ethical perspective, we must be constantly vigilant that we are not taking actions that undermine the values and selfhood senior residents possess.

It is that equilibrium we strive for in selecting a long-term-care institution. You want a place that maximizes autonomy, where life is the least regimented, and that permits the greatest degree of privacy and choice—whether it's bedtime, activities, or mealtimes. Ideally, residents could keep possessions from their lifelong homes, such as a favorite chair or dresser. They should be encouraged to make their own decisions about health care for the present and for the future.

Institutions don't have to be rigid to be good institutions. They actually work better—for employees, owners, and residents alike—when they are set up to maximize, rather than curtail, their residents' freedom and autonomy. One place that comes closest to this ideal is an innovative nursing home in Maine, called Sandy River. Sandy River is different from the ground up, starting with the fact that many of its residents have family members on the staff, giving the institution a communal feeling. Sandy River doesn't enforce rigid hours for bedtimes or mealtimes; if you want to stay up, you can, and a room is open all night for residents to sit in and read or watch TV. Meals accommodate personal schedules as much as possible.

Its architecture reflects Sandy River's commitment to the ethics of autonomy: rooms are built into a cloverleaf design, allowing residents to wander in and out at leisure, providing a great deal of freedom within a secure setting, yet never allowing residents to stray too far out of range of the staff's watchful eyes. They provide private rooms for people to have intimate time together, recognizing seniors' need for privacy to do precisely the things that those of us who live in our own homes take for granted.

From its physical plant to its humanitarian outlook, Sandy River has managed to do much of what nursing homes say is impossible, with the explicit goal of nurturing their residents' sense of self-control and dignity. Unfortunately, Sandy River is the exception.

Far more common are institutions where the residents' needs seem to come far down the line after the smooth operation of the institution. One way such institutions keep control is with restraints, physical and chemical. According to the joint House-Senate Committee on the Elderly, well over half the people in long-term care in this country are kept under some form of restraint. Research shows that of the nearly one half million Americans who are restrained with belts, vests, and jackets, at least two hundred of them will die choking deaths this year. Records from a Minnesota study show that in one year, fully one-third of nursing home patients younger than seventy were given chemical restraints to make them easier to manage. More than half of the patients classed as "disruptive" are given anti-psychotic medication, despite the fact that these medications when used for nonpsychotic patients often make them worse. In Europe chemical and physical restraints are almost never used.

There are times, to be sure, as with my mother, when restraints are a necessary part of a short-term, focused medical plan designed to reverse the effects of illness or accident. Often, however, they are habitually used as powerful means to keep people docile. As such, they are shortcut substitutes for intelligent, humane, and sufficient management, the lazy alternative to proper staffing, training, supervision, and appropriate programs for residents. Anyone who has spent much time around such places knows that most long-term-care institutions go much further in restraining, requiring accommodation, and curtailing autonomy than is absolutely necessary. In the words of an editorial in the *New York Times*, "the overwhelming majority are restrained or sedated because it makes them easier to handle. . . . Heavy sedation or straps so diminish the existence of vast numbers of patients that they are robbed of the freedom and vitality that can make life worth living." In the worst cases, restraint and sedation degenerate into horrifying instances of abuse and neglect of the residents.

The serious problems of abuse have created both good and bad news for older persons. The good news comes in the form of a law passed by the U.S. Congress in 1987, the Nursing Home Reform Law, that established a set of explicit rights of nursing home residents. Among them are the following rights:

♦ To gain access to their own medical records within forty-eight hours of a request.

♦ To have thirty days' notice before a room change.

♦ To be provided with private areas for visits or solitude.

♦ To have private use of a telephone both wheelchair accessible and usable by hearing impaired and visually impaired persons.

- To know any deficiencies in their institutions found by state regulators.
- To share a room with a spouse or companion.

If some of these concerns seem commonplace, they are an eloquent reminder of the sobering state of affairs that they were drafted to correct. Perhaps the most important new right is to be free from the use of unnecessary physical and chemical restraints. Physical restraints can only be used if doing so will enable the resident to attain or maintain the highest level of mental, physical, or psychological function. The institution must exhaust and assess all less restrictive measures, and the resident or his legal representative must be involved with consultations with health professionals about the decision to restrain.

In terms of chemical restraint, residents may no longer be treated with psychotropic or antipsychotic drugs unless this specific therapy is necessary to treat a specific condition. In all cases the chart must document the reason for using this particular medication and the dangers of using the medications must be clearly spelled out. This newly established set of rights attempts to balance the scale somewhat, to make sure that the values and dignity of the individual are not being inhumanely sacrificed to lack of professional expertise or to institutional convenience.

The Nursing Home Reform Law has had some good effect. In 1988, the New Hampshire Health Care Association began urging nurses to gradually lessen restraints on their elderly patients. The number of patients under sedation shrank more than fivefold, from 66 percent to 12 percent. Patients have become more alert and social; their muscle tone and mobility have improved; family visits and nurse and patient morale have climbed—all without having to change the number of nurses.

At the same time these regulations have brought much-needed reform, they are also part of an increasing trend toward greater regulation of nursing homes, practiced by armies of state and federal regulators, inspectors, and oversight agencies. That trend, unfortunately, has had some unintended effects. For one thing, it has created a highly adversarial relationship with nursing homes, giving all long-term institutions an undeserved black eye, creating anxiety for patients and families alike.

For another, negotiating death in a nursing home can be a bureaucratic nightmare. Not long ago, when death was a frequent and tolerated visitor to most nursing homes, we spoke of pneumonia as "the old man's friend," understanding it to be a merciful end to life's most difficult transition. But with our society's mounting concern, even paranoia, over nursing homes, death's inevitable arrival increasingly came to be seen as the result of neglect or abuse. It became harder and harder to have a dignified, appropriate passing. For now it became the institution's goal to intervene aggressively, sending patients off into the medical machine, so nobody would charge neglect. For their part, regulators and bureaucrats helped fan that flame, creating what many nursing homes call the "bouncing ball syndrome," as patients bounce from hospital to nursing home to hospital and back.

Nursing homes, by definition, are not acute-care hospitals, lacking the hospital's advanced tools, techniques, and highly trained medical staff. Until recently, they have not even been required to have a physician on staff, and many were run only by a director of nursing, with the result that many such homes had woefully inadequate care. But even at their best, nursing homes are very rarely equipped to do full-scale resuscitation, and if more advanced care is required, the person must be moved to a hospital.

At that point, the older person and her family have come to a crucial crossroads; once she is transferred into an acute-care hospital, all involved are on the slippery slope of ever-increasing care.

Here again is a place where the proper advance planning can spell the difference between a merciful and a miserable death. It involves a tool that is only now being discussed in ethical and legal circles. It is the DNT—for "Do Not Transfer"—or DNH—for "Do Not Hospitalize"—order. Like a DNR order, a living will, or a durable power of attorney for health-care decisions, a DNT order is another tool in your arsenal of personal choice, a way for you to help assure that your wishes will be heard and heeded when the time comes.

Like a DNR order, which applies to the specific medical act of resuscitation (usually in a hospital), a DNT order precludes the specific act of transfer to a hospital where resuscitation or other aggressive procedures would occur. DNT's are complicated. There are certainly times—when a person is in pain, or if she has an acute injury such as a broken hip that could be repaired, letting her regain independence and functioning—that going into a hospital for treatment makes sense. Often, however, transfers happen in all the wrong ways for all the wrong reasons. When a person is terminally ill or in the process of dying, when aggressive medical interventions would be unsuccessful in providing renewed health, then this tool can mercifully prevent someone you love from being sacrificed to the maelstrom of the hospital. That is why the best DNT orders allow for some discretion. As such they loom just over the horizon, as ethicists, caregivers, administrators, and attorneys struggle to strike a proper balance.

When an older person requests not to be transferred to a hospital, we should ask the same questions we face with a DNR order: Is that appropriate medically? Does it reflect clinical depression? Does this seem to be a well-considered, consistent decision? Does the person seem at peace with herself or fearful? Does she want to be transferred for comfort care, but not life-sustaining interventions? If others are making the decisions for her, what is the basis for their right to decide and which standards should constrain their choices? DNT orders—like all the advance-planning tools we have discussed—are a way to make sure you won't be stuck in a life you don't want to live.

Hospice: Hope at the End

There is one last venue where we may spend our final days, one that has come into its own only recently: the hospice. Hospices differ radically from a nursing home or a hospital. They are the antechamber of an uncontested death, the place we go to die with full knowledge and no apologies. The stated goal of hospice care is not to combat mortality, but to ease its arrival. Rather than focusing medical hope and energy on cure or treatment, the hospice exists to make your life and body as comfortable as possible as death approaches, to help you retain as much hope as possible until death occurs, and to help you and your family to experience death as peacefully as possible.

In general, comfort and palliation of suffering are the goals of hospice care. Hospice staff often talk in terms of rejecting "aggressive" therapies—those meant to reverse the process of the underlying disease—in favor of "gentle" ones, those given to increase the comfort, and alleviate the suffering, of the patient. The distinction turns not on *what* the specific treatment is, but on *why* it is being done. Invasive surgery, for example, would normally be considered highly aggressive. But in a person with terminal cancer who comes down with an emergency inflamed appendix, the appendectomy would likely be done— not with the goal of removing the underlying cancer or prolonging life, but to relieve the pain of the appendicitis. Likewise, a blood transfusion given in the hopes of stopping the underlying disease is "aggressive"; the same treatment offered to give the patient more energy to enjoy her final days would be "gentle."

In hospice care, the medical arts have come full circle, acknowledging that just as there is a time to resist death's blandishments there is also a time to accept the inevitable. Because the assumptions of the place are different, it frees doctors and nurses to go about the work of keeping their charges as comfortable as possible. Both in expertise and expectations, hospice caregivers bring a wholly different attitude than do their in-hospital colleagues. In hospitals, doctors and nurses are rarely versed in the art of managing pain; they may even be reluctant to do so, fearing that pain medications will mask symptoms and obstruct their ability to deliver care.

In the hospice setting, caregivers are specifically trained to minimize pain. More important, they share a deep philosophical and ethical commitment to doing everything possible to keep people comfortable—without being distracted by worry for their long-term prognosis.

Hospice is less a place than it is a philosophy of care. You don't have to be in a hospice to use its ideas. Often, the primary function of a hospice is to coordinate home care where the person stays at home and the hospice sends out visiting nurses and even doctors to help the family and patient move comfortably toward death. Above all, hospice tries to fit care to the patient's values, wishes, and circumstances. Hospice is designed to give patient and family maximum control over the details of one's final time and even the quality of death. As part of that view, hospice programs encourage open discussion of the process of dying. But where acute care focuses solely on the needs of the patient, hospice supports both the patient and the family. Hospice respects, first and foremost, the rights of those most involved in seeing this human life through to a dignified, appropriate death—however they themselves may define it.

That means that what is or is not appropriate in hospice varies by circumstance. Two years ago, my bioethics team was called to consult about Edward, a ninety-two-year-old man dying from liver cancer. At peace and ready to die, he contracted pneumonia. Normally, in a hospice, that would not have been treated with antibiotics; he would just have been kept comfortable as the lung infection took him. But in this case, he asked for treatment; his favorite granddaughter was getting married in ten days, and he dearly wanted to attend the wedding. Our discussions with the hospice staff led us to a unanimous conclusion: the man was ready to die, and soon would. Treating his pneumonia would not affect his underlying liver cancer, but given his deeply felt wishes, we thought it was entirely appropriate to provide treatment that a hospice normally would not. It was, in our eyes, a way to let Edward die in dignity and peace and to permit what was most important to him.

In a high-tech age, hospice represents a conscious return to the roots of medical tradition: a way to comfort and care rather than diagnose and defeat illness. For those comfortable with it, hospice offers a compassionate alternative. There are, however, a few practical impediments. First of all, hospice is a new development, and some doctors may be unacquainted with its goals, or reluctant to transfer someone to an institution committed to comfort rather than cure. Families and patients may also be unfamiliar with the idea of hospice and mistrust its less technological approach. They may be very ambivalent about relinquishing the struggle for cure or uneasy about the propriety of accepting death. No matter how resigned or well prepared, none of us can be indifferent to the idea that we are going someplace to die.

Finally, hospices in this country are a phenomenon of the last two decades; they remain a rarity in most places. There are only some eighteen hundred hospices nationwide, including units in private hospitals, and a smaller number yet of Medicare-licensed hospice programs. Private insurance generally does not cover hospice care, although Medicare does under certain circumstances. If you think a hospice may make sense for you or someone you love, there are some straightforward questions to pose:

♦ At this stage, is this person's medical condition amenable to medical or technological treatment that will allow him to retain his present condition or to regain higher levels of functioning? Is the available treatment of substantial benefit not outweighed by its attendant burden?

♦ If not, does your community have a hospice program available that can ensure that pain and suffering will be controlled as much as possible?

Given the problems we have seen with mindlessly aggressive medical intervention, hospice does offer a humane and supportive way for those we love to spend their final weeks or months. For the patient who lies beyond cure, the hospice movement is the place to temper the headlong rush of the technological imperative with the oldest of our human virtues, compassion.

As we have seen, the choices we will have depend in large part on where we find ourselves, and those we love. But whether we are in a hospital or at home, in a nursing home or hospice, it is often hard to hear the voices of those who are ill, and harder still when they are also old.

To help us do that, here are a few tips that have been adapted from *Effective Counseling of the Elderly,* published by the American Bar Association Commission on the Legal Problems of the Elderly.

◆ Hold discussions at times when the elderly person is most alert and comfortable. For example, if you know that the person has morning bathroom difficulties, that would not be the best time to help the person to focus on difficult and complex issues. Be certain that the person is comfortable in the chair or bed before you begin the discussion. Ask, for example, if he needs a pillow or a glass of water.

◆ Take time to explain all of the issues slowly and carefully. Questions of health and the possibility of dying are emotionally loaded and hard to deal with. Do not make important points quickly and in passing. To be sure that the person has grasped the importance of the discussion, talk about it for a bit, without being condescending.

Organize your discussion carefully so that your points are clear and follow in a logical manner; thus, don't talk about death before you talk about health-care decisions in general. You may even try, if there is time, to spread your discussion over a few visits.

◆ Be direct, not bashful. All older people, and especially those with health problems, and most especially those in the hospital, have thought about death. If they don't want to talk about it, you can be sure they will be clear and forceful. Often, a lack of response simply reflects their concerns for the sensibilities of their family members and loved ones. Try not to communicate the idea that you are uncomfortable with these topics.

◆ Work to listen carefully. Many older persons talk slowly and respond precisely to questions. They have a lifetime's worth of experiences and values to consider when crafting an answer.

◆ Be aware of their limitations. To compensate for hearing loss, try to reduce or eliminate background noise. It may help to sit so that the person can see your face and especially your lips. Speak in a low pitch, slowly, enunciating clearly.

To compensate for vision loss: double- or triple-space all written materials and type them in large type, if possible, or in all capital letters. Allow ample time for the person to read the materials, and let them read without facing a source of glare such as a shiny tabletop, desktop, or window.

◆ Be prepared. Bring documents relevant to the person's care and be prepared to leave them for a day or two for the person to read and contemplate before actually arranging for signature. Of course, sometimes his condition may not permit this leisure, but if possible, it will make it easier for the patient.

These suggestions may be more or less help for any given older person. They, like all of us, differ enormously, aging at different rates and in various ways. Trust what you know about the person to judge her strengths and weaknesses, so you can both work together to make sure her decisions are the best ones possible.

For all of us, whatever our age, there are many reasons why it is hard to hear the voices of the elderly, particularly when they are also ill. In our culture, age and sickness conspire to create a double jeopardy. All of which makes the moral of this chapter an easy, and by now a familiar, one: we keep most control of our lives by thinking ahead. If we are to steer our own fate, at least where our health care is concerned, we do well to chart our course, know our options, and make our decisions while we are still able to.

8

INNOCENTS LOST

DECIDING FOR NEWBORNS

We all expect, at some time, to face the death of a parent. Many of us, as well, will endure the serious illness of a spouse or loved one. But the worst nightmare we can face comes when the person in bed is a child. Since the medical issues they encounter differ from those faced by adults, the next three chapters deal with what happens when the patient is too young to make decisions and balance options, and the various players, and questions that arise starting from the very moment of birth.

Tyrone was one of those babies who never get a fair chance at life. Up until a few years ago, he would not have survived his first few days; in Montefiore's state-of-the-art pediatric ICU, he had spent every day for five and a half months lying alone in his bassinet, fighting a losing battle for life.

When I saw him, Tyrone lay immobile, scarcely sixteen inches long, so small he could fit in one large hand. His skin was a sickly gray, his breath coming in shallow puffs from a ventilator next to the bassinet through a tracheostomy tube connected to a hole in his neck through a collar. He was completely unresponsive, so still that you had to look closely to see that he was breathing at all. One eye was closed, the other a slit, barely open, unfocused. One of the pediatricians gestured at the tiny inert form. "This is Tyrone at his most active." As I stood there, he stabbed a button on the panel of the heart monitor and a nearly flat green line wobbled across the bottom of the monitor screen, the feeble trace of this child's failing heart activity.

Tyrone's short life history was captured in his bulging medical chart. Born to a twenty-one-year-old diabetic mother who had already lost three babies in miscarriages, he was the sad result of her fourth try. He had twelve serious birth defects. All the organs of his abdomen and chest—heart, lungs, liver, stomach—were flip-flopped in left-to-right mirror image of their usual placement, as though some malign surgeon had taken his vital organs out and put them back in precisely backwards. The left side of his heart was underdeveloped, the blood vessels connecting it to the circulatory system grossly distorted, and the artery going to his lung seriously narrowed, dramatically reducing this vital blood flow. Two main valves in his tiny heart were malformed, and two large holes—the ductus arteriosus and the foramen ovale—which normally seal themselves around the time of birth, had not done so. The combination meant that blood was leaking and backing up seriously, both within the chambers of the heart and where the heart meets the circulatory system.

In addition, Tyrone was microcephalic, his head grossly underdeveloped, which suggested brain malformations; he had a marked weakness—medically, a "palsy"—of the seventh nerve controlling one-half of his face; his left eye was small and malformed, and his right ear lower than his left. The combined problems suggested that he had either a severe genetic abnormality or had perhaps suffered an infection in the womb about the sixth week of development; no matter their cause, his problems were severe and irreparable.

On Tyrone's second day of life, surgeons made a desperate

attempt to increase blood flow to the lungs, but the overlapping effects of his other problems made further surgery impossible. Now, five months later, it was clear that his brain had become severely damaged, its higher centers atrophied. He could not play or interact with anyone, could not even swallow, and required feeding through a tube running into his nose and down to his stomach. He had contracted pneumonia twice, battled five other major infections, and required resuscitation more than twenty times. On these occasions, his lungs would begin to fail, he would gasp for air, turn blue, and require the nurses to "bag" him—fitting a manual ventilation bag over his nose and mouth to force oxygen into his lungs and stabilize his condition. In addition to all of this, on the day I was meeting with this team, they had learned that Tyrone had been exposed to chicken pox, so he was isolated to protect other babies in the ICU.

Fourteen members of the pediatric intensive care unit— medical students, ICU nurses and assistants, social workers, house staff, and physicians—attended this meeting; in his short life, Tyrone had touched a lot of people. A senior pediatrician presented the medical facts, explaining why Tyrone's days had degenerated into an unbroken dirge of pain. "Each time he is bathed or changed, touched at all, he starts to arrest, turns agitated and blue; his heart slows and he gasps for air." He shook his head sadly. "This baby is trying to die."

A nurse quietly agreed: "Every time I bag him, I apologize to him for making him suffer another day." One doctor proposed they remove him from the ventilator and let nature take its slow but ultimately humane course. At least, a Do Not Resuscitate order would make Tyrone's next cardiac arrest— they now happened at least daily—his last. Fourteen heads nodded in agreement.

Normally, such a painful decision is made by and with the parents, but Tyrone had no known father and his mother was, in the words of an intern, "checked out." Only twenty-one, she had attempted suicide twice since his birth and did not seem to understand her son's worsening condition. She visited him once a week or less, sometimes disappearing for several weeks at a time. She had recently gone to visit her family for three weeks without informing anyone taking care of Tyrone. The day she reappeared she stayed less than five minutes and left without even asking how her son was. Several times she had come and gone without even visiting Tyrone at all.

Several members of the team described her detachment as bizarre, virtually unprecedented, way beyond the kind of denial they often encounter. They felt that her own desperation seemed to have blinded her to her infant's obvious misery. She asked when he would "get better and come home," and seemed not to hear when doctors gently told her "never." One intern termed her thinking "magical." The nurses worried that her sporadic visits did not give her any real appreciation of her son's continuous suffering. Tyrone's mother insisted on the most aggressive treatment and would not even consider the alternatives.

The team was anguished. They feared violating the most basic ethical rule of "do no harm." The other key ethical principle—"let the patient decide"—was of no help, for any newborn is a tabula rasa, with no history of desires or preferences and no capacity to create them. In general with children, the rule is that parents decide, in consultation with physicians, what is best for the child. As a society, we let parents make decisions for their ailing children because we presume they have the child's best interests at heart and will act as the child's best advocate.

But sometimes, as in Tyrone's case, parents betray that most fundamental trust, either intentionally or through their own inability to deal with the situation. Then we encounter the dilemma the pediatric team was now facing: whether this uninvolved mother should indeed be given the authority to decide without some concomitant responsibility to care, or at least to know the facts of her child's situation and prognosis. Because

Tyrone's mother had not been willing or able to act knowledgeably for him, should it fall to this team of dedicated strangers to analyze the issues, fashion the options, and choose the best solution? Was it their job to do what was right?

As we talked, their reluctant consensus grew clearer: medical efforts were futile. Tyrone would never be better, so there was no medical justification for continuing treatments that caused him further pain and could promise no compensating benefit. Merely extending this life of pain with no prospect of recovery, growth, or development was not a benefit. Tyrone would never experience pleasure, nor relate to others; medicine or surgery would only prolong his suffering. Tyrone's mother might have the legal right to decide whether her baby should be resuscitated, but had she forfeited that right by her seeming indifference and lack of involvement? Did the physicians and nurses have to continue what they felt to be a harmful and inhumane care plan? After all, they knew, as members of the pediatric intensive care unit, their prime duty lay with their young patient who slept fitfully in his bassinet, mute and helpless.

Could they act on their own? Was it appropriate to override the mother? Was her decision to continue care, and with it suffering, valid? Was that best for Tyrone? Or would death be a more humane alternative?

Not long ago, when our society routinely handed physicians sweeping powers to decide, such determinations were made more easily. Today at Montefiore, as in many progressive teaching institutions, we inculcate in doctors the practice of listening to and honoring the wishes of patients and families. We train them to include others in decisions and obtain their informed consent. Tyrone's case was troubling precisely because it made physicians and nurses wrestle with their own roles and their ethical responsibility to provide the best care for Tyrone; the difficulty is deciding what is "best."

Wearing my lawyer hat, I explained that the law does not

require us to provide futile treatment for a child who is suffering and is close to death. Nor does it demand that we slavishly follow the demands of a parent if that entails increased pain and suffering with no attendant benefit. The sad fact was, this baby was trying to die and we all agreed he should be permitted to do so. That situation, in itself, posed neither ethical nor legal problems. Supporting life does not require senseless procedures that merely prolong suffering.

But although Tyrone was the primary patient, all of us were also concerned to help the mother. What was our obligation to this young woman with her three miscarriages and two suicide attempts? Surely, it was her right to know the basic truth: that every tool of modern medicine could not keep her son alive, that her baby was in the process of dying, that all we could do was to prolong that process. She must hear, as well, that we could not comfortably and ethically continue care that brought him agony simply to pacify and placate her.

We agreed that the senior pediatrician would again attempt to talk with the mother and would ask for a meeting with the bioethics committee. In addition, he would try to convene a small meeting with her, other family members if she agreed, and a social worker, to try to arrange for some psychological support. We would ask her if she wanted to hold Tyrone in her arms in the final moments, so she could know she had been with him. As best we could, we would give her the comfort she needed.

Six days later I learned that the baby's pediatrician had contacted the mother several times, trying to explain the circumstances. She had, however, declined to come to the hospital, either to meet with the care team or to see her son. With the agreement of the ethics committee, the team assigned Tyrone a "Do Not Resuscitate" status. The next day, he began his usual cycle of falling into cardiac distress. It progressed into a full-scale cardiac arrest, from which he was not resuscitated. Tyrone died two days before his sixth month of age.

Yes, parents have rights, but if they conflict with what is best for the child, what happens? Who should decide? Who does decide? Sometimes the price of doing the right thing is incredibly high. Sometimes we can do no better than to provide what medical ethicists call "the least worst alternative."

Some time ago, a friend, by then a successful practitioner of obstetrics and gynecology, described the first time he delivered a baby on his own as a medical student in the 1950s. The fetus that emerged was grossly abnormal: few of its external organs were in the right place; its internal organs were plainly visible in an open abdominal sac; it was not even breathing. Shaken, he reached to swat the baby's behind as per the textbook delivery protocol when he felt the hand of the obstetrical nurse, a twenty-five-year veteran of the delivery room, gently stay his arm. "Don't rush," she said quietly, her eyes locking with his. "No need to rush."

In those days, some babies didn't make it out of the delivery room. But the process of deciding was no process at all. Physicians and, less often, nurses made decisions based on what they thought was right; neither parents nor other professionals had any formal opportunity to consider the options, the issues, or decide for themselves. Physicians knew that they were making value judgments, and tried to do so according to principles of beneficence and kindness. They attempted to spare parents the anguish and pain of confronting life-and-death decisions about their offspring. Most of the decisions favored life for the "normal" child, but neonates with congenital anomalies—the imperiled newborns—often didn't leave the delivery room alive.

Physicians, by and large, viewed this as appropriate. There was even a famous article published in the prestigious *New England Journal of Medicine* that argued that these decisions properly belonged to physicians, although parents could, under some circumstances, be consulted. In part this was because, medically, there was little that could be done anyway. Without the tools of modern microsurgery, synthetic antibiotics, infant ventilators, and resuscitation available in the modern neonatal intensive care unit, doctors had no choice but to let these imperiled babies die naturally. Now, for better or worse—and in a hospital you learn it is definitely both—there is just such a choice.

The doctors and nurses who deal with these cases know only too well that treatment can be both a benefit and a burden. It can inflict extraordinary suffering and pain on baby and family for the scant benefit of a few days or months of purely biological existence. There has long been a tacit understanding among medical professionals that some young lives are simply better off not prolonged. That means that certain newborns, as much as we might wish otherwise, are simply not appropriate subjects for medical interventions. But some will grow and thrive and experience lives of pleasure.

At the moment of birth, however, it is very difficult, if not impossible, to know which babies fall into which category. Making a mistake at that moment leaves no possibility for recovery. Thus, alongside the "don't rush" rule a new rule began to emerge for physicians in the delivery room: "treat first, assess later." Although with newborns, and sometimes with children, the best thing to do may be to permit a merciful and quick death, our increasing ability to keep babies alive forced us to confront the question of when this is the ethically proper course. Our medical skill has brought with it the ordeal of selection, and required us to consciously opt for life or death. Our increasing sensitivity to the complexity of ethical dilemmas demanded that doctors include the parents in these agonizing decisions.

Traditionally, once the determination was made that a baby was hopelessly imperiled, it fell to physicians to make the actual decision not to treat, often within a matter of seconds. Parents, it was felt, not only lacked the experience and knowledge to make complex medical decisions, but were typically in a shattered, emotionally vulnerable state. It was considered far more humane for the doctor, knowing the parents' and community's morals and values, to relieve the parents of a tragic burden and make the decision alone. The physician, with his greater skill and detachment and the experience of years of practice, felt it a duty to shoulder these hard choices.

Then, in the 1960s and '70s, that view began to change from two directions. The growing patients' rights movement argued that patients and their families, rather than doctors, had the right to decide about their care. While, obviously, the newborn could not decide, the next most closely involved party, the parents, could and should decide what happened to their baby. At the same time, the disability rights movement challenged the accepted wisdom that the lives of some people—babies with Down's syndrome, the mentally retarded, those injured in car accidents or war, victims of diseases like cerebral palsy—were somehow of less value to society. They stood up for the idea that people with disabilities were valuable, their lives worthwhile, and that they were every bit as entitled to care and treatment as anyone else. Issues once medical were becoming political.

Matters came to a head on April 9, 1982. That evening, in an operating room in Bloomington, Indiana, a baby boy, Baby Doe, was born. He had Down's syndrome, a genetic abnormality that is irreversible and leads to some retardation and some altered facial appearance; he also was born with esophageal atresia (a blockage of the esophagus), a reversible condition. Because of his genetic condition, the baby's physician did not recommend he be subjected to the succession of surgeries, first to place a feeding hole in his stomach and subsequently to open the esophagus, that would allow the baby to eat and therefore survive. Instead, his parents and doctors chose a different course: they decided to put the baby in a corner of the hospital ward to be allowed to die as his congenital deformities took their natural course.

That child's life would last only a few days; but it would spark off a fire storm of debate that would forever change American medicine. It began when a nervous hospital administration, reluctant to simply let the baby die, brought the case to court. The parents testified that the child would never achieve even a minimally acceptable quality of life. The trial court upheld the parents' right to make the decision and the Supreme Court of Indiana upheld that decision. Meanwhile, intimate facts about Baby Doe's life and death were splattered across newspapers from coast to coast.

It began a legal-medical-ethical free-for-all, for it turned out that a number of groups had powerful reasons to care about what happened to this Baby Doe in particular, and to other babies like him. The first to weigh in were lawyers from the Reagan administration's Justice Department, reflecting the political agenda of pro-life activists and a personal commitment to children with Down's syndrome. Their concern was that Down's syndrome babies would be left untreated when they could be helped, which they argued was a form of discrimination against the disabled. To prevent that, the federal government issued regulations based on laws prohibiting discrimination against the handicapped. These regulations mandated that no infant could be "discriminatorily denied food or customary medical care" and, for a period, required signs in every hospital nursery and pediatric unit saying: "Discriminatory failure to feed and care for handicapped children in this facility is prohibited by federal law." They even set up an 800-number hot line to facilitate reports of violations.

The federal regulators were joined by disability advocates, who saw in the case a watershed for the rights of disabled people to medical care. They pointed out that babies with Down's syndrome had, for centuries, been shoved into asylums and back rooms. Yet the mere fact of Down's syndrome,

per se, does not make an infant imperiled, nor does it irrevo-
cably sentence her to a hopeless, "useless" life. Our modern
understanding and treatment of the manifestations of Down's
syndrome show that a sizable percentage of these children can
go through life as functioning and productive people. With
proper medical management and adequate social support from
the family and community, many of them lead quite productive
and fulfilled lives.

Physicians, for their part, were wary that the Baby Doe
furor had the potential to lead medical care in worrisome new
directions. Most of them agreed that Baby Doe should, in fact,
have been treated, that his physical problem was easily reme-
died and his genetic condition did not preclude meaningful life.
From their perspective on the front lines, they saw in him a
symbol of the struggle to protect their small patients from the
prejudice of some parents and physicians. But they also feared
that in the haste to protect some babies, a policy of "treat at all
costs" would emerge. That, they knew, would be as terrible as
permitting discrimination. Many physicians argued that, just
because they had great success with one very specific kind of
infant—Down's syndrome babies—that should not influence
treatment of other seriously imperiled, multiply handicapped
newborns. They worried that hospitals were applying the lessons of Down's syndrome babies too broadly, that it was becoming mandatory to treat, and overtreat, infants with the most
extensive physiological and neurological problems regardless of
what parents, families, or doctors believed was right.

Smack in the middle of the debate were the medical ethicists. It was clear that our society needed to sort out our attitudes about hopeless, multiply impaired children, who were the
by-products of our burgeoning medical expertise. More important, physicians needed to distinguish between two very different kinds of infants: imperiled children whose overwhelming
medical problems precluded a chance at a meaningful life, and
those who were disabled or retarded but who had a chance of

growing, communicating, giving and receiving love. Clearly, what was at stake was very different for these children. Society also had to decide, in case there was a contest between parents, physicians, hospital administrators, and the state, who had the ultimate authority to render judgments on life and death. More and more children with handicaps were surviving infancy—that was a success story. But our ability to think clearly about the decisions that surrounded their lives seemed mired in conflict, confusion, and politics.

It was also clear, as the discussion ensued, that different parties were talking at cross-purposes. To some, "handicapped babies" meant functional Down's syndrome or merely retarded children, where others meant the hopeless, profoundly damaged infants who would never get off life-support machines. Surely there was a middle ground that would respect the rights of both.

Over the next year the issues raised by Baby Doe were dissected, argued, and analyzed in meetings and symposia, in the courts and the Congress, in hospital nurseries and academic medical centers. A coalition led by the American Academy of Pediatrics went to court to challenge the federal government regulations. The federal judge was finally to rule that the regulations were improper; the warning signs were removed and the hot-line number disconnected. When the dust settled, local hospitals were not obliged to follow these hastily conceived regulations. The process reminded us all of the old adage, "For every problem there is an apparent neat and tidy solution, which is simply wrong."

The national debate raised a series of deep questions. Did infants, no matter how disabled, have a right to life? Was it a foregone conclusion that treatment was always appropriate? Did the fact that it was technically possible to maintain these tiny bodies mean it was ethically or legally mandatory that doctors do so? Was it the role of the federal government and regulatory agencies to create inflexible, hard-and-fast rules that would bind parents and caregivers? Were parents and caregivers really the enemies of their newborn babies, so that society needed to protect the infants by law and regulation?

Into the midst of this maelstrom came another severely and multiply handicapped baby—Baby Jane Doe. She was born on October 11, 1983, in a Long Island hospital and soon transferred to the neonatal intensive care unit at the University Hospital at Stony Brook, New York. Lawrence Washburn, the right-to-life activist from Vermont, went to court to force the parents to consent to treatment to close an opening in her spine. The New York court effectively told Mr. Washburn to butt out, that the decision whether or not to treat the baby was a decision for the parents in consultation with their doctor—not for a stranger with a political agenda.

Next the federal government joined the fray, demanding to see the hospital records to ensure that no violation of the baby's rights had occurred. They threatened to remove funding for the hospital—a matter of some $20 million—if the hospital did not comply. What had been a personal tragedy was now making front-page headlines as political activists, courts, hospitals, and the federal government lawyers all jumped in. At the heart of the battle lay a question for society: who actually has the right to decide about the care of a child?

The federal government brought its own loud views. Reagan administration representatives saw in this an ideological war. They seemed unable or unwilling to distinguish between two very different kinds of infants: those with disabilities and those with only the slimmest likelihood of surviving, whose conditions sentenced them to lives of pain and suffering. It was these children who were most at issue. It was for them this battle was being fought.

After extensive negotiations between medical associations, regulators, federal officials and advocates, it was agreed that failure to respond to an infant's life-threatening conditions would be an illegal withholding of treatment unless:

A. The infant is chronically irreversibly comatose;

B. The provision of such treatment would
   i. merely prolong dying,
   ii. not be effective in ameliorating or correcting all of the infant's life-threatening conditions, or
   iii. otherwise be futile in terms of the survival of the infant; or

C. The provision of such treatment would be virtually futile in terms of the survival of the infant and the treatment itself would be inhumane.

This language was eventually codified by the United States Congress in an amendment to child abuse legislation, giving us a formal yardstick to measure the medical, ethical, and legal acceptability of any decisions to withhold or withdraw care from newborns. For many of us, the words "virtually futile" and "inhumane" were the magic here—they allowed a place for human judgment and compassion. None of us ever wants to see a baby die who could live and gain human satisfaction from the contact and love and comfort of others. But, equally important, no one wants decisions about real people's suffering to be made by the impersonal scythe of federal bureaucrats and regulators—most especially not in the ever-variable world of medical care and the human experience between parent and child.

But through it all, history had been made. For the first time, America had held an extraordinary national conversation, conducted in our newspapers, our newscasts, our churches and courts, and in the halls of Congress. We sought, as a nation, to forge an ethical vision concerning our society's responsibilities to its youngest, most vulnerable members. It brought together, for the first time, advocates and caregivers, religious representatives, advocates for disabled rights, the federal Department of Health and Human Services, the American Academy of Pediatrics, judges, and politicians. When the smoke cleared, bioethical decisions about the lives of children had gone public. As a nation, America had gone on record about these agonizing issues. We said, first, that we considered the biological accident of certain conditions—Down's syndrome, mental retardation—as no barrier in itself to treatment for a correctable problem, any more than might be the biological accident of red instead of black hair. In effect, the consensus made such conditions in general, and Down's syndrome in particular, medically and morally neutral in considering treatment decisions for newborns.

We also officially recognized the wide variation in the lives of neonates. We acknowledged and distinguished between cases when babies could and should receive proper treatment, and cases when infants dying with profound and multiple handicaps should not be subjected to medical intervention that is inappropriate or cruel, or that causes or prolongs suffering. Our new legal-ethical approach is a "child-centered" ethic. It requires that such decisions not be based on classes and categories—that this is the "type" of child society wants or doesn't—but rely instead on a clear-eyed evaluation of this individual child's capacities, pain and suffering, and medical particulars. Always we recognize that maximizing life span for any child is an ethically and medically reasonable goal if it produces pleasure and satisfaction for that particular child. It is also recognized that there is a sphere in which it is ethically appropriate for parents and physicians together to exercise judgment and make decisions.

Most important of all, the discussion had shifted our ethical compass, moving the child to its appropriate place at the center of the discussion. It was agreed that life-and-death decisions could not be made only by taking into account the wishes of the parents or the convenience of the family, but must take into account the well-being of the one most intimately involved: that helpless baby in the bassinet.

In their short lives, Baby Doe and Baby Jane Doe brought these issues to the public in a way that had never happened before. Other events, such as the Quinlan case, had raised similar issues for discussion; but these discussions had in no fashion resolved any of the crucial questions. In contrast, the discussions of Baby Doe and Baby Jane Doe had defined boundaries that we as a society are willing to accept: first, that you cannot decide not to treat based merely on the fact of disability; second, that you cannot insist every infant in every condition be treated no matter what. Now, at least, the poles of the discussion were fixed. To be sure, the agonies of each individual case had still to be weighed. But now, at least, we had some help, for society had set the limits of what is permissible.

Montefiore has for ten years had an Infant Bioethics Review Committee charged to help resolve the special issues encountered with newborns. The brainchild of Dr. Alan Fleischman, the director of the Division of Neonatology and an able bioethicist, it includes physicians, neonatal nurse practitioners, social workers, lawyers, risk managers, administrators, and bioethicists from Montefiore and its three affiliated or associated institutions. Over the years, this committee has distilled three clear guidelines that help us keep the interests of the child at the center of our thinking:

1. If a child will absolutely and clearly benefit from an intervention, then the committee urges strongly that the parent not be permitted to refuse. We communicate the discussion and the decision to the primary physician and suggest that she request the hospital to appeal to the court if necessary.

2. If treatment will clearly not benefit a child but will merely prolong or increase suffering, then the committee urges strongly that the parents not be permitted to insist on it. The final decision rests with the attending pediatrician and the hospital administration, but the committee's analysis and recommendation weighs heavily in the ultimate decision and provides invaluable support for the care team if there should be conflict with parents.

3. In the great majority of cases in between, where there is

real uncertainty about the outcome, the committee is comfortable reemphasizing the principle that caregivers should be guided by the parents' wishes and values.

Such rules seem simple, and they are; it is applying them that becomes so hellishly complex. Erin was one of those rare children clearly born without a future. She suffered from a chromosome defect called Trisomy-13, creating an overwhelming series of defects. She was profoundly retarded, with several deep abnormalities of brain structure. She was blind, her ears were abnormally shaped and placed, and she had a severe cleft palate. Most threatening was a condition called gastroschisis, where the abdomen does not close and its organs are exposed; this condition requires a long, complex, and very painful operation to repair. Trisomy-13 is invariably fatal, and the great majority of such babies die within their first year.

Her parents, devoutly religious people, seemed unable to accept the gravity of her condition. They felt that they "spoke to God" frequently in prayers, and their faith in God told them Erin would be "just fine." Unfortunately, God needed a bit of help from our surgeons; if the gross intestinal abnormalities were not corrected, Erin would soon die of overwhelming infection. To the parents, the course was clear: for their daughter to have any chance they needed an operation as soon as possible.

The pediatric surgeons, however, refused, and the neonatal team agreed with them. This shattered baby was not, in their medical view, a candidate for surgery. If she even survived the operation—by no means certain—it would only prolong her suffering until the constellation of her profound problems took their lethal course. This small person was one who, they felt, had no option; to inflict further pain and suffering on her, for no real medical benefit, would violate their solemn professional ethic to do no harm. As much as we usually try to respect parents' wishes, in this case the team agreed we could not. Parents have the right to request treatment on behalf of their children, but not to demand that a doctor provide care the doctor thinks is medically inappropriate. Erin was kept warm and comfortable, and died within forty-eight hours.

A growing number of doctors will not provide or continue treatment they think is counter to the best interest of the child. Our evolving ethical understanding tells us that nobody, not even a grieving parent, has the right to prolong the suffering of a hopelessly ill, severely disabled and suffering child. We could not accept a solution that would require treatment when it would not clearly lengthen life span or provide a meaningful benefit. It is true that there is nothing harder than telling a desperate parent no, and Erin's case was one of the hardest. Yet our highest ethical obligation was to her, not to her parents. For Erin, our littlest constituent, the care team had to feel sure we were doing the right thing.

Newborns like Erin often present many of their own questions and complexities. For one thing, the medical realities of taking care of newborns is that decisions often have to be made very quickly; because neonates are just developing, the first year of life really finishes off the process that began in the womb. For another, even medical experts are often very uncertain about outcome. Medical science may be able to intervene to extend life, but that gives no guarantee that a given baby will grow into a being that can relate to others, experience pleasure and love, or function independently. That means that these decisions carry enormous long-term consequences. When you deal with newborns, you aren't making decisions simply about a patient or a condition, but about a whole lifetime, for the baby and its family. You are dealing with the highest possible stakes.

All of these elements were at work with Viola, a twenty-two-year-old Hispanic woman who first appeared at our emergency room late one July night. She was about midway in her pregnancy—eighteen weeks or so—and her membranes had ruptured. Five decades ago, before powerful modern antibiotics, this would have spelled an inevitable abortion. Mother and child were both at certain risk for massive, even deadly, infection, which would almost certainly cost the life of the fetus, possibly making Viola sterile; even, perhaps, threatening her life. In the last twenty years, Viola herself would have had a somewhat better chance. Since her fetus was far younger than the twenty-four weeks minimum for survival, Viola would have been given a drug, oxytocin, to terminate her pregnancy. She would lose the baby, but live and perhaps be able to bear another.

But in 1991, in a high-tech sophisticated obstetrics service, Viola had new options that only made things more complex. More and more in cases like this one, doctors employ a strategy called tocolysis, a combination of intravenous fluids, sedation, an inclined bed, and antibiotics to stop the process of labor, sometimes for many weeks. They hope, in that time, to give the fetus time to mature enough to be able to survive outside the womb. Then, although gravely premature, it may have at least a fighting chance at life.

Viola, however, refused to stay in the hospital for several weeks; on her second day she checked out "AMA"—against medical advice. Her care team was disturbed: as an adult, Viola was within her rights, and they could hardly stop her. Yet, they knew, two things were certain: they would see this young woman again, and when they did, things would be worse. They were right on both counts.

Viola was back in early September, by then in what appeared to be about her twenty-third week. That, of course, was the roughest sort of guess. Often, if women have not had adequate prenatal care, neither they nor their doctors may know how far along they are. The only way to be absolutely certain is in cases of in vitro fertilization, when conception takes place under the medical eye. Real people in the real world are often dealing with a few-week window of imprecision, and Viola, like most mothers, didn't know exactly when she had conceived. In addition, so late in pregnancy, sonogram tests are notoriously imprecise—they present the most accurate pictures in the late first or second trimester.

Yet the difference between a twenty-one-week and a twenty-five-week fetus is the difference between life and death. The twenty-one-week-old cannot survive outside the womb; four weeks later, it has a slim but real chance. The obstetrician's best estimate put Viola's fetus at twenty-three weeks—about a week short of what is widely accepted as the earliest age of survival. In the antiseptic language of obstetrics, this fetus was not "viable" today, yet, at least theoretically, would be in one week.

That placed Viola squarely in the grayest of middle grounds, her fetus perched just the wrong side of life's first perimeter. A doctor could neither know that it was doomed nor promise it would survive. The only certainty here came from the team's experience with thousands of babies, and from obstetrical textbooks: "Premature rupture of membranes before twenty-four weeks is known to have a terrible outcome for the fetus and substantial risk to the mother."

Her care team faced three options. Choosing the first meant doing nothing. Medically, that was legitimate; ruptured membranes before twenty-four weeks is widely accepted as a diagnosis of inevitable abortion. If they did not abort the fetus, nature probably would. Legally, once a pregnancy has gone so awry, doctors have great discretion as to when they deliver the baby, taking into account the risk to mother and fetus. They knew that every day they waited put Viola at risk for infection.

Second, they could hasten delivery, ending her pregnancy, to protect Viola's health. It was remarkable that she had made it without infection for a month from her first admission; but she was clearly on borrowed time, and there was no guarantee that would continue. Some on the team believed that they had a legal and ethical obligation to terminate the pregnancy to save Viola's own health, even her life.

Their third option was to medically delay labor, hoping to

keep the fetus alive long enough to become viable. But this is rarely done in cases of premature rupture. It is usually used in borderline cases of premature labor, from twenty-eight to thirty-two weeks, to buy the extra little time necessary to increase the odds of delivering a viable fetus. It is not recommended in cases at twenty-four weeks, when a fetus has such negligible chances of survival.

The attending neonatologist from the pediatric ICU recited the grim facts: fewer than 10 to 20 percent of twenty-four-week babies even survive, and those that do have overwhelming medical problems. Fully half have severe, life-threatening problems of brain damage and inactive lungs. He spoke bluntly: "In the vast, vast, vast majority of cases we lose the baby after enormous medical energy and resources are spent and after much trauma for the mother. If it were me, I would recommend we terminate this pregnancy." Behind his firm words lay the medical reality: such tiny creatures are probably not meant to survive, and usually don't. But sometimes they do, with generally horrible consequences.

The care team discussed the situation with Viola at length to be sure she understood what might lie ahead: the risks to her fetus, the usual poor outcomes for baby and mother alike, the risk to her own health. They explained that waiting put her at risk for serious infection—a risk that had to be weighed carefully by caregivers and patient.

For her part, Viola described how much she wanted to go through with the pregnancy. Despite her young age, this ill-fated attempt was her third try at pregnancy. But what the care team knew, which she could not, was just how grievous it can be when a baby has such a poor prognosis. The horrible pain and suffering, the endless emergencies of hope and despair, the soul-draining sorrow and grief of caring for these struggling beings, all can wreak psychological devastation. What lay ahead, they knew, would be harder than Viola could imagine.

Yet the young woman wanted more than anything to go

through with her pregnancy, and would hear of nothing else. Given that, and since there was no sign of infection, the team decided to honor her decision. Reluctantly, they began tocolysis to buy her whatever time they could.

Nine days later, Viola went into labor. Her baby boy came out bigger than expected, looking like a twenty-six-week child. But the good news stopped there. He had both severe jaundice and a large hemorrhage in the brain, which promised significant neurological problems. His underdeveloped eyes might become blind and his immature lungs were unable to breathe, so he was placed on a ventilator immediately. The neonatologist's prognosis was grim: this baby was one of the "lucky" 20 percent who survive. But it might be a terrible survival. He would need a ventilator for at least another month—if he lived that long. After that, he would be tied to an oxygen tube for several months longer, would experience severe respiratory problems throughout the first year or two of life—and perhaps forever— and would likely return to the hospital several more times. He might be sentenced to live out his life in one of the few facilities that can treat ventilator-dependent children. He would certainly suffer lifelong, severe problems from asthma and lung infections. Even more troubling, he might never know or recognize or respond to those who loved him. The team knew that this would probably mean his abandonment to a life in an institution. For even the most loving families with emotional and financial resources can rarely stand the daily, hourly confrontation with a breathing child who is not really there in any human sense of the term.

After one month, Viola's baby still weighed only three and one-half pounds. His medical situation remained precarious. What had changed was Viola's attitude. Confronted with the full effect of the baby's enormous medical problems, and his grave prognosis, she had grown more ambivalent. This was not the baby she had envisioned. She visited less and less often, and spoke of wanting "all of this over with." During a recent visit, as she looked down at this tiny being held in a web of tubes and wires, she told a nurse that she wanted "no more machines" for her baby.

For the care team, it was all sadly familiar. In the best of faith, they had made a decision, with Viola's and the baby's best interests at heart. Now they faced an irreparably ill and disabled baby who might well not survive. He had no real prospect for a healthy life, and a mother uninterested or unable to care for him. In his first month of life, enormous resources of time and energy, and tens of thousands of dollars, had been spent, resources in increasingly short supply. The baby was suffering, but not—yet, at least—at risk of dying immediately. Instead, he passed time in a limbo of tubes and wires, drugged out of pain into a near-continuous sleep, each breath pumped into its damaged lungs by a machine. Faced with the overwhelming uncertainties of such situations, the care team had gambled. This time, as often happens with newborns, nobody really won.

Guidelines with Newborns

Happily, the great majority of pregnancies proceed uneventfully from conception through delivery, ending in one of life's great miracles—a healthy newborn baby. But not always. This section is presented to help you think through your options if something seems amiss or goes awry.

Lack of adequate prenatal care is the single greatest risk factor for physical and neurological problems in a newborn baby. Alcohol and smoking also contribute to low-birthweight infants, and low birthweight usually accompanies neonatal problems and the need for ICU care. Thus, the need for regular prenatal care is the single most important lesson for all of us.

Genetic counseling can also be important to help inform prospective parents about their chances for a healthy baby. Genetic counselors are highly skilled advisers trained to interpret the complex genetic picture presented by any couple and to provide information that is, to the greatest degree possible, based on medical facts. The job of a genetic counselor is to provide nondirective counseling on the possible risk for a genetic disorder. It is up to the couple to decide if they are willing to assume this risk. The genetic counselor is a crucial person for couples deciding whether to have a baby.

Amniocentesis and CVS—chorionic villus sampling, a test done early in pregnancy that samples placental tissue to examine chromosomes—provide prospective parents with specific information about their fetus. They can help determine if the fetus has specific genetic problems and let them choose whether to continue or to terminate the pregnancy. Sometimes, however, when problems are discovered later in the pregnancy, usually through the use of ultrasound, it is no longer possible to terminate a pregnancy. It then becomes critical to discuss all of the possibilities with the obstetrician and neonatologist in the medical center.

Physicians have their own values, style of practice, and ways of discussing the options for care. Some physicians and hospitals have a stronger tendency to treat aggressively than others do. Some have a greater history of parental involvement and are happy to share with parents how their own conclusions were reached. In the vast majority of cases, if the medical outcome is uncertain, the values of the parents will primarily determine what care is given.

If you should ever confront such issues, it may help you to refer to this summary of the guidelines of the Infant Bioethics Review Committee:

♦ If treatment will clearly help the baby, physicians feel legally and ethically bound to treat. If necessary, with institutional support, they will be willing to go to court for legal permission to proceed over the parents' objections.

♦ If the treatment will clearly not help the baby, if it is likely to die imminently with or without the treatment, some physicians will refuse to proceed no matter what the parents' wishes; other doctors, however, will feel bound to follow the course the parents choose. Which choice the physician makes will depend on whether she sees herself as the physician for the child or as the caregiver for the family.

• Few physicians will treat aggressively if that treatment causes pain and suffering and promises no benefit in terms of lengthened survival time or increased potential for pleasure for the baby.

• If the prognosis is uncertain, as it usually is, if the chances of benefit are between 10 and 60 percent, with similar chances of long-term serious disability, then the physicians and parents will struggle together to balance the imponderables and reach consensus. If you find yourself in such a situation, you are well within your rights to ask for specific information, when available; ask to read some of the key articles in the pediatric literature about the condition or any material they have specifically geared to your baby's problems. Don't be afraid to ask the physician what he thinks is the proper thing to do and what he plans to do if you and he disagree. You may also want to ask for a second—or third—medical opinion.

Always, no matter what the odds or the circumstance, the best tool you can have is an open relationship with the neonatologist and frank discussions between the parties. Only then can all of you reach a decision that will be the most humane, fair, and compassionate resolution for all concerned.

CHOOSING FOR OUR CHILDREN

A "child," as we know it, is a recent invention. Not biologically, of course. But the legal and social notion of "child"—a formal entity worthy of special treatment, regard, and rights—is a modern invention in the broad arc of the world's cultures. For most of human history, children were legally viewed as their parents' property. Mere chattel, they could be disposed of, sold into slavery, or disciplined unto death, with no questions asked. In many societies, it was common practice that babies—especially females—were left to starve lest they drain a poor family's purse. Families too impoverished to pay the dowry necessary to marry off a daughter might simply leave their girl child on a hillside or river's edge to die.

In eighteenth- and nineteenth-century Europe, babies were commonly "sent to the farm," a euphemism for being put out to die. (Such infanticide appears to continue in many parts of the world today, most specifically in China, where it is tacitly encouraged by the government policy of one child per family.) So high was infant mortality that historical memoirs chronicle mothers who consciously avoided bonding with their infants until the end of the child's first year, to avoid the pain of likely loss. Some countries codified that idea, establishing that children below the age of one year had no valid legal claim or rights. Those children lucky enough to survive infancy were viewed and treated as diminutive adults. In the London of 1710, for example, the seven-year-old caught stealing could expect to swing at the gallows alongside his thirty-seven-year-old father.

Not until the closing years of the last century, with the growth of the social welfare movements, did this view start to change. We began to recognize that the Dickensian conditions under which children lived were incompatible with our society's evolving sense of welfare obligation. At the same time, the newly created profession of social work—largely staffed by women—and increasing numbers of women entering the working world, gave concerns of children and family a higher place on the national agenda.

In 1899 America redefined childhood. That year the state of Illinois passed the nation's first Family Court Act, proposed by practitioners of the budding science of social work at Jane Addams's Hull House in Chicago. The law was the first to establish that society had a special interest in children, and that children needed to be offered special protection in an adult world. It specifically outlined three distinct classes of children:

First among these was the "delinquent"—a child whose actions, if performed by an adult, would be a crime. By virtue of their age, the law said, these young lawbreakers would not be charged with formal crimes and prosecuted in criminal courts. Instead it created a new "family court" characterized by informality, privacy, and concern for the welfare and social and moral development of the growing child.

The law also recognized a second kind of child, the "status offender." These were children who did something that would not be a crime if an adult did it: staying out past a parent's curfew, for example. Under the newly developing law, these children would come to have many names: Persons in Need of Supervision (PINS), the Unruly Child, the Ungovernable Child. The law fashioned special punishments for them: they might receive a stern lecture or warning from a judge, or might be given restrictions that, if broken, would lead to incarceration if they reappeared in court; they might be directly placed in a "reformatory," as they were then called. Clearly, however, this category was something of a catchall: one classic study showed that the person most likely to be labeled a "PINS" was a young woman, fifteen years old, who was sexually active and whose grandmother lived in the house with her. Obviously this label, devised for truly troubling behavior, could be and was overapplied to ordinary clashes of evolving values, conflicts among generations, and routine family conflicts.

But it was the third category of the law that would shape medical decisions from then on: the neglected child, whose parents, although they were financially able to do so, were not providing proper food, shelter, or medical care. For the first time, the law established conditions that could place persons other than parents in the position of deciding what was right for a child. It also assumed that there exists a right answer for problems presented by raising a child, a proposition that many beleaguered parents might dispute. Over the next thirty-five years, every state would adopt similar laws to deal with these new legal entities called children. Then, as now, the children seen in these courts were overwhelmingly the children of poor people and disproportionately nonwhite; today family court primarily serves those whose domestic and family problems are inseparable from their perch on the lowest rung of the economic ladder.

Over a few short decades, our society had forged a brand-new class of citizen. We conceived a new vision of our youngest members as people deserving special protections. More important, for thousands of youngsters, we created a new set of caretakers, parties other than the child's parents, who are seen as having ongoing authority, responsibility, and standing to act in support of that child's welfare. Today, those "someone elses" are active in hospitals, doctor's offices, and communities across the country.

They are involved in a new undertaking: identifying and combating "medical neglect." Sometimes, when they recognize child abuse and save the child from harm, even death, society applauds their efforts. Sometimes, when they remove a child from the home and place him in the virtually nonfunctioning foster care system, reasonable people may shake their heads and wonder if any good cause has been served.

Medical neglect, itself, is a new idea. As medicine has grown ever more sophisticated and successful over the last decades, its practitioners have grown quite confident that there are certain conditions they can reliably improve and sometimes cure. So then, if a parent, for any reason, refuses that care, what should happen? Should society apply the principle that children, as less than fully capable beings, should be protected from harm? How do we balance that with other principles giving parents the responsibility and right to make decisions about the lives of their children and all people the freedom to practice their own religion according to their own dictates? Issues about the care of children usually involve reconciling some or all of these thorny issues.

In earlier chapters, you met the many parties who are engaged in decisions about adults: patient and family, caregivers, and hospital staff; even, at last resort, judges. But when the patient is young, a new player steps to the bedside: the state. It is represented not only by the black robes of justice but also by agencies that have been set up in the last decades to deal with and supervise less fortunate children. ("Less fortunate" here should have little to do with poverty or privilege. Despite the mistaken view that it is only poor people who neglect or otherwise harm their children, recent research on child abuse, especially sexual abuse, makes it clear that this problem ranges across all segments of society. But it is among the poor that society's mechanisms are most able to uncover and address child abuse through the long and powerful arms of state child protection agencies.) In the person of child welfare workers, agency representatives and state and federal regulators, the state plays a visible and ubiquitous role in many decisions made for and about children.

Death by Faith

Normally it is assumed that parents have the best interests of their children in mind, and therefore are the best advocates for their children. Ninety-nine times out of a hundred, it makes sense that parents should decide about medical care for their children. But sometimes that is not the case, and that is when things get difficult.

Cecil, now fourteen years old, had been feeling poorly for three months before he came to the hospital, with increasing fatigue, weight loss, fevers, and night sweats. The doctors in our Division of Adolescent Medicine saw in his symptoms the classic hallmarks of Hodgkin's disease, a type of disseminated cancer.

His mother, referred to by staff as "the Mom," was not a typical concerned mother. She seemed less worried about Cecil's welfare than she was alarmed that he might require a blood transfusion. That, she explained, was a gross violation of her religious principles. Agitated, she brought the subject up as soon as she met a new staff member.

Once Cecil's diagnosis was confirmed by biopsy, the physician, a pediatric cancer specialist, sat down with the mother. He explained that this particular type of childhood cancer, when it is diagnosed as early as Cecil's had been, had an excellent prognosis for remission, even for full recovery—if chemotherapy began immediately. But at some point in Cecil's treatment, he explained, it was possible that the drugs would dangerously depress Cecil's blood count and put his life in jeopardy. If that happened, he would require an immediate transfusion of blood platelets or red blood cells to save his life.

The doctor later said that he felt she was only half listening during their talk. Where most parents would have been shocked, or hopeful that Cecil had a real chance to survive, she seemed not to focus on her son's illness or prognosis. She was far more concerned that he never receive blood. "That won't do," she kept repeating. "It is an abomination for a Jehovah's Witness."

The physician knew from prior experience that Witnesses strictly forbid the use of blood or blood products. He also knew that this severely limited the care team's ability to cure Cecil; he could not, in good conscience, accept a limitation that endangered his patient's young life—and told her so. She simply became more adamant about refusing blood products—despite the fact that she admitted she had lost another child some fifteen years before, a child two years old, leaving Cecil her only remaining child.

That night, floor nurses saw the mother and another church member walking Cecil to the elevator. They confronted the mother, who produced a letter purporting to dismiss the physician. She explained that she planned to take the child to a doctor in South Carolina who "is a perfectly good doctor"— and a fellow Witness. He, she believed, would be more sympathetic to, in accord with, and respectful of her religious beliefs.

After a long discussion, the staff and mother finally agreed Cecil should stay until morning. In a note in his chart, the social worker recounted the evening's events and left specific instructions: if she, her family, or any Witnesses tried to take Cecil, security should stop them and Special Services for Children should be alerted. The next day, Special Services for Children (SSC)—the child-protective agency for the city of New York, responsible for neglected and possibly neglected children—was warned of the potential danger to this child.

They placed a "hold" on Cecil, so he could not be removed from the institution. In addition to their legal role, they can also play a psychological role. Sometimes, when an uninvolved third party like SSC takes responsibility for the decision, it removes that responsibility from the family, which can then bow more comfortably to authority, saving face in their church community.

It was now Friday. By Monday, the physician said, he needed to start treatment because every day was lowering Cecil's chances of cure. On Monday, the doctors felt they could wait no longer and treatment began. The mother had been unable to secure any medical expert in all of New York who would agree to treat Cecil and promise not to use blood if, at some time during treatment, it was required.

That week, Cecil went into kidney failure from the chemotherapy and was transferred to a special kidney unit at an allied hospital. After six days of dialysis, his kidneys improved, but then his overtaxed lungs started failing, and he was put on a respirator. Cecil was returned to our pediatric intensive care unit where his vital signs, breathing, and kidney function could be carefully monitored. At this point it was growing increasingly clear that he might need a blood transfusion.

Cautious, the pediatrician asked the hospital to go to court to obtain an order that would permit the team to administer blood if Cecil fell into a life-threatening crisis. Again, the physician met with Cecil and his mom. He explained that he would only use blood if it was absolutely necessary and only after she and the elders had been notified, if at all possible. But he repeated, if there was an immediately life-threatening crisis, with no time to notify her or the church elders, he would do whatever was necessary to save Cecil's life.

Cecil himself presented conflicting opinions and attitudes during these discussions. He was always very respectful of his mom and quick to mirror her theological statements. He simultaneously maintained, however, that he did not want to die.

Furthermore, the staff sensed neither real commitment nor intensity in his dutiful protestations of religious preference.

Now the drama moved to court. Attorneys for the Jehovah's Witness religion were representing the mother. They explained the belief of Jehovah's Witnesses that using blood or blood products pollutes the body, condemns the person to endless purgatory, precluding that person's entrance into the Kingdom of Heaven. This is a deeply held belief, a fundamental belief in the theological system of the church. Given that, they argued, the First Amendment to the Constitution protected the free exercise of religion and that meant protecting the mother's right to make decisions for her child in accordance with her—and presumably her son's—beliefs.

On the other side lay the medical facts. Cecil would probably recover with treatment; he would probably not if, in a crisis, blood products could not be used to reverse the damage done by chemotherapy. Blood transfusions are relatively simple, they last a short time, and their results are largely predictable.

The judge's role was clear: to weigh the state's obligation to protect its most vulnerable citizens, its children, against a parent's right to educate and rear a child in the traditions and the belief systems of her choice. For it is, after all, one thing for a parent to choose for herself, and a different thing altogether to choose for another human being. In this case, the judge felt the court was obligated to protect Cecil's welfare until such time as he was able to choose his religion and rationally assess the dangers he would court in its observance.

She ruled to permit blood transfusions to be administered "as necessary," and ordered the physician to notify the mother and church elders beforehand if possible. If there was not time, however, the doctors were to save the life first, and inform later. The doctors did eventually have to give Cecil four units of blood, and he was able to complete his chemotherapy. Today, two years later, Cecil is thriving, playing in the band at his school, and apparently fine.

The fundamental issue here is establishing the proper hierarchy for competing principles and values. This same issue lies at the core of a classic New York legal case, *In re Seiferth,* which concerned the proper care and treatment for a child with a cleft palate and a harelip. The father of the child believed in faith healing, as apparently did the child, and so surgery was refused. The physicians were understandingly skeptical about the ability of any miracle to repair this congenital, although fully reparable, problem. A psychologist testified in court that the disability and its accompanying deformity interfered with the ability of the child to learn in school and made him the object of ridicule by his classmates. The judge decided to honor the wishes of the father and the child, noting that the father and child were very close and imposing care might split their alliance. Besides, he reasoned, the child could always choose surgical repair once he had reached adulthood.

My pediatric colleagues are always horrified by this case. How, they wonder, could a judge permit the child to suffer the pain of a reparable deformity through childhood and adolescence? How could he fail to understand that pain can be as much emotional as physical and choose to sacrifice this child's sense of self on the basis of such clearly deluded beliefs? I respond by asking who among those pediatricians would want the responsibility of choosing the surgery and assuming responsibility for the inevitable risk that surgery presents? Who would want to separate the child from his father and bar the man from the hospital until the surgery was completed? Would our answers change if the child were five, or ten, or fifteen years old?

The larger question here is whether our mutual social contract—the larger, stable, broadly held values of society—override parents' legal and moral bases for making decisions about their children's lives. We recognize that parents have quite wide latitude to decide how their children will be raised, according to what values, in what religion, with what specific sets of moral rules. Even if some of us would choose differently, society generally cedes this realm of choice to the parents. But what if parents choose a religion like Christian Science or Jehovah's Witness, which rejects some of the basic tenets of modern medicine? Does society want to accept that freedom of worship is the most important value at stake, and therefore defend parents' rights to make critical health-care decisions according to their beliefs?

Most bioethicists, and almost all the judges who have ever considered the problem, argue that the life and well-being of the child must be protected independently even if it means defending the child from the parents' decisions. They support the use of modern medical interventions, if the chances of success are statistically high. In one way or another, they reject the idea that freedom of religion permits a parent to deny a child life-sustaining or life-enhancing care.

Lurking in this choice is the bias of a secular society that values the body over the spirit. If the courts and bioethics scholars really believed that the child's soul existed independently after death and would be condemned to eternal damnation, they might not order blood transfusions over the objections of parents. Perhaps if this were a popular religion observed by vast numbers of faithful, with politically powerful and well-connected lobbies, the result might be different. But in our secular society, judges have unanimously agreed to rank the danger of eternal damnation below the possibility of death. In our society there is an implicit agreement to safeguard the lives of our children until they reach adulthood—at which time they may choose the religion and the tenets of their parents, or not.

Judges often cite the state's *"parens patriae"* obligation—literally "parent of the country" but now used to refer to the governmental obligation to protect persons under some disability as, for example, when a court orders guardians in childhood. They have, in effect, recognized a primary American ethic to nurture and protect our young, above and beyond our responsibility to always respect parents' wishes at all costs.

Far more often, however, society allows parents the right to decide, for obvious and sensible reasons. Most of us would agree that, by themselves, most young children have neither the maturity, judgment, insight, or wisdom to decide complex questions about their treatment. They cannot balance present pain and discomfort against future, abstract, possible benefit. When my now generally rational adolescent son, Josh, was two years old, he could not be convinced that getting a needle in his arm at one moment was justified because it would confer protection against measles or mumps at another, later moment. There was really nothing to do but hold his outraged and screaming person until the assault was over and I could present whatever bribe I had brought along for the occasion.

Since children of this age cannot decide alone, it is usually recognized that parents are best equipped to decide. They will, we assume, hold the child's best interests at heart. But what if they don't, and what if they don't decide based on a principled set of reasons? Generally, our legal and ethical system supports the parents' right to consent to care on behalf of their children. But when they refuse, as Cecil's mother did, for reasons that are peculiarly important to them, we medical ethicists become much less comfortable. Parents have the responsibility and right to consent to care on behalf of children, but have less latitude to refuse care; this too is the law.

When doctors and family agree on the care to be provided, all parties are somehow comfortable that is the right decision. The combination of the concerned relative and the disinterested professional best ensures that the decision chosen is the right one—a built-in check and balance that, in general, leads to the best outcome for the most people. When familial and societal values collide, it is then that the state intervenes. Its role is to support a treatment plan giving the child the greatest likelihood of recovery. How that ends up may depend on what state you live in, for some state courts are more committed to parents' rights to decide than are others. So, for example, the New York court that decided the Seiferth case about the boy with a harelip also decided in the case *In re Hofbauer* that parents could continue with relatively unconventional treatment for Hodgkin's disease if it was sponsored and supervised by a "licensed physician"; yet in a very similar case, a Massachusetts court ordered more conventional medical treatment over the objection of the parents.

By ordering treatment over parents' objections, courts are actually protecting a child's right to hold different beliefs than its parents do, safeguarding a young life until the child is old enough to decide for herself, based on her own values about medical treatment. In doing so, these courts have taken the next logical step in our century-long evolution from viewing children as property to viewing them as beings with independent rights that must be protected until adulthood—if necessary, by the state.

When doctors and parents fall on opposite sides of the treatment fence—say, a child has leukemia for which standard and customary chemotherapy has an 85 percent cure rate, but the parents prefer the magic power of crystals, which have no scientifically demonstrated cure rate—parents will often lose, as judges virtually always rule in favor of doctors and hospitals. We as a society are on reasonably firm ground when the medical issues are reasonably clear-cut.

The questions arise in the uncertain middle, when medical matters are less clear. Perhaps the treatment the child needs is not so benign as a blood transfusion, nor the outcome so certain. When there are several possible alternatives, or when the risks of medical treatment are high and the outcome uncertain, or in cases when the child's life is not immediately threatened, courts feel more comfortable endorsing the legitimate sphere of parents' authority to decide. In general, when parents and doctors disagree over a relatively uncontroversial treatment, it can be said that doctors usually win; the more uncertain the medical treatment, the greater the chance that the courts will support the parents.

But even parental authority goes only so far. The parents in Bloomington who didn't want their baby treated simply because it had Down's syndrome ignited controversy because they exceeded the limits of what our society has now agreed to permit. In the time since Baby Doe hit the news, it has been agreed that disabled children who have medical problems that are amenable to medical intervention, where the success of the procedure is relatively certain, are entitled to the treatment. We as a culture have now agreed that disability, by itself, is not a reason to deprive a child of treatment that could help it. In this case, where there is a painstakingly forged social consensus, parents do not have the right to breach it, no matter their wishes.

Who Knows What's "Best"?

For parents and caregivers alike, it can sometimes be very difficult to determine the "best interest" of a child. It is particularly anguishing when one of the decisions would permit the child's death. Anita was one such poignant case. At thirteen years old she was severely retarded, with the mental age of a preschool child. She was obese and physically imposing, with strength far exceeding the norm for a young teen. She also had osteosarcoma of the leg, a cancer that could kill her if it spread throughout her body. The standard medical treatment was clear: amputation. But that would be enormously hard for Anita. She did not possess the mental faculties to understand what was happening to her or to cooperate in any way with her care. Although mentally little more than an infant, her adult size and strength would preclude the physical restraints the pediatrics team can usually impose on a small child who cannot understand or tolerate the discomfort of treatment. This powerful disparity between mental age and physical stature weighed heavy in any balance of the care options.

What she had managed to do was to thoroughly intimidate her mother. Anita would hurl herself at her mother and other adults when she wanted attention, a toy, or food. Unable to express herself clearly, her frustration would explode in raging tantrums. In addition, Anita hated being touched by unfamiliar doctors and nurses. Having her as a patient would not be easy for her, or for us. The staff also worried that losing her leg would remove one of the greatest pleasures of her life, unrestricted movement. Nonetheless, her virulent tumor left little choice, so with her mother's permission, the decision was made to amputate.

To everyone's surprise, Anita came through surgery with flying colors. She was given a walker and wheelchair, which she learned to use with astonishing speed and agility. After several weeks convalescing on the unit, the nurses noticed something wonderful starting to happen: this young woman, with a lifetime of terrible problems, began to blossom.

Here, under the loving care of a dozen nurses and doctors, in the company of other children, Anita began acquiring new language and communications skills. As she felt increasingly comfortable with the staff, much of her hostile negative behavior melted away. She began to respect the limits set by the nurses; she learned not to grab items from other children, but to ask that they be given to her. She began to sit sociably with the other sick children and appeared to enjoy their company even if she could communicate only haltingly with them.

Her stay stretched from days to weeks to months. Each time the care team made plans to send her home, Anita's mother found a reason to delay, quite clearly terrified. Finally, it became clear she didn't want Anita at home, so the team's social worker had to begin the long task of finding an appropriate placement facility for her, which stretched Anita's three-month stay to six, then to eight. As the months rolled by, Anita's verbal and social skills were developing more than they had in the thirteen years previous. Delighted, the nurses patiently worked with her in each shift, teaching her new skills and new words to communicate her newly acquired perceptions. She became adopted as a favorite patient on the unit, zooming around in her wheelchair, playing games with the nurses. Over the course of almost a year, before our eyes, Anita had bloomed into a happy and contented, if moderately retarded, thirteen-year-old. She was a testament to the miracles that can occur when medicine and love combine.

But it was not to last. In her eleventh month on the ward, Anita developed fevers. Tests confirmed our worst fears: her cancer had metastasized. It was now widespread, with masses in her right leg and, worse, her chest cavity and lungs. The news shook even our most veteran doctors. This time, they knew, Anita's surgery would be very different. As well as taking her other leg, complex and painful chest surgery was required. Recovery would require an extended time in the pediatric ICU connected at first to a ventilator and, later, to a web of monitors and tubes. More seriously, her survival would require cooperation. Immediately after surgery, she would need to cough, exercise, and breathe to clear her lungs to avoid life-threatening pneumonia.

This child, we all knew, would have no way to make sense from the pain and confinement she would face. She would only experience frustrating, painful challenges to all she held dear: her mobility, her freedom, her relations with the care team and other children. Even given her terrific relationship with the nurses, Anita still hated getting any kind of needle. A special behavior modification program by the nurses had not changed this; each time the staff had to draw blood or administer a shot Anita had to be held down. The physicians couldn't even rely on an in-dwelling catheter to eliminate the need for frequent needles; Anita didn't understand it and always found a way to pull it out. The prospect of intravenous lines in her arms was as horrendous to the staff as it would have been monstrous to Anita. The nurses could keep her sedated for her entire stay in the ICU, but that would interfere with her ability to follow directions to properly clear her lungs.

It wasn't even clear what the chances were for remission even with aggressive surgery and chemotherapy. Some doctors argued that, given the progress of the disease thus far, the speed of the recurrence, and the particular type of tumor, Anita would not likely be able to last another year. And it would be a year of sheer torture.

Others were more optimistic. They cited some little-known studies suggesting such a child, with such a tumor, had a much greater chance for recovery and a number of untroubled and entirely satisfactory years. Anita, they pointed out, had surprised all of us before, healing, learning new skills, and adjusting magnificently to her disability. They felt that her history and her phenomenal growth and development during her year on the ward all added up to giving her another chance at life.

The team was deadlocked about whether or not to recommend to the mother that the surgeons proceed with an operation. The basic division was over what, in the language of ethics, *was* in Anita's "best interest." If medical science could offer even a 25 percent chance of recovery to a level of function that would allow Anita enjoyment and pleasure, there would be no question in the minds of most of the caregivers to proceed (although her mother might be another, separate, matter). But for her, the odds were far lower: maybe 10 percent, 15 optimistically. As always, such low odds are not very precise. But the entire care team knew the chance that any good would come out of treatment was remote; even with surgery and chemotherapy, the doctors could probably do little to help Anita.

In most pediatric cases, the physician comes to the parents with a suggestion for a plan of care, allowing them to choose one option from among several. The ethical doctrine of informed consent does not require that the physician have no opinion about the best route to follow, but simply that she explain all the options with their risks and benefits. Most physicians, either when asked or as part of their presentations, give a personal opinion about which route they recommend and why. After much discussion, it was clear that although the team was evenly divided, the senior treating physician strongly favored proceeding.

Anita's mother met with the attending physician, the pediatric oncologist who had been treating the child, the nurse who knew her the best, and the social worker who had been involved since the beginning. The mother was clearly overwhelmed by the decision before her. She spent several days talking with her family and her priest, even returning with a few family members to revisit the discussion. During this time debate raged in the ward. Those opposed to the treatment argued that the chance of a happy outcome was so slight and Anita's pain, disorientation, and suffering would be so enormous that the burdens clearly outweighed the benefits. The opposing camp cited her newfound communication skills, her trust in the staff, and her growing relationship with them. To them, Anita's shot at a few more years of life justified the pain and suffering that would certainly occur. They did not wish to deny her an opportunity for survival that would have been available to her had she been of normal intelligence. All of them, no matter their view, used the same language and saw their solution as in her "best interest."

Ironically, those were the very words Anita's mother would use to describe her decision two days later: she would take Anita home for her last days. She felt that she could not bring herself to inflict pain and suffering on her child. Several staff were clearly and vocally upset. They felt that the mother's discomfort and fear of her daughter might have affected her ability to choose treatment—certainly the scarier of the two routes—but that option only offered, and did not promise, longer life. Facing such massive uncertainty, Anita's mother decided that it was in her child's "best interest" to lead her to an earlier death. Although some of the team were saddened by the decision, they helped to make it possible, first arranging for home care and later for hospice care to make Anita's life and her death the most comfortable possible.

Anita's case was one of the most difficult that I, and the pediatric team, had ever faced, but it was, at least, resolved cooperatively. Her mother made up her mind with full consultation, information, and support from the team. Harder still are the cases where it is not the parents, but the care team, who ultimately must weigh the elements and decide.

At four years old, Noel had lived in our pediatric intensive care unit for all but a few weeks of his life. He had been born six weeks prematurely, mildly retarded, with several medical problems, the most serious of which required him to be on a ventilator. Over the next months he endured surgery after surgery, fought off a series of devastating infections, fighting his way inch by inch into the land of the living. Despite his retardation, he was an engaging boy, loving and good natured, who always greeted his doctors and nurses with a great big smile as he tolerated an endless stream of tests and procedures. After a few months, it became clear that this plucky little boy would be on a ventilator the rest of his life. But, at least, he would have a life.

The bigger question now seemed to be his mother. When he was born, she had been a scared, overwhelmed, but devoted seventeen-year-old. She had visited Noel every day when he was first admitted to the pediatric ICU. After six months she had tried to take him home, which ended in failure as he was rushed back to the pediatric ICU in a life-threatening emergency. For the next few months, she visited very regularly, watching her son grow up into a sweet and appealing but mischievous little boy. Noel's most serious "trick" was that he had learned the quickest way to get attention, especially when the nurses were busy with a very sick new admission, was to disconnect his respirator, triggering alarms of ringing buzzers and flashing lights. The cacophony brought nurses running, to his delight and their aggravation.

Since he could not go home, the team tried to transfer Noel to a long-term facility designed for chronic-care children. The first place they tried had children far more disabled than he was; Noel hated it, pulling out his respirator every hour or so. After three days, he came back to us. The social worker found another place which had less sophisticated medical facilities, but after a week there, Noel developed pneumonia and was rushed back to the ICU. After that his mother refused to discuss placement. She had decided that the best place for him was in our pediatric ICU.

For her, maybe, that was true. Her behavior had clearly changed over the years. She now visited once a week or less; sometimes a whole month elapsed between visits. When she came, she didn't linger. She would say hello to Noel and chat with him briefly, but she almost never picked him up or played with him, and never came in the daytime when they could have gone for a walk outside—in a wheelchair with a portable respirator. More ominously, she was clearly not eager to get him home, and would always offer long, drawn-out excuses why now wasn't "the right time." Between his recurrent medical needs and her reluctance, the months turned to a year, then two. It was clear his mother was either disengaging or already completely disengaged.

What she could not give him, the pediatrics team did. Noel had become a beloved member of the Montefiore pediatric family. The animals in his crib were all presents from the nurses. They played with him and taught him, gave him birthday parties, and when it was sunny took him out in a wheelchair on a portable ventilator during their lunch hour. Noel hated being alone, and was gleeful when the unit was full of other children. He yearned to play with them, and tried to cheer them up when they were sick. They—and we—were the only family Noel ever knew; as unorthodox as it was, he loved his family very much.

The clearer it got that Noel was not heading home, the

clearer it became that he had to go somewhere. The pediatric ICU, as welcoming as it is to its small charges, is an unnatural, stressed, and violent place. It is also a scarce resource for those babies who truly need its services in an emergency to save their lives, and so cannot be filled with custodial charges like Noel. Most of all, Noel needed a life; if not at home, and not with us, then somewhere. For a year, the social worker had pressed his mother to visit the nearest facility that would take retarded and developmentally delayed children like Noel who needed a respirator. That would offer him the best life; he would be with other children, able to socialize and learn with them; he would enjoy maximum independence and mobility, yet get the medical care he needed. Unfortunately, the nearest such facility was two hundred miles away, in Pennsylvania, and when doctors asked Noel's mother to go look at it, she repeatedly backed out. Once, the hospital even sent a car to take her and wait for her, to no avail.

As Noel approached his fourth birthday, the social worker came to feel that the mother's bond with him was more than purely maternal. She confirmed her suspicion that the mother had never informed the city administrator that Noel was living in the hospital. That meant for four years she had been collecting money for his support at home while, at the same time, Medicaid was paying for his care with us. It was in her interest to keep things this way forever—but not in Noel's, and not in ours.

Since his mother was so clearly opting out of her son's life, it fell to the ICU team to balance the delicate calculus of what was "best" for Noel. They knew that moving Noel would mean the end of Noel's relationship with his mom. She barely visited him when he was less than a mile from where she lived; she would clearly never make it to a facility two hundred miles away. Balanced against that loss was Noel's ability to live with other children and go to school. There was also the prospect of a wonderful contraption that would permit him to move about despite his ventilator: the facility specialized in creating one of these splendid machines for each of its children, giving them the chance to live a relatively normal life outside of the oppressive confines of the ICU. No more would Noel miss his physical therapy sessions because he'd been kept up all night by a sick child and was too tired. No more would he feel lonely and abandoned when the ICU was empty, or look longingly over to the few children who were too sick to play.

Finally, the team agreed that the loss of his mom, already occurring on its own, was less terrible to Noel than his long-term isolation in the pediatric ICU. In their view, as painful as it might be, moving to a facility able to meet his needs was more supportive than occasional visits from an increasingly detached mother. Finally, the social worker put in the call and began the process of determining medical neglect.

Almost as difficult as the decision itself, was the fact that the care team was put in the position to have to make it. Pediatric staff are used to empowering parents and helping them to decide—that is the role they are trained for. In general, pediatricians try to be very attuned to the needs of the child within the family. As "primary care" physicians, they tend to have the skills necessary to relate to parents and children, to translate the risks and benefits of medical care into comprehensible language, and they know how to lead parents through the complex evaluation of various treatment options. Ideally, as they work with parents and family, they forge a consensus on the best plan of care. After all, both parties want the child to get better, to allay the child's fears, to make him more comfortable, and speed his recovery. But that all breaks down when there is no parent to whom to relate. Then it falls to strangers to decide what is in their young charges' best interest. In the case of Noel, they did, and it worked. At least for a while. He lived for about a year but his medical problems were, it turned out, really too complicated to manage outside of the ICU. A year after his transfer he died. A recent photograph of Noel now hangs in the pediatric

ICU nursing station. His smile reminds us that even for the most skilled professionals determining the best interest of a child is a complex business.

In most cases, deciding for children is not as difficult as it was with Cecil, Anita, or Noel. The vast majority of medical issues that parents face for their children are within the comfortable capability of those parents to decide. But for all of us, such questions remain a work in progress, for we live in a society that is continually redefining the role and rights of its youngest members.

10

TREATING
OUR
TEENS

Teenagers, as every parent knows, are an awkward species. Not surprisingly, they raise serious questions for those responsible for their physical or educational well-being, and those who care for them. If medical care questions seem complex for newborns and children, they grow murkier still when the child matures into that perhaps most misunderstood of creatures, the American adolescent.

The central ethical question we face with teenagers looks like one we have encountered before—"Who decides?" But with teens, there are some special variations on the theme. Adolescents, with one foot still in the land of the children they were, the other in the realm of the adults they will become, inhabit a challenging niche in our culture. Are these beings great big children, or little adults? In fact, they are both and neither—and therein lies the confusion.

A few years ago, I was called to another New York hospital to consult on the case of Ramon, a seventeen-year-old Argentinean boy. He had undergone surgery for a brain tumor four years earlier, and now was back, suffering a sudden and life-threatening recurrence. The boy's only hope, said his surgeons, was more surgery.

His mother, a highly educated professional, desperately wanted the surgery if it meant her son would live. Ramon, however, was equally adamant. He had endured the pain of the first operation, and had then lived under its cloud for four years. More than anything else, he knew he did not want to be forced to endure another operation. Although only seventeen, he made an extraordinarily touching plea to be spared surgery. But his mother would not relent, and finally, over his objection, Ramon was dragged, literally kicking and screaming, into surgery. There was to be no happy ending, unfortunately; he came out of the operation totally insensate and died four agonizing months later.

Ramon raised a raft of troubling questions. Should the surgeons in this case have accepted his mother's judgment over his firm opposition? On what basis did they decide to heed her wishes, and not Ramon's? Her status as "mother"? Her strength of presentation? The fact that she agreed with the doctors? It seemed a most difficult decision to disregard the voice of this young man. He was, I argued, so close to being an adult. Did the magic number eighteen really preclude the need for a hard confrontation with his wishes and needs? At age seventeen he knew far more than we strangers ever could—and probably as much as any adult patient ever would—about what this operation meant to him. Perhaps his adolescent nature overwhelmed his ability to reason about his care. Perhaps his experience equipped him uniquely to choose for himself. In any event, his thoughts, preferences, and values mattered and should have been given greater weight. For just that reason many adolescent medicine physicians will not treat over the refusal of the patient, but prefer to wait until agreement has been reached before proceeding.

In reality, there are real limits in the search for agreement. Let us assume that a child does not concur with a particular treatment for a treatable tumor. The teenager may be responding to a number of forces in his life. First, he may not be "crazy" but may be reacting to overwhelming anxiety or to the conflict with a parent. Second, he may be mentally ill or suicidal. In either event he is making a health decision contrary to his best interest. Waiting for agreement may well be futile—the agreement may simply never emerge and the search for it will come to be an insuperable barrier to care in the child's best interest.

Ramon presented the central questions caregivers and parents face with all teenagers: when and whether to respect the autonomous values and wishes of the adolescent patient. Are the adults certain that his judgment is less mature and informed—even though it is he who must live with the consequences? Are adolescents capable of giving truly informed consent? Or should the care team rely on parents' greater life experience, wider perspective, and presumably better judgment—despite the fact that they are not the patient and, indeed, their values, morals, and perspective, may have little in common with those of their teenager. How should the health-care providers resolve any disagreement? Must one assume that lack of maturity is the cause of the disagreement, and that the child will necessarily evolve into a clone of the adult? How old does a person have to be to be old enough to decide? Does that depend on the specific decision? Is there a difference between a sixteen-year old girl choosing contraception or treatment for sexually transmitted diseases, and choosing abortion, sterilization, or major surgery? What is the responsibility of the physician to whom she turns for help?

Such questions vex us precisely because our society is profoundly confused about the rights and autonomy of adolescents and because adolescent development is such a moving target. We recognize that adolescents have emerged from the protective chrysalis of childhood, but have yet to don the full mantle of an adult. Nobody—not adults, not the courts, and certainly not teenagers themselves—can agree on just what capabilities they do, or should, have.

In general, society is torn between permitting teenagers to decide and permitting the parent to decide even over the objection of the adolescent. We let teens go to war and vote for president, yet in most states they cannot drink alcohol. In California, prosecutors have attempted to hold parents responsible for the gang behavior of their children. In New York, on the other hand, adolescents who commit horribly depraved and shocking crimes are now tried in adult criminal court where they cannot hide behind the curtain of protection of the juvenile justice system.

This same confusion runs through our health laws. In Alabama, a fourteen-year-old can choose her own medical care; in Oregon, she must wait until age fifteen; in most other states she must be eighteen; and in Nebraska and Wyoming she is not legally able to do so until she is nineteen. Many states recognize a variation of the "mature" or "emancipated" minor doctrine, and so permit certain teenagers, such as a young woman who has borne a child, to make decisions about medical care. Legally and psychologically, relationships between adults and their maturing children are a patchwork, confused and ambivalent. Our legal system reflects the fact that even the most normal teenager goes through ups and downs, flashes of insight and moments of utter self-delusion, the vagaries that often characterize adolescence.

Our legal system, like other societal institutions, struggles to keep pace with the massive social changes our culture has undergone. Never before have so many adolescents made their own decisions, lived apart from parents and families. Tens of millions more are independently engaging in "adult" behaviors: earning money, having sex, conceiving and bearing children, using and abusing drugs and alcohol.

As with adults—only more so—their decisions may or may not be rational, consciously explored choices but may instead reflect enthusiasm, rebellion, peer pressure, or insecurity. Yet such decisions carry medical implications. They raise complex questions for doctors, nurses, and social workers, questions that arise every day in our clinics, doctor's offices, hospitals, and courts.

Cindy was a young woman with severe progressive kidney disease. At age fifteen, she had been diagnosed with kidney problems, treated in the hospital, and released. Now three years later, at age eighteen, she was brought back to the hospital by ambulance in a severely debilitated condition. Her failing kidneys were no longer producing a substance called erythropoietin, a natural body chemical that stimulates the production of red blood cells. As a result, her red blood cell count had dropped and, as she grew gradually more anemic, her heart was forced to pump ever faster to circulate enough oxygen to her body's organs. Now her heart could no longer stand the stress; untreated, she was at high risk for a fatal cardiac arrest. At this crisis stage, the only remedy is an immediate blood transfusion to relieve the burden on a failing heart.

Unfortunately, it was not to be so easy. Cindy's mother was a Jehovah's Witness and refused to grant permission for a transfusion. Cindy also refused. Her doctors felt an increasing sense of desperation. Without an immediate transfusion, they knew, this young woman would die. Technically, Cindy was eighteen and therefore legally empowered to make the decision for herself. However, ethically they did not feel comfortable simply colluding in the decision to let an eighteen-year-old woman die a preventable death.

Certain members of the care team had grave reservations for another reason. They felt Cindy was being heavily influenced by her mother and by the steady stream of church elders who took turns staying in her room at all times. The staff felt this presence might be influencing Cindy's decision unduly, that perhaps the young woman was being coerced by this community of faithful. The care team would have felt more comfortable if they had had some opportunity to talk with the young woman alone, but time, visitors, and her condition had conspired to make that impossible.

Was Cindy, they wondered, making this decision after a full examination of her own values, weighing the risks and benefits of the decision, or was she merely responding to a catechism inculcated into her as a child and reinforced by her visitors? Is there really a difference? When does teaching become belief? Hers was certainly a legally respectable decision; was it also ethically respectable? Should her hospital care team stand firmly behind her decision and stand silent, or was there some overriding ethical reason to contest this decision? Was hers a refusal that should be respected?

The physicians and the care team could not know if the limits being drawn here reflected her adult wishes or her childish loyalties. Several nurses worried that they had been wrong to allow the elders' constant attendance at her bedside. Had they unwittingly allowed something improper? A physician voiced the concern that, even though Cindy was legally old enough to decide, if she had been four months younger and only seventeen, the hospital might have petitioned the court to permit the transfusion. Should the care team simply abdicate responsibility for what, in a younger child, would be medical neglect?

Ultimately, the decision was taken out of our hands. By early evening, Cindy fell into a coma. At that point, her father arrived. Although he had not seen her in many years, he was clearly deeply concerned at the turn of events, and distraught over his daughter's worsening condition. When he learned the situation he immediately went to court to get an order for her treatment. At 2:00 A.M. that same night, a judge was awakened and granted the order. A blood transfusion was given immediately, but to no avail—the young woman never regained consciousness, and died shortly afterward.

In Cindy's case, everybody lost. Her wishes, and those of her mother, had been violated by the transfusion. For her father, his only daughter had died needlessly, the victim, as he saw it, of a community's belief and medical neglect. Our medical staff was also devastated: they worried that by delaying the transfusion they had let this beautiful young woman die, her life sacrificed on a mere technicality of secular law. But they also worried that they had provided insufficient support for her faith. In a very real way, Cindy was a casualty of our collective confusion.

In an attempt to clarify matters, our courts have tried to carve out areas where adolescents are legally recognized to have rights protected by law, including certain rights to decide for themselves. I date the real growth of adolescent rights from the case of *Brown v. the Board of Education,* in which the United States Supreme Court found separate schools for black and white children inherently unequal. But, more importantly for this discussion, it said that the constitution applies independently to children as well as adults. The next step came in a case, *Gault v. Arizona,* where a teenager was sentenced to seven years in reform school without ever knowing the charges against him, or confronting the witnesses, or having a lawyer. Calling it a "kangaroo court," Mr. Justice Goldberg extended the protections of the constitution to these younger defendants, even if they were called merely charges or wards.

These rights extended to medical care with the Supreme Court case of *Carey v. Population Services,* in 1976. At issue was the teenager's right to contraception. There, the judges wrote that: "Constitutional rights do not mature magically at adulthood." The message was clear: teens can choose to use contraceptives without parental consent. Under a combination of state statutes and regulations and federal law, they may also receive treatment for sexually transmitted diseases and gain access to family planning and drug and alcohol treatment. In many states, they have access to abortions without parental notification.

It is no accident that so many of these questions involve questions of sex; in our culture, the combination of sex, teenagers, and adult attitudes makes a volatile mix. Another such explosive debate has raged in New York City. Here, as in many cities, studies show that approximately 80 percent of eighteen-year-olds are sexually active—often without the knowledge or consent of their parents. Given those overwhelming statistics a political fire storm exploded over whether public schools should make condoms easily and confidentially available to students, and whether parents could exclude their own teenagers from such a program. The rancorous argument pitted the Catholic archdiocese, some other religious organizations, and conservative parents groups against the school chancellor, AIDS and health activists and educators, and a coalition of worried parents.

The dispute embodied all our deepest discomfort about our teens. Beneath the lurid headlines lay the same basic tensions that occur so often: How much do these decisions rest with parents, how much with teenagers, and how much does the State have a real interest in the public health and personal welfare ramifications of such decisions? Some argued that it falls to the parents to control what happens to their children, others that society has such an overriding interest in their welfare that it should allow teens to override parental wishes. At root lay the fundamental question: Are teenagers old enough to make decisions for themselves? More accurately, this was not one question but a series of questions: Is supplying condoms in the interest of public health? Has that interest overwhelmed our proper concern for adolescent behavior? Does providing condoms encourage promiscuity or merely protect those who have already decided about their personal sexual code? Do schools send any overt or covert messages about sexuality when they distribute the paraphernalia of "safer sex"? Is it a good thing or not for our view of education if the school acts to distribute condoms and not to teach about them?

Given the statistics, and the scary fact of a city with more AIDS cases than any other, sex presents the clear and real danger of death. The decision to have sex—no matter what moral value one may assign it—carries with it the medical imperative to encourage the use of condoms. For at this moment, prevention, education, and the use of condoms and clean needles are our only tools to fight this epidemic. The prevalence of AIDS shifted this discussion from one of morality to mortality; no longer was it simply a matter of comfort for parents, or respect for religious views, but a decision whose consequences are no less than life and death itself.

The specter of HIV-related disease has made things more complex around adolescents and sex. Where once these decisions involved only the teenager and the family, in the age of AIDS they involve our whole society. Personal health now blurs into public health, which raises the stakes enormously.

Jim was nineteen years old, and infected with HIV from a blood transfusion he had received five years before—a fact unknown outside his care team. He was a patient in our adolescent AIDS service where, one day, he accidentally ran into Raymond, a high school friend, working at a summer job in the hospital. Jim stuttered that he had come "to visit my sick grandfather"; Raymond, knowing there were no grandfathers in the adolescent unit, reasoned that Jim was likely there for a far more serious, and personal, reason.

The next day, Raymond cornered one of the social workers, very upset: "Look, I know it's none of my business, but my sister's best friend, Lisa, went steady with Jim two years ago. They slept together. Does that mean . . ." His implication hung in the air. Jim's most personal secret was out, an unknowing young woman could well be infected with the lethal virus, and both of those pieces of deeply private information were now known to an unrelated stranger. The chance meeting of two young men, it was clear, held extraordinary consequences; like a pebble dropped in a pond, its ripples would spread, touching many lives.

That afternoon, I was called to a meeting of the adolescent

AIDS team: its medical director, two attending physicians, several PGY-1 and PGY-2 physicians, nurses and nurse practitioners, and three social workers. Juanita, Jim's primary doctor, began: "He's sexually active, but I don't feel confident that he's telling his partners." Leon, Jimmy's social worker, nodded his head: "Last year, Jimmy disclosed his status to a girlfriend, and she broke off with him. He thinks he'll never find another girlfriend if he tells, and he's desperate. He's even convinced that they'll know he's positive if he says he wants to use a condom."

In the silence that followed, I sensed one thought on everybody's mind. Sally, a nurse practitioner, spoke first: "Her life may be in danger, without her even knowing it. In my heart I want to just call her and say 'go get tested.' If she's HIV-positive, she could get help. She has the right to know, and get treatment."

Yet telling her, the care team knew, opened a Pandora's box. First of all, Lisa's getting the news from us could be immensely traumatic. That would have to be handled carefully, and she would have to be well supported—not necessarily easy when nobody on the team even knew her last name. She would also infer who had put her at risk, which meant the physicians would have breached their professional obligation to respect Jim's confidentiality. If Jim heard about it—as he undoubtedly would—his trust could be shattered. Feeling betrayed and ashamed, he might well drop out of the program; then he would lose his treatment, and the program would lose any chance at all to influence his sexual behavior. Another nurse spoke up, obviously frustrated: "Look, he might leave, or he might not—that's his choice. But how can we protect this girl, when her life may be at stake?"

Unfortunately, all of us knew, Lisa's and Jim's were not the only lives at stake. There were forty-five teens like them in our adolescent AIDS service. Some live on their own, others are street teens for whom Montefiore is their sole contact with adult authority. These are the hardest sort of kids to reach: their young, brutal lives, often involving sex as a commodity for exploitation, have taught them deep distrust and suspicion of strangers. For such teens, with few moorings to family or community, we were all they had.

For five years this team had worked to win their trust; step by agonizing step, with honesty, fairness, and scrupulous respect for confidentiality. All of us knew, too, that for these kids, their HIV status was the deepest, darkest secret they carried. If word got out on the street that the clinic doctors had "fingered" Jim—even to help Lisa—the effects could easily backfire; dozens of these skittish patients could be driven away from the only health care available to them. For although other places in the city provide some care for these kids, Montefiore is one of the only ones to actively seek them out as patients. Losing their confidence would also mean losing our ability to stop them from potentially infecting hundreds of others.

But what about this young woman? One PGY-2 spoke, hopefully: "Look, they're not together now. It's not like they are still having sex, where our silence would put her at risk for infection." If Lisa had contracted the virus from Jim, it had already happened, she argued. Did that change anything?

The team agreed that our duty to warn would be stronger in situations where the risk is continuing. I cited a precedent-setting legal case in California, where a psychotherapist was held to have a duty to warn a specific third party who was in danger from the therapist's patient. Some wondered if this obligation existed in New York and, if so, was Jim's case analogous? Was Jim's doctor like that therapist?

The law aside, the unit psychologist wondered what would be served by telling Lisa—would that help or hurt her? Not so long ago, that was a real question, for people with HIV could only worry and wait. Now, however, she could take any of several drugs to postpone or prevent the onset of the infections that can kill people with AIDS. As professionals, they knew that fully one-third of the teens they treat have no symptoms, and are able to take these drugs to keep themselves healthy as long as possible. Knowing her status meant Lisa could get new medical treatments as they became available, and possibly avoid fatal illness.

Then there was the issue of transmission to others. Although women seem to transmit HIV less easily than men do, Lisa's knowing her status might help stop her from infecting others. Statistics suggest that fewer than one in one hundred of the HIV-positive teens in our city know their status. If Lisa did, perhaps she would take precautions for herself and her present or future partners.

Finally, there was the concern about transmission to future offspring. In addition to living in the middle of the AIDS epidemic, Lisa was also living in the middle of an epidemic of teen pregnancy. While it is not yet clear exactly what percentage of the babies of infected mothers actually contract the virus, research data indicate anywhere from 12 percent to 30 percent. Whatever the actual number, some significant proportion of these babies will have the AIDS virus and will die from it. That should be a factor in the minds of women who consider pregnancy, Lisa among them.

The team was torn among so many risks—to Lisa, to Jim, to the other patients in the program, to their past, present, and future sex partners. Jim's doctor asked if, by breaking confidentiality in this case, the team would be on a slippery slope: "Does this make it easier to do it again for the next kid?" she challenged us. "What about our sworn professional ethic to not disclose, and our obligation to the other kids in the program?"

As we talked, it became clear that our question was not whether to tell Lisa, but how. Donning my public health lawyer cap, I reminded them of one other option. Through what is termed "partner notification" the New York City Department of Health could inform Lisa anonymously. Like hundreds of other people around the country, she would simply receive a call from a "partner notification" officer, requesting a visit. Then, face-to-face, she would be informed that she might have been exposed to HIV infection. Absolutely no further information on the source of the infection would be given; but she would be urged to get tested and, if she wished, even given an appointment for a counseling session at that time. She would not necessarily connect it specifically to Jim, or to us. It minimized our breach of Jim's confidentiality, and the risk to our other young patients. There remained some risk, however. Public health law required the doctor to tell Jim that she was going to notify Lisa, so he could tell her first if he wished. Yes, there would be some risk of alienating him, but it was a risk the team felt to be justified for the greater good.

"What about him?" One PGY-2 shook his head. "What about the ethics of taking this young guy with a fatal illness, who will likely die from it, and simply treating him so he can go back on the street to spread his fatal illness? Where does he change from a kid who needs help to a madman going out killing people—and what's our responsibility in that? That's why I don't sleep at night." Several heads bobbed in unison.

Perhaps, said the attending pediatrician, this was our chance to get through to Jim. "We've got to make him see his obligation not to spread the virus. If he knows he may have given it to someone, maybe he'll realize he needs to take responsibility. This could work as a lesson to kids who know they are positive and aren't taking responsibility."

Perhaps, someone suggested, Jim needed the "Hornlab" treatment, named after one of Montefiore's most admired and effective practitioners. This wise and compassionate doctor, having practiced medicine for fifty years, has seen every variety of human foible and obstinacy at least twice. His tactic is simple: "You just badger the hell out of them till they come 'round."

Sometimes, when dealing with adolescents, there is a responsible parent or adult to whom doctors can appeal for help when the adolescent behaves destructively. But for street kids, there is not. Jim's own doctor said that she felt comfortable telling Jim that if he didn't stop putting partners at risk, she would call the public health authorities and have him jailed. Ethically and pragmatically, of course, she could not easily have played that trump card—I half wondered, in fact, if the suggestion was made tongue-in-cheek. But Jim wouldn't know that. For our part, all the team knew that, given the possible harm to others from Jim's continuing this behavior, they had to get through to him any way possible, even if that meant raising the stakes.

Often, adolescents' newfound right to make sexual and health decisions outstrips their willingness to take responsibility for those decisions. Where once that meant "shotgun weddings," today it can mean death. Jim's behavior was ethically horrific, no doubt. But the available options—surveillance, threats of incarceration, intimidation—pose a deeper, ultimately more destructive, terror for a free society.

Our society has few good answers for HIV-positive teenagers—or adults—who refuse to practice safe sex. So the caregivers on the front lines use what tools they have: education and information, partner notification and persuasion—and when there is no choice, ruthless badgering has its place. Here, as they do so often, the AIDS team was struggling to find a combination of approaches that might approximate what happens when a reasonably happy adolescent goes through some trauma in the context of a stable and loving home. In this discussion, we were in effect trying to provide the support of family to kids without it. Most of all, as this dedicated team goes about its daily work, they hope to encourage in their young charges the most powerful motivator of all, a caring human conscience that takes responsibility for the results of their behavior.

It isn't just the teenagers who are changing—so are doctors. As they do, they are rethinking their relationships with their young patients. Traditionally, teenagers were treated by a pediatrician, whose primary loyalty and relationship lay with parents. In the last two decades, however, a recognized medical subspecialty, adolescent medicine, has developed. These doctors may be pediatricians or family practice doctors with special training in teen health care. They tend to approach problems somewhat differently from some of their pediatric colleagues.

Many adolescent medicine doctors will likely tell parents and the teenager that what happens between the child and the physician is confidential unless the child is in direct physical or psychological danger of harm—in which case the protections for privacy will be breached and the parents involved. More and more, these adolescent medicine specialists tend to see the child as their patient, and put less emphasis on their relationship to parents. Accordingly, most adolescent medicine physicians will treat teens over fifteen without parental consent if the treatment is relatively uncontroversial, and if it is exclusively for the benefit of the child.

Things get complicated in adolescent medicine concerning the question of who pays. Those doctors who work on a fee-for-service basis are less likely to assume the care of the teen without the parents' agreement to pay. Only in clinics and specially funded programs can care be delivered free to the teen without parental involvement. Thus even though increasing numbers of physicians see no absolute ethical or legal barriers to providing at least some kinds of care, the constraint is often economic, and it is real.

Most adolescents, however, are cared for by physicians with no special training in adolescent medicine: pediatricians, family practitioners, and gynecologists. Happily, this is starting to change: Most residency programs in pediatrics, family medicine, and obstetrics and gynecology now formally address the special medical, social, developmental, and ethical problems that adolescents present. Specifically, they address the changes of style and practice necessary to provide appropriate care for our emerging adults. The doctor's attitude and approach are central to the success of adolescent medicine. Physicians treating teens must take seriously their responsibility to talk to teens and to listen carefully and respectfully to their comments and answers to questions. They should also be acutely aware of the tensions between parent and child, striving, if possible, to mediate those tensions.

And, as every parent knows, dealing with adolescents can be difficult even in the best of times. In my house, as my children came into adolescence, my husband and I liked to say that we "communicated mainly by rumor." (We also commented to each other that rather than having a door to close, some of us now had doors to slam.) What all parents know is that adolescents are private and guarded—precisely those characteristics that make the delivery of care impossible. Good medical care must be based on a complete physical history accompanied by a personal narrative that gives it all meaning. Monosyllabic grunts don't go far in sketching out relevant personal medical history.

Despite the still-spotty specialty training in adolescent medicine, parents should not be surprised to discover physicians and nurse practitioners who have rules that differ from standard pediatric practice. These doctors will fold the emerging maturity of the adolescent into the calculation that determines when to involve parents or others in the care of a particular teen. Not only do thirteen- and seventeen-year-olds have different medical issues, they are in different developmental stages. This awareness is central to providing them with appropriate care.

AIDS has made it even more complicated. The disease does not present new questions but does bring existing questions into sharper relief. The same matters of confidentiality and payment, privacy and access to care, and the right to decide remain central. But added to them have been the factors of public health and the transmission of the virus to sexual and drug-sharing partners and to newborns. Adolescence complicates the already complex world of doctor, patient, and society.

The clear trend is to honor confidentiality with teenagers, as with any other patient. This is particularly true of physicians who treat adolescents in big cities. Generally the teenagers are encouraged to involve their parents, but if they refuse to do so, they will be treated anyway—especially if the treatment is uncontroversial, such as a course of penicillin for gonorrhea.

The situation may change, however, if the doctor feels that the teen is in danger from the behavior he or she has chosen. A teen who has diabetes, who is neither monitoring blood sugar nor restricting her diet, is putting herself at risk for diabetic coma and death. In this case, even if she is being treated confidentially, if her doctor fears her behavior will not change, he will likely contact a parent in the interest of protecting her health. Almost certainly, however, he will inform the child of his intent before he contacts the parent.

In a hundred ways, medical care for adolescents is a terrain of shifting sands. Most adolescent specialists would treat an eighteen-year-old girl with a sexually transmitted disease without telling her parents. The same might be true if she were seventeen or sixteen. But what if she is fifteen? If she is fourteen, thirteen, twelve years old, where do they draw a line and go to the parent? Considering that young age, a doctor must weigh the possibility of sexual abuse, in which case the parents would be dealt with differently—as possible suspects—and authorities notified. Each case requires careful judgment calls. Running through all of them, however, is a clear and growing social consensus that teenagers have the same rights our society values for adults. They have the right to participate in their own decisions, to confidentiality of their personal information, the right to privacy from parents, and the right to receive necessary, uncontroversial and appropriate care. (Given the economic realities of adolescence and the rising cost of medical care, however, there is no assurance that our teenagers will be able to afford the care to which they have a "right.") Increasingly, medical ethicists argue that a teenager's informed opinion and consent should be respected in decisions made about their health.

It also makes pure medical sense to try to include young people to the degree that they can participate. The twelve-year-old with leukemia may not properly be the sole decider about whether or not to take a course of chemotherapy, but can and should have a role in making certain decisions about treatment. She has every right, for example, to choose whether treatment sessions should occur in the morning or evening, in her bedroom or in the pediatric library (assuming that all of these are medically possible). Involving chronically ill youngsters in decisions about their care greatly enhances their own sense of autonomy, makes their treatment easier to bear and correspondingly easier for the staff to administer, and often makes treatment more effective.

This principle of inclusion is particularly true for older chronically ill children and teenagers. These young patients are often remarkably wise and perceptive. They alone know the pain and suffering that disease has brought into their lives, and this knowledge can powerfully inform their decisions. It is clearly unrealistic to expect that all teenagers at all times will be capable of making such decisions—just as it is unrealistic to expect that of adults. But it is equally wrong to think that the mere fact of their youth should automatically disqualify their views or deafen us to their wishes.

America has come a long way from the days when a child was considered a parent's property, to be dealt with, decided for, and disposed of at the parent's whim. Collectively, we still wrestle with the roles of parent and child, struggling to assure our newborns, children, and our youngest adults of the rights they deserve, while affording them the protections they require.

WHO GETS THE KIDNEYS?

WHEN THERE'S
NOT ENOUGH HEALTH
FOR EVERYBODY

Throughout this book, I have put the interests of the patient, family member, or loved one squarely at the center of each decision. But sometimes this cannot be the case—nor should it be. In this chapter, we confront specific limits—ethically appropriate limits—to a patient's ability to determine what happens to him. These circumstances arise around what ethicists term "scarce resources," and they are a hard and inevitable fact of the way we practice medicine in this country. Because you may encounter them, you'd best know how they work, and why.

A medical resource is classified as "scarce" whenever demand exceeds supply: when, for example, a hospital has one more patient in respiratory distress than it has available respirators, a respirator becomes a scarce resource. The medical assets in demand may be intrinsically scarce, such as transplant organs; they may be scarce because they are expensive, like intensive care beds in a hospital; they may simply be expensive, like highly technological devices called "fluidized air beds." Yet in each case, scarce resources confront caregivers with a lifeboat calculus where they must weigh which patient will benefit most from the resources available, and then choose. Often, that becomes a decision of who shall live and who shall die.

What makes scarce resources different is that, in such circumstances, patients, and those who love them, are not the right ones to decide. Quite the contrary: patients, spouses, or family have one specific individual's interest at heart. They cannot be expected to balance that interest against the possible greater needs of another person for the same resource. To ask them to do so is both unrealistic and inhumane. When there is not enough to go around, caregivers have an ethical obligation to balance more than one patient's interest to determine who will benefit most. That means you may not get to decide about your care, you may not get what you want, and there is probably nothing you can do about it. Moreover, such a state of affairs is completely appropriate—or would be if all else in our health-care system were fair, equitable, and just.

Three specific circumstances where you are most likely to encounter this problem are: when you need an intensive care unit (ICU) bed; when you need an organ transplant; or when you require a specific medical asset in short supply. Such assets may include an "air fluidized" or "liquid fluid" bed, which prevents bed sores in immobile patients; a nutritional treatment called Total Parenteral Nutrition, or TPN, which replaces the complex amino acids and minerals needed by patients who cannot gain sufficient nutrients through taking food orally; and many other costly and scarce medical interventions that are multiplying in medicine's headlong rush to progress. Because each of these kinds of scarcity poses its own concerns, we should look at them in turn.

Intense Decisions in Intensive Care

When most people think of hospitals, they think of the ICU, with its beeping monitors, high-tech machines, and dramatic lifesaving techniques. But this vision of a hospital is a very recent invention. What we now think of as the modern ICU was born of catastrophes in the 1940s and '50s that would forever alter how we conceived the work of the physician. One of those occurred in 1942, the tragic Coconut Grove nightclub fire in Boston, which presented doctors with the urgent need to treat large numbers of critically burned and injured people. Around that same time, physicians, fresh from their battlefield experiences of the Second World War, developed and experimented with radical new techniques of resuscitation, sustaining bodies by maintaining vital functions of heartbeat and breathing. This expertise would prove invaluable only a few years later, as they found themselves facing a devastating polio epidemic and thousands of people needing mechanical assistance—"iron lungs"—to breathe.

By the late 1950s, the external defibrillator, with its shock paddles to jump-start the failed heart, was invented. The 1960s brought a cascade of new wonders: the introduction of closed-chest CPR, the invention of a permanent shunt making kidney dialysis practical. Even the space program contributed, as the same miniaturized technologies used to monitor body functions of astronauts in space were adapted to monitor vital signs of the desperately ill in our hospitals. By the end of that decade, more than 95 percent of American acute care hospitals had established critical care units. Only recently has this young and growing field come of age: the first certifying exams for physicians specializing in critical care medicine were not given until 1987.

The medical pioneers of forty years ago could scarcely recognize the awesome place the modern ICU has become. Night and day are lost in perpetual fluorescent light, computer probes continuously track the vital signs of every patient: breathing, heartbeat, blood flow, blood oxygen and chemical balance, even brain activity. The ICU team is trained to cheat death on a daily basis. They command machines that shock the failing human heart back into vigor, drugs that vanquish infection, chemicals that restore lost blood pressure and revive the damaged brain. ICU technologies co-opt the human body's most intimate functions—breath and pulse, sustenance and elimination. The ICU revolves around the hope, often unavailing, that by defying otherwise certain death, we can sustain a body long enough to allow its systems to resume their own work.

The ICU has become the stage on which are played out many of the most heated ethical debates occurring in medicine today. The ability to mimic the cardiac, respiratory, and renal functions of healthy organ systems has blurred the line between life and death and challenged our most bedrock assumptions about life, its quality and length. Our wondrous technological capacities have spawned knotty dilemmas: when should we apply these interventions to patients? To which patients? Who decides, based on what rules and principles? When do we call it quits—and who decides that? What appeal is there, and to whom, if you disagree with any of these decisions? Are there different rules for children? For retarded persons? For the severely demented elderly?

Some of those dilemmas arise simply because such intensive care is intensely expensive. It costs $2,500 each day to staff a modern ICU bed with the almost one-on-one nursing ratio each patient needs for twenty-four-hour care. ICU's now consume $14 billion to $20 billion a year, one-fifth of all hospital resources and fully 1 percent of the nation's gross national product. The facts of hospital economics dictate that any hospital can support only a limited number of ICU beds. These beds are a resource made scarce by economic design, limited by policy decisions of hospital administrators and state regulators. Ultimately, we could control this and create more, but that would involve a long process of market research, economic forecasts, hospital planning, capital improvement, and staff development. At some point in every hospital, whether it has five ICU beds or fifty, there comes a moment when one too many sick people need one too few beds. In that instant, for that person, that bed has become a truly scarce resource. Now someone must make a hard decision.

Over the years, physicians and nurses specializing in intensive care have struggled to find a fair way to decide who gets those beds. Some proposed a first-come-first-served system, but often the patient who gets there first needs the ICU less, or stands to gain less by aggressive care than another who happens to come later. Some planners suggested choosing by lottery, but the most severely ill people, or those most likely to benefit, are not necessarily the ones with lucky numbers. Once again, under these systems, ICU care could go to those who wouldn't benefit from it most. Over the years, therefore, ethicists and physicians have generally rejected both such approaches, in the search for a system both fair and rational.

At sixty-four, Jenny Parfort was active, vital, an artist and tireless community volunteer. One day, as she was chatting on the phone to her forty-two-year-old daughter, Susan, the younger woman heard her mother's voice become strangely slurred; before she could ask what was wrong, the phone clattered to the floor and the line fell silent. Upset and anxious, Susan sped to her mother's house and found her unconscious on the kitchen floor. She was rushed to our emergency room, where initial examination showed a massive cerebral hemorrhage involving a significant portion of her brain. The ER team stabilized Mrs. Parfort's vital signs and moved her to the ICU for observation. There, after several days of constant monitoring with no perceptible change, the consulting neurologist wrote a note in the chart: "Profound, bilateral brain damage." Mrs. Parfort's prognosis, he concluded, was "hopeless."

That evening, the ICU resident sat down to break the news to Susan. "There is nothing more we can do for her," he explained sadly. They talked for a few minutes before he asked her: "Would you agree to have your mom transferred out of the ICU tomorrow to a regular floor unit?" Her answer, he knew, would have significant repercussions. A patient simply cannot be monitored as closely on a standard nursing unit as in the ICU. Mrs. Parfort's ventilator, the pressor drugs maintaining her blood pressure, and the intravenous lines maintaining her blood chemistry, all worked well only as long as they were constantly adjusted and monitored. On a regular nursing floor, the calibrations would slowly drift until Mrs. Parfort's body could no longer sustain even its current high-tech imitation of life.

Medically, we had come to the point where the ICU was no longer the best place for this patient. ICU's exist to mobilize medicine's most aggressive efforts in support of life. Traditionally, we have viewed the "best" care as the most intensive, high-tech treatment—but sometimes this is just not so. The ICU is a perpetual assault, an unending procession of tubes, lights, noise, stress, alarm, pain, and indignity. Although the nurses work tirelessly to maintain principles of compassionate care and address the patient as a whole person with dignity and privacy, the focus of care tends to shift inexorably to maintaining organ function. For efficiency, patients are often only draped, not clothed; if restless, they may be naked; they are often completely helpless or deeply sedated.

In such circumstances, caregivers know that there comes a moment when continued medical manipulation of a body will not make the patient any better. Then it falls to the director of the ICU to make the decision to discharge or transfer a patient.

The director of the ICU had reviewed Mrs. Parfort's case and decided that, for her, the ICU was now a venue, not of hope, but of prolonged dying. In her case, a transfer out was simply the next step in an inexorable journey that began when the artery exploded in her brain. It would allow nature to take its course, and allow her to die the most natural death possible in a hospital. Besides, given the shortage of ICU beds, this wasn't just a case of what was best for one woman. From the director's professional perspective, this was one life among many in his care. That is why decisions about allocating ICU beds properly fall to the director, for it is by definition a decision requiring a broader, neutral perspective from a professional who can balance competing needs.

ICU directors tend to be a special breed of practitioners. They are technically trained to walk the fine line that separates death from life. They bring to the job a deep mastery of the science of maintaining organ systems, and, usually, a deep loathing of conceding defeat to mortality. Thus when the ICU director reaches the decision that this person can no longer benefit from ICU care, you can be quite sure that the decision was reached only after a struggle.

Several elements entwine in such a decision. In our ICU, as in most, it is policy not to keep patients who cannot benefit from care, meaning that their physical functioning or their mental status cannot improve. When that is the case, it is an inappropriate use of the bed to have someone there. In the days before hospitals began to struggle for their financial lives, many tried to leave one empty bed in the ICU at all times, so the next critically injured or ill patient would have a place to go immediately upon admission. That way the hospital could avoid a contest between two people for the same bed, a contest that could take hours or days to resolve, in situations where delay can cost a life.

On this day, our last bed was filled by Mrs. Parfort, whom we could no longer help. She would likely not be moved out unless there was someone more needy; but in the meantime, she had to be identified as the next patient to move if and when the contest for the bed emerged.

Unfortunately, it fell to the ICU resident to give Susan the news she didn't want to hear. She listened, clearly enraged that her mother might be taken out of ICU. Growing increasingly hostile and abusive, she demanded to see the administrator on call, and threatened to call the president of the hospital and the press. "Who are you to play God?" she spat at the doctor at one point. It was an ironic question: nobody complains when doctors play God by attaching a person to life-support machines in the first place. Removing Mrs. Parfort from this exquisite monitoring was merely conceding that the time had come to stop moving mountains for this one patient and to consider the needs of other possible patients. Moving her out of the unit did not affect her dismal prognosis, but it did diminish her chances of satisfactory organ maintenance, pointing toward a more rapid death. The meeting was adjourned with no resolution, and I was called to come up to the ICU to meet with the staff later that afternoon. Then, if we all felt it was appropriate, I would meet with Mrs. Parfort's family.

In that meeting, several things became clear: first, as incredible as it seemed, nobody had clearly explained to Susan—or more likely, Susan seemed not to have heard—the hopelessness of her mother's condition. She seemed to think her mother might still recover, and saw the suggestion to reduce her mother's care in that light. It might at first seem impossible that nobody had really discussed the prognosis with her, given how many physicians and nurses swarm over the ICU. Yet in a decade and a half, I have learned that such lapses are dismayingly common, particularly in large teaching hospitals, particularly when medical events move as quickly as they do in the ICU. Equally common, however, is that the discussions occur but families do not hear them.

After our meeting, the physician tried to help Susan understand the extent of her mother's brain damage. He explained that she would not get better, despite the high-tech ministrations of the ICU. The more we talked, the clearer it became that it was this basic prognosis that had so angered Susan. She was unable to accept the news that her mother was gone—had, in fact, been effectively gone since she collapsed in her kitchen. We were witnessing a grieving daughter coming to grips with the prognosis she did not want to hear.

But there was another element in her reaction as well. When the physician had asked her to consent to moving her mother, Susan felt she was being forced to make the decision to stop care for her mother. To say yes, she felt, would make her responsible for her mother's death. "How could I live with myself?" she sobbed.

The attending physician gently explained that in fact the decision to move her mother from the ICU was not Susan's to make. Ethically, he stood on firm ground, for given unlimited demand for limited ICU beds, these decisions can only be made by staff. We cannot, and should not, put family members in the position to make such agonizing decisions. It would be unrealistic and cruel to ask Susan to forfeit her mother's life for that of a stranger. Instead, in such times, having others decide can make it much easier for family members to accept the inevitable.

We tried to help Susan understand that her mother would be moved out, but that it was not her decision, and she could not affect it. Ethically, our obligation was to balance the needs of many, as yet unidentified, against the wishes of one. For that reason, such decisions are usually final. We had done our best to explain clearly to Susan her mother's status and prognosis, to listen carefully to her concerns, and to support her in what was an emotionally traumatic process. But we could not give Susan what she wanted: her mother back. The woman who had stood chatting in her kitchen yesterday was gone forever.

Susan's case also raises another principle, allied to these others and yet distinct: patients and families have in general no right to demand care that physicians judge medically or morally inappropriate. Just because they demand care does not mean they are entitled to it; the physician must be the one to judge if the request, or demand, is for medically appropriate intervention. Often this judgment occurs before the patient or family is even presented with the option. If the care is not medically appropriate, the doctor is not ethically required to provide it. Physicians have no obligation to respect irrational, unjustified demands for care, whether made by family members or by the patient himself.

This, like so many ethical questions, is drawn in shades of gray. Some ethicists argue that when the patient herself makes a request as a "dying request," there is a special ethical burden to honor it—even if it qualifies as "hopeless" care. Intuitively, we might agree that being at death's door gives one a different moral standing to demand things. Thus his doctors allowed my friend Joseph, dying of terminal cancer, to request resuscitation that was, in their judgment, medically futile, as it could not reverse his underlying condition. Note, however, that for Joseph it was not futile. The physicians acted out of respect for Joseph and his religious beliefs. Similarly, AIDS patients, who are clearly dying, who are often young and angry, may be provided with care that the team knows will neither postpone death nor improve the patient's lot simply because the anguish at the end is so overwhelming. By general agreement, requests coming from the patient himself are seen as presenting a more powerful claim on resources than requests from the family.

So while they don't have to, doctors can give care beyond what they might view as medically advisable—provided it does not interfere with what another patient might get or need. But that is a wholly different matter than a principle requiring physicians to follow deathbed wishes slavishly, with no possibility of their own dissent. Medicine has explicitly identified limits to empowering the patient to decide.

Transplants: Who Gets the Kidney?

There is a big difference between things that are merely expensive and those that are truly scarce. If ICU beds are difficult to come by because they are expensive, transplants involve a more intransigent kind of scarcity. Here, the limits are not fiscal, but biological and societal. Biologically, there are a finite number of donor organs due to a finite number of bodies whose organs are acceptable for transplant. Socially, there is widespread unwillingness of many individuals and families to donate organs. Combined, these factors mean that, in any given month, twenty-three thousand Americans are waiting for new hearts, kidneys, lungs, livers, and pancreases. The supply of these organs is somewhat beyond our control, regulated by the lives and deaths of others.

The biological shortage is made more acute by the fact that only a small fraction of available organs actually make their way to patients in need. Medical experts estimate that as many as fifteen thousand people could potentially be donors each year; today, only four thousand are. So it is both pure availability and limitations of the consent process that actually control organ supply. Some ethicists have suggested that organ donation ought not to be an individual decision but rather one for society—that all organs that could be used, should be used. This idea, however, has not yet moved even to the stage of discussion let alone to a popular consensus.

Scarcity is not limited to kidneys. Transplant organs today include skin for burn victims, hearts and lungs, corneas, livers, pancreases, bones and bone marrow. All of these organs have one thing in common: there are not enough to give to all who need them, and we cannot get more of them simply by paying for them. Eventually, we may be able to do so through public education, but for the moment they are the purest sort of scarce medical resource.

Fifty years ago, such a scarcity, indeed the notion of organ transplants at all, was pretty much inconceivable. It was not until 1953 that a medical team from the Peter Bent Brigham Hospital in Boston stunned the world by announcing that they had performed a successful kidney transplant on a patient who actually lived to leave the hospital. Shortly thereafter, the same hospital announced the first kidney transplant between identical twins; this patient would live for over eight years, rather than the few months of his predecessor. In the nine hours these two operations required, transplants had moved from science fiction to science.

The next three decades brought a torrent of transplant breakthroughs, each more hopeful than the last. In the 1960s, growing expertise in kidney dialysis allowed more people to live long enough to receive kidney transplants. In 1967 came the first human heart transplant, by Dr. Christian Barnard. Scientists around the world worked to perfect the science of tissue matching to reduce rejection of transplanted organs. The next big boost to organ transplants came in 1983 when Sandoz released the new immunosuppressive drug Cyclosporine, which greatly reduced the risk of organ rejection. With that development, transplants really took off; by the late 1980s, more and more hospitals boasted transplant teams.

Now society was facing a new problem: skyrocketing demand for organs, especially kidneys. That meant that research breakthroughs from the laboratories were not enough. We needed to match them with public policy initiatives if we were to manage our new medical miracles. In the early 1970s, all fifty states passed laws based on the model of the Uniform Anatomical Gift Act, permitting legal donations of organs by individuals and family members. States devised organ donor cards and sent them to everybody getting or renewing a driver's license. Americans were proclaiming on the back of their driver's license their intent to help others in the event of death—just in case.

By the early 1980s, most states had passed legislation recognizing "brain death" as a legal standard, so doctors could "harvest" organs from one patient while they were still vital and useful for another patient. That was followed in many states by "required request" or "routine inquiry" laws. These statutes attempted to increase organ supply by requiring hospital staff to approach families at the time of death for permission to transplant their loved one's organs. In 1986, Congress gave that effort a push when it passed legislation requiring all hospitals receiving federal Medicare or Medicaid funds—which amounted to virtually all hospitals except a few "for-profit" institutions—to routinely request donor organs from families of patients who have died. These laws provide legal encouragement for doctors to have these most difficult discussions at the most difficult of times.

Yet despite the best legislative intentions, there have remained far more people needing organs than bodies providing them. Three decades of scientific progress had moved transplants from stunning breakthrough to commonplace need. It had also created our newest scarce medical resource: pieces of the living human body. This new scarcity bred a new litany of questions: Who would get these scarce organs? Who would decide? How would they decide?

The questions go beyond simply the donor organs to a series of related technologies and treatments. In the early years of kidney transplants, for example, questions arose over who would get the kidneys themselves, but also who would get access to the dialysis machines to keep them alive long enough to receive a donor kidney. Those questions came to a boil in a famous case in Seattle in 1971. The Northwest Kidney Center, like most dialysis facilities of the time, had many more patients needing lifesaving dialysis than it had time available to provide it. To bridge this gap the clinic created a committee of citizens, whose identities were kept secret, charged with choosing the "most appropriate" dialysis candidates. Struggling for a fair way to screen applicants, the committee came up with a complex set of criteria, including the patient's ability to take an active role in the care plan, his ability to live a "useful life," and his capacity to withstand the stress of the treatment. The committee also considered such elements as the patient's education, work history, income, and number of dependents. One of the patients needing dialysis was a man named Ernie Crowfeather.

In the eyes of the committee, Crowfeather, who was half Sioux Indian, was a ne'er-do-well, a chronic alcoholic who had served time in reform school for a failed robbery attempt. The committee rejected him as an applicant, citing medical reasons. But it was clear they had also considered his lack of money, his "unstable home life with a common law wife," and his criminal record. After being denied dialysis, he managed to enroll himself in an experimental program and received a transplant kidney, which his body rejected. As procedure after procedure failed, Ernie became more and more uncooperative, discontinuing treatment abruptly and seemingly without reason, but always eventually coming back for more help. His criminal activity continued, he attempted suicide, and soon his records labeled him a "sociopath." Again, he applied to the Northwest Kidney Center for dialysis; again, the committee refused him further use of the scarce resource that time on the dialysis machines represented.

The committee record states that an "evaluation of the medical, social, and rehabilitation reports revealed a long history of recidivism . . . he was again in custody at the time. Mr. Crowfeather has been historically uncooperative in his medical management . . . [there is] little hope for successful reform and a highly probable inability to manage home dialysis." At root, they were using what ethicists term "social worth criteria," trying to allocate access to lifesaving dialysis based on an individual's worth to society. That approach is deeply flawed in many ways.

First, the process cannot help but reflect the biases of its participants. Those deemed most "worthy" tend to be those who are "responsibly" employed, not too old, with dependents, in otherwise good health, enjoying a certain rank in their family, at work, at church, and civic groups in surrounding society. In other words, the group of people who most closely resemble the profile and embody the values of white, married, middle-class, heterosexual males. Under these criteria, a huge swath of people would be excluded.

Such facile judgments obscure the value of our intrinsic human worth, which we all share equally, viewing people instead as a means to an end: productivity, wealth, or status. Decisions couched in these terms often mask a hierarchy, valuing some human lives more than others. They also presume that any one individual is capable of judging the human worth of another, and of deciding that another person deserves to live or die. That, in itself, does extraordinary violence to our notions of the common dignity of humankind.

Ernie Crowfeather came to a sad end. After the Native American community raised $23,000 to keep him on dialysis, that money eventually ran out. With just a few treatments left, Crowfeather gave up. He skipped treatments, drank heavily, tried to rob a Hilton Hotel, and finally disappeared, in the words of his sister, "to drink himself into oblivion."

By the time his life ended in an emergency room a few weeks later, his legacy had already become a part of American medical history. In 1971, in response to the demand for expensive dialysis treatments the United States Congress found itself debating a bill to permit federal dollars to pay for kidney dialysis. One story, perhaps part of urban mythology, is that a dialysis patient, in his hospital bed and connected to his machine, was wheeled onto the floor of Congress to dramatize the plight of would-be dialysis patients. Clearly, the fact that dialysis centers were becoming the newest for-profit medical enterprises, and knew how to employ lobbyists, played no small role. Whatever the reason, lawmakers were flush with enthusiasm for the promise of this burgeoning technology. In 1972, they established the "End-Stage Renal Disease" program (ESRD). Under federal law, Medicare would henceforth cover dialysis or a kidney transplant for every single American who needed it. For the moment, for kidney disease at least, there would be no more Ernie Crowfeathers.

That noble decision would turn out to be enormously costly. By 1987, 147,850 patients were being kept alive on dialysis at a cost to the federal government of $3.3 billion each year. Experts predict that number will rise to 245,000 patients by the end of this decade, with costs expected to exceed $5 billion each year. Unfortunately, even the august powers of the United States Congress cannot mandate as much as one new kidney into existence, so the larger problem—too few organs for too many people—remains unsolved, particularly since even a new kidney often offers only a few-year hiatus in the downward spiral of ongoing renal disease. Besides, with medicine's increasing transplant expertise, kidneys were but one of the human spare parts in increasingly short supply.

Ernie Crowfeather left his mark on our ethical consensus. The discussion his case engendered led physicians and ethicists to uniformly reject "social worth" criteria as an ethically unacceptable way to apportion our scarce resources. Unfortunately, we have been less than successful at finding a rational and fair alternative. A number of systems have been proposed by health planners, health economists, and ethicists. Some argue that organs should go to the candidates who need them most. Others say gravely ill people are poorer risks for surgery so our precious organs should go to healthier people with the greatest likelihood of recovery. Troubled by any human judgment in the process of selection, some favor a first-come-first-served system, with organs going to those who have waited longest. Yet, some argue that this fails to calculate which patient is in greatest need; one person waiting two years may be stronger than another who has waited six months; so which of them should rightfully receive the organ, and which should wait? Ethicists have also argued for the impartial fairness of a transplant lottery, where recipients are chosen randomly. But as we have seen in the ICU case, that does not take into account the medical need, severity, or prognosis of the particular individual. So, at present, chaos reigns. Those in greatest need, who have waited for years, may die while far less sick people receive organs, and those who could most benefit receive nothing while those who are so sick they are likely to die anyway get the few precious organs.

This remains an ethical tower of Babel, with competing voices clamoring in confusing and quarrelsome debate, the stakes nothing less than life itself. Despite the debate raging in scholarly journals, university medical centers, and academic think tanks, every transplant still involves many levels of human judgment. Some of those judgments are straightforward and medical: every transplant center in the country rigorously screens potential recipients about their medical history, disease profile, and risk factors. Although it is much less commonly discussed, recipients are also screened for certain psychosocial criteria—not least of which is the ability to pay. True, the more blatant examples of social worth judgments are no longer used—at least not openly—but we are a far cry from a fair and equitable system. This is little comfort to the hapless twenty-three thousand people awaiting transplants today. There exists no central registry, no systematic standard, no national standard, no formal communication link or shared rules to ensure a just and equitable matching of people with organs.

A new kind of institution has sprung up to meet the need, organ procurement agencies—"OPA's," as they are known in the industry. Like the procurers that are their namesake, they often play by their own rules. Some OPA's are hospital-based, giving their own patients first crack at any organs they procure, and others are "independent" OPA's offering their precious organs to many different transplant centers.

In the meantime, a ferocious free market applies to organ transplants. But in it, as in most "free" markets, some players are more equal than others, and those who are well connected, wealthy, aggressive, and articulate often have a distinct advantage. The prospect of survival gives an overwhelming incentive to manipulate the existing systems. It is hardly surprising that we see distraught parents parading on television to publicly beg for organs for their dying children, desperate recipients mortgaging houses to pay for the costs of care.

Nor is it surprising that those with money have learned how to take advantage of the lack of centralized clearing systems to, in effect, jump the queue. They may travel to a dozen different transplant centers, from Seattle to Miami. In each they are seen by experts, put through a full medical workup, and put on the waiting list. This way, they get a shot at a donor organ that becomes available in one of a dozen cities—the medical equivalent of buying more lottery tickets. Playing the medical odds this way means some people get an extraordinary second chance at life. Conversely, those who can't afford it are simply less likely to be on the list at a given location when a given organ becomes available.

Given the efficiency of market systems, it should come as no surprise that there is a growing market for the sale of organs to the highest bidder. This is most commonly the case for kidneys, and has been widely documented in India. But there are many, many cases of poor people in Third World countries making money by selling organs to those in richer Western countries. It would be a new low for ethical standards if these organs for sale were permitted to enter the legitimate realm of transplant decisions. There should be some things that cannot be bought and sold.

But other transplant issues are by no means so clear. We have for years accepted the concept of family members restricting their donation to another family member, especially for kidneys, bone marrow, and increasingly, for lung and pancreas tissue. In such cases, we allow the donor to give a recipient sole claim to this organ. Principles of family loyalty and support, and the special moral relationship between the parties, place these transactions outside of the reach of nonrelated others.

Recent events have taken us one step closer to actually creating an organ for the explicit purpose of transplantation. Newspapers and magazines report on women who have chosen to become pregnant so that precious bone marrow can be transplanted from this new life to save the life of a prior-born sibling for whom no matched donor could be identified. As a mother I can empathize with that decision. Many ethicists, however, argue that a child should only be conceived when that child is desired for itself and not for any other motive—despite the fact that a motive often contains numerous elements. We can all expect such debates to deepen as medical technologies advance.

Few people would argue that what presently exists is an ethically defensible system. Most would agree that there should be a more equitable way to allocate precious medical resources. We do not want to give patients and families incentive to manipulate the system, nor do we want decisions to be subject to undue patient influence. Decisions about transplants, like other decisions about scarce resources, should be made by people who weigh the greatest good for all. Just as clearly, however, such a system is a far cry from reality. Until this changes, people will continue playing the system as though their lives depended on it—for the simple reason that they do.

Secret Scarcities

ICU beds and transplant organs are not the only scarce medical resource. "Secret scarcities" is a term for all those medical assets in chronically short supply around our hospitals. Unlike ICU beds or transplants, they are secret only because most people don't know they exist or are unaware that administrative cost-cutting decisions form the basis of hospital survival.

Some of those scarce resources are machines. You may never have heard of a liquid-fluidized bed—but your doctor probably has and your nursing supervisor certainly has. Such a bed is a high-tech marvel. Using a computer and air compressor, a liquid-fluid bed constantly changes the pressure among hundreds of air cells or air-fluidized silicone beads below the surface on which a person lies. By inflating first some pockets, then others in a constantly changing sequence, it relieves the constant pressure of lying immobile on a regular mattress. It was designed to be very comfortable and its manufacturers assert that patients in such beds are at lower risk for the terrible pain and life-threatening infection bedsores can create. In fact, studies don't prove the beds do prevent bedsores, and some patients seem to find them uncomfortable.

If their medical value is unproven, their expense is not. Liquid-fluid beds cost about $33,000 each to buy, or $65 per day to rent, and require sophisticated maintenance that few hospitals can provide. It generally falls to the nursing budget to cover the cost of the rental. Today, as nursing salaries rise to attract ever-scarcer nursing staff, such optional "frills" as liquid-fluid beds are increasingly being edged off the economic menu. That means that today these devices have been effectively lost from the doctor's or nurse's arsenal. The liquid-fluid bed has become so scarce that in many hospitals today it is not an active option.

Other secret scarcities are human ones. You or a loved one may require a private-duty nurse for twenty-four-hour supervision. Most hospitals have a very limited number of private-duty nurses available. With the growing nursing shortage, they may become a truly scarce resource like transplant organs. Or they may just become very expensive, in which case you may be able to get a private nurse by contracting through an agency on your own.

When my mother was in the hospital, reeling from her falls and unable to follow directions, we faced a choice: for her own safety she could be restrained with a vest, which she hated, or we would have to get a private-duty nurse to watch her constantly. But nurses were a scarce resource at the hospital, so if we wanted it, we had to pay for it ourselves. Even hospitals like Montefiore, which used to provide special one-on-one nursing when required, can no longer do so given the economics of today's health-care system. Floor nurses are all the hospital could afford. It used to be that when a doctor moved a patient out of the ICU he could demand private-duty nurses for the patient; no longer, for the money is simply not there. Thus, in my mother's case, if we couldn't pay the extra charges, that was simply too bad. When health care is seen as a commodity, sometimes care goes to the highest bidder.

Sometimes the scarce resource is a kind of treatment. One of these is TPN—Total Parenteral Nutrition. TPN is "food in a tube," a completely artificial diet that is infused through an intravenous line. It bears scant resemblance to any popular notion of "food." Rather, it is a delicate balance of amino acids and glucose, fat, and electrolytes like sodium and calcium. Formulated by a physician and pharmacist working in cooperation, it is tailored to meet the specific nutritional needs of a particular patient.

TPN is also a last resort, because the human body was not designed to be fed intravenously, and it can be very dangerous. If the formula includes too much glucose, for example, a patient won't heal well, a particular danger if she needs surgery. Side effects of TPN can include infection, fever, blood clots, back pain, liver problems, and occasionally nausea and headaches. When this procedure is necessary and executed successfully, TPN improves a person's nutritional status, and health, enormously. It can help people resist open skin sores and infections, make them more mentally alert and physically energetic, and can improve the ability of antibiotics and drugs to work in their bodies. Before TPN, a patient's failing nutritional status could block her getting well; today, sophisticated TPN gives her a fighting chance.

TPN is enormously expensive. Because every individual's formula is individually concocted every day, it requires a lot of highly skilled doctors' and pharmacists' time. The physician must initially formulate the necessary mix of glucose, protein, and other elements, taking the patient's age, weight, and diagnosis into consideration. All this information is then fed into a computer system for reference and monitoring, so the physician can change the formula rapidly to compensate for bodily changes. The pharmacist must work closely with the physician, reviewing the formula each day to make her own suggestions for changes, which must then be approved by the physician, the proper paperwork filed, and the computer updated. Some of the TPN formula is so delicate that the final balancing of electrolytes must be done in the half hour before the patient receives it. Such immensely complex monitoring and adjusting means that most hospital pharmacies can fill only a limited number of TPN orders. In most places, TPN is a scarce resource that must be scrupulously rationed. At most public hospitals, it simply does not exist.

Ira was a ninety-two-year-old man who, until a year before, had remained active and independent. In the last year he had virtually stopped eating, had weakened and deteriorated, although his doctors had discovered no reason why. He had also consistently expressed his readiness to die, had written a living will stipulating that in the case of a "terminal illness" he wanted "no heroic measures," and had reiterated his wishes upon admission to the hospital. Now he had been admitted to our pulmonary intensive care unit with pneumonia. His daughters seemed not at all ready to see him die, and told the staff to "do everything possible" to treat him. His pneumonia, they knew, was not necessarily a terminal disease, but might be cured with antibiotics. Gently, the medical staff explained that Ira was so greatly debilitated from months of not eating that there was little likelihood antibiotics would work. One of the daughters then demanded he be "tube fed." After all, she argued, neither TPN nor antibiotics were "heroic treatment" like resuscitation.

Ira presented a classic scarce-resources problem: did it make sense to use one of a limited number of TPN slots for a man, ninety-two years old, in failing health who had basically stopped eating? Ira had clearly stated to his family and to care-givers that he had lived a good life and was ready to die. His living will specifically excluded aggressive treatment, although it did not address—either way—the issue of TPN. It was clear that the daughters were reluctant to lose their father; but that did not give them the right to demand a scarce resource, which would mean some other patient would not get it. After a long, hard discussion with the TPN team, the physician in charge of the case decided. Bound to respect Ira's living will and mindful of the resource at stake, the doctor determined that Ira would not get TPN; six days later Ira died.

The issues raised by scarce resources affect some of our most cherished assumptions about medical care. Throughout this book I have argued that physicians and care staff have a duty to tell patients of all their options. But when an option has been considered and rejected on the grounds of scarce resources, there is no ethical imperative to disclose that it might have been available. No doctor should have to say, nor should any patient have to hear: "Mr. Smith, you need an ICU bed, but you can't have it because someone else needs it more." Full disclosure, when a decision is out of your hands and you cannot influence it, is not supportive and it can be destructive.

It is not a service to patients and families, for example, to explain that the hospital does not do "ECMO"—extra-corporeal membrane oxygenation. This is a process where a heart-lung machine is connected to the patient as a last-ditch effort to give the failing heart a rest. This machine is often used during surgery, but to use it at the bedside is so labor-intensive, and thus so vastly expensive, that it is prohibitive for most institutions in this era of cost containment. Nor does it help to tell a family that another antibiotic might better help their ailing baby but the pharmacy doesn't stock it because it costs ten times as much as the next best and makes only a marginal difference in a very few cases. It does no good to tempt patients and families with the possibilities of a world of unlimited medical resources, for that is not the world that they—or any of us—live in.

The increasingly hard reality is that cost steers availability, and that trend will only increase. The patient's only recourse—a feeble one, at best—is to try to select a hospital that has not yet had to make too many of these hard decisions that limit the availability of its high-tech, high-priced care. But one's ability to choose depends almost completely on one's discretionary wealth. If you have no choice but to go to a public hospital, you will feel these effects most acutely, for at these hospitals resources are most limited and "standard" care is most curtailed.

Most of us aren't doctors or nurses, and we can't be expected to know about all the available medical options. What you can know, however, are some ways to clarify what is going on if you are in a scarce resources situation, and what, if anything, can be done. It may be useful to at least pose the questions:

♦ Are there any other options that might be available for my care, but for the fact that they are a limited resource?
♦ How does this decision get made?
♦ By whom?
♦ Are there any things I can do to influence the outcome of this decision?

In some circumstances, it is true, allocating scarce resources is done on the basis of connections, privilege, or prejudice. You may feel strongly that you might want to discuss or challenge such a decision, to be certain that it is being made on a fair and equitable basis. In that case, be aware of the fact that you are treading on one of the most tender areas of medical privilege. By even raising questions about scarce resources, some doctors or administrators may feel that you are challenging their authority and react in a hostile or dismissive way. Indeed, this may be the only section in this book that will get you thrown out of someone's office!

But it doesn't need to be that way. Above all, your knowing to ask these questions marks you as an educated medical consumer, and may give you more appropriate access to the discussions. Because, so often, scarce resources concern matters of life and death, you may feel you have nothing to lose, and everything to gain, by raising the issue. Most of all, your doing so increases the odds that these questions will be dealt with in an open, aboveboard manner. That way, even if the result is not what you would prefer, you will have the best chance to understand it.

At first glance, it might seem that of all the kinds of scarce resources, those in this third category are the most tractable. After all, to increase the number of organ donors requires a society-wide effort; building and staffing new ICU beds takes many years and millions of dollars and several years. But it would seem rather simple to pay four extra pharmacists to formulate twenty more TPN solutions a day, to hire more private-duty nurses, or to buy a dozen more liquid-fluidized beds.

Unfortunately, it is not as easy as it appears. For those scarce resources are merely the most visible cracks in a medical edifice fast crumbling down around our ears. More and more, our entire health-care system is becoming subject to the same rules that used to apply only to a few specific scarce resources. To more and more Americans, health care itself is becoming a scarce resource—a fact with profound implications for all of us.

With Liberty and Scarcity for All

It is an increasingly open secret that our country, one of the world's most advanced, remains primitive when it comes to health care. Most modern democratic governments recognize certain obligations to their citizens: national defense, police and fire protection, education, infrastructure of roads, bridges, and sewers. Recognizing a minimum level of income, we have federal and state welfare; recognizing the need for some income after retirement, we have social security. In virtually all developed Western nations except ours, those fundamental obligations of government include basic access to health care. The British have their National Health Service. France, Germany, and Canada each have systems that ensure all citizens access to medical care. America and South Africa stand as the only developed nations that recognize health care neither as a fundamental right of their citizens nor as a fundamental responsibility of government.

Instead, what we have evolved as our health-care system is more accurately a nonsystem. Americans spend 171 percent more on health care per person than do the British, 124 percent more than the Japanese, and 38 percent more than Canadians. Indeed, Canada spends only 6 percent of its GNP on health care, and all citizens have access. We spend twice that percentage—nearly 12 percent—of our GNP on health, yet thirty-seven to forty-two million people have no health coverage and as many as seventy million more receive inadequate care. In 1990, we spent $666 billion on health care—$2,664 for every man, woman, and child. Yet for those billions of dollars, we rank sixteenth in life expectancy, twenty-third in infant mortality, and twenty-fourth in the percentage of normal-birthweight babies—behind Bulgaria, the Soviet Union, and Hong Kong.

These dismal statistics are an inevitable result of the American view of health care as a market commodity. We have secured the dubious liberty of allowing our citizenry to either afford health care or not. Increasingly, many can't. With health costs rising faster than any other sector of the economy and the increasing demands of an aging population, access to health care is itself becoming an increasingly scarce resource. The same factors we saw in microcosm with ICU space, transplant organs, or TPN solutions are increasingly at play in the macrocosm of our entire health-care system.

Creeping scarcities affect us all, for they limit our ability to choose and direct our care. One way that happens is through setting limits or rationing, which, one way or another, already affects you. Recall the phantom we met in Chapter 3, DRG's. Diagnosis related groups describe a mean for your hospital stay according to the medical problem, and create incentives for the hospital to discharge you "quicker and sicker." They are a powerful way the public sector—government and regulators—tries to control rising health costs. Private insurers also use a variety of systems to control costs. When you find you are required to call before you go into the hospital, when specific medical conditions are excluded, when whole categories of people find themselves excluded from coverage, we are watching private rationing at work.

We are not the first nation to face limits. Every country with an organized health-care system has had to directly confront decisions about rationing care. Under the British system, you simply don't get placed onto kidney dialysis after age fifty-five. Other people wait up to three years in a strict queue for a hip replacement surgery; there, the patient who can't walk at all takes precedence over one who can walk, even with great pain. Such are the decisions they have made to ration scarce resources. We have made different ones: government rules denying health-care access to large portions of our population, especially the poor; private insurance regulations that screen out those who are most likely to get sick.

The state of Oregon made national headlines in 1987 when it attempted to devise an explicit rationing system for their Medicaid-covered patients. Their goal was noble: to try to spread the state Medicaid dollars to give the maximum number of people access to care. They proposed to do it in a way no other state had tried: in effect, they ranked medical treatments—from routine office visits to open-heart surgery—and then drew an absolute line. Certain expensive treatments, including bone marrow, pancreas, heart, or liver transplants, would simply not be covered, the money being used instead for prenatal care for fifteen hundred women. For the people suffering from those diseases, it meant the end of the road.

The policy made headlines in the anguished case of Coby Howard, a seven-year-old boy in Gresham, Oregon. Coby was refused Medicaid coverage for the liver transplant needed to save his life. His case was paraded before state bureaucrats and legislators, newspapers raised a great public outcry, his parents even launched a desperate campaign to solicit private funds for the $100,000 the transplant would cost—all to no avail. After several months, Coby died. Public opinion would lay his death at the door of the Oregon state legislature; it is an irony of the case that there is real question whether the boy was, in fact, medically eligible for a transplant, even had funds been available. The legacy of Coby Howard stands to remind us of the very human costs of the decisions we are forced to confront when there isn't enough health to go around. The policy remains in effect.

No matter whether rationing occurs with the government, state health regulators, your own private insurer, or your hospital, it is indisputable that scarcity reduces your options. In the big picture, as in the little one, the scarcer the resources, the more likely it is that decisions will get removed from patient and family and handed over to cost cutters, regulators, administrators, and physicians. Scarcity's tremors are being felt at the very foundations of medicine, shaking some of our most basic assumptions about how we seek and practice healing. This new austerity has even affected one of the most sacrosanct medical domains, the doctor-patient relationship. For most of medical history, we have taken it as an axiom that the physician was an unambivalent advocate for the individual patient's well-being. He brought to the bedside his devotion to identifying the best option that could possibly help, and his skills in implementing it.

Scarce resources are changing that. As medical care has grown more expensive and its structure has changed, the basic relationship between physician-advocate and patient-consumer has grown far more complex. You may have heard of, or may belong to, an HMO—a "health maintenance organization." These are prepaid subscription organizations that provide health care based on the principle that the greater needs of some balance the lesser needs of others—they are among the most fair and equitable systems we have. The formula attempts to provide affordable health care for all its members while giving doctors an adequate living. In that setting, if every doctor provides the most extensive care for every patient, the organization will go bankrupt—or his contract will be terminated.

The doctor, then, must balance what is best for this patient while maintaining a pattern of practice that will permit the fiscal health of the organization (and escape notice by auditors hired to monitor which doctors order which tests and procedures). Practically, this does not pose an irreconcilable conflict, for as we have seen, the most extensive and expensive care is not necessarily the best care. But in principle, this raises troubling questions: is the physician comfortable stopping short of suggesting, prescribing, and providing treatment that would help the individual for the greater good of other patients, the larger institution, and, ultimately, himself? Is there an inherent, unavoidable conflict between the doctor doing what is best for any particular patient and trying to conserve resources for the next patient? Does that compromise the doctor's professional standing and role?

Jack was a thirty-three-year-old man with a long history of intravenous drug abuse. Like most people who shoot drugs, he had suffered a series of serious infections, including several bouts of hepatitis and two distinct episodes of endocarditis. That disease is caused when bacteria carried by unclean needles infect and damage the heart valves. Untreated, the condition usually kills. Twice before, Jack had come to the hospital in distress with advanced, life-threatening endocarditis. Each time, his life had been saved by valve replacement surgery.

The kind of heart surgery Jack had twice undergone represents an enormous drain on resources—for the hospital, insurers, and society. It includes the $65,000 cost of the operation—and follow-up care part of which was covered by Medicaid. The eight-hour operation diverts the time of several highly skilled surgeons; requires an elaborate cardiothoracic surgical team of surgical nurses and anesthesiologists; takes a long time in the operating facility; requires an array of specialized equipment that must be prepped, cleaned, and refitted; includes long stays in the cardiac intensive care unit; and often weeks of protracted in-hospital recovery and rehabilitation time. All told, such procedures are among the most expensive undertakings in any hospital. That huge cost, however, is usually balanced against its clear benefit: such operations, by themselves, save lives, pure and simple.

Less simple, however, is what happens next, when the patient leaves the hospital. If he continues to shoot drugs, as most do, it is a virtual certainty that the new valve will be reinfected. For that reason, some cardiothoracic surgery units have adopted a firm policy: active intravenous drug abusers are not candidates for difficult and expensive heart-valve replacement.

To Jack, who would otherwise die, the operation meant the difference between life and death. From the doctors' perspective, operations for chronic drug use are a useless waste of their expensive, precious, and scarce resources. They argue that it makes no sense to give a third such operation to a patient who continues to shoot drugs, putting the new valve at risk for infection. They know, too, that IV drug users are more likely to be infected with the HIV virus, thereby putting surgeons at greater risk in operating on them.

The doctors argued against squandering enormously expensive, scarce resources, even possibly placing physicians at risk, for Jack, who had had the operation twice before and was here again because of his own behavior. This debate would not happen in most places, for the great majority of hospital surgical units observe the unwritten rule: one valve per patient, no second valves—and no valves at all for intraveneous drug users or the terminally ill. In Jack's case, we were debating his third.

To rule him ineligible, of course, would be to step onto a slippery slope. Would we then take the next step and agree that patients in final stages of inoperable cancer or AIDS should be removed as potential candidates for other expensive interventions? Today hospitals and health planners, constrained by fixed budgets, are juggling the increasing needs of patients. They are desperately engaging in a process of allocating what resources they have in a manner both fair and rational.

Similar questions arise at life's beginning. You can walk

into our neonatal intensive care unit on any given day and see several gravely imperiled newborns being kept alive by massive efforts. The great majority of them will die despite those efforts; most will live with some substantial disability. It is not uncommon for such a newborn's hospital stay to cost more than $150,000, ranking neonatal intensive care among the most expensive medical procedures, along with heart or liver transplants. Often, those costs are borne by the public through Medicaid.

Are we at the point in society where we can continue to accept that if there is only a tiny statistical likelihood of a child's surviving, we nonetheless devote to that child one hundred-plus thousand dollars and several months of precious ICU nursery critical care? Given that we are dealing with ever-more-finite resources, what is our obligation to all the other children, less gravely impaired, who have a better chance to benefit from care they are not getting? We know that the best way to prevent the birth of these very small, premature, or low-weight babies is to provide adequate prenatal care—at a cost of about $164 per woman. Could we not better allocate these massive amounts of money and time spent in our prenatal care ICU's for thousands of children to better avoid beginning as such imperiled babies?

Rationing decisions have become an unavoidable feature of the medical landscape, and will only grow more urgent. But that doesn't mean they have to be made—or should be made—by individual doctors at the bedsides of individual patients.

Mr. Chankoff was an eighty-year-old patient. Both he and his wife had survived the concentration camps before coming to this country in 1946; unfortunately, no one in their family, including their two children, had been so fortunate. Once in the United States the couple began to rebuild their shattered lives, eventually raising two sons and a daughter. They managed to finance their children's education in the New York City college system, and watch them grow into a clinical psychologist, a special education teacher, and an accountant.

One sizzling summer day, when the temperature went over one hundred, Mr. Chankoff had not been feeling well and went to see his doctor. The doctor said he was fine, probably had a virus, and counseled him to go home and rest. Later that day, the effects of the viral syndrome, his age, and the heat contributed to more serious heat stroke, and he began to have seizures. He was rushed to the hospital and moved quickly into the ICU. He stayed weeks in the ICU, going downhill despite all efforts. After that time, the director of the unit explained to the family that Mr. Chankoff was no longer an appropriate patient for the unit; his chances of medical recovery were essentially nonexistent, his brain irreparably damaged. When his temperature had climbed to 107 degrees, it had destroyed his brain forever, and with it his ability to regain consciousness and relate to others.

We found ourselves at a familiar juncture. We could maintain his existence by scrupulously monitoring his organ functions, but Mr. Chankoff's real being would never come back. Beyond the ICU's ability to help, he was being transferred to a bed on the regular medical floor. The family was medically sophisticated enough to know that move would diminish his chances of maintaining even his current level of organ function.

Unwilling to face that, his family demanded that he be kept in the ICU. When that demand was refused, a decision supported by all of the hospital personnel they consulted, they shifted tactics. While they had no choice when the ICU director had moved him, they were now going to fight, unwilling to accept what they saw as a death sentence. Their next step was to demand that the hospital keep staff at his bedside when he was moved.

The physician in this case had been the family physician for years, and was deeply sympathetic to the family's demands. He, too, came from a family of Holocaust survivors and understood the exquisitely complex pressures that the children of such families experience: to be the perfect children, to protect themselves and their parents, to ward off the discussion, let alone the fact, of death. Other family members and their rabbi continued to emphasize the necessity for the most vigilant and aggressive care possible.

Matters boiled over one evening when Mr. Chankoff's blood pressure dropped suddenly. The family ran screaming to the nurses' station demanding immediate attention. It just so happened that there were a number of very sick patients that evening, so the medical staff had their hands completely full treating these other patients—patients who, they knew, had a greater chance of recovering than the hopeless Mr. Chankoff. Accordingly, they refused to leave these other patients until their crises had subsided. The Chankoff family became abusive and disrupted the staff's ability to maintain the entire ward.

The next day, the house staff and nurses, in an uproar, called an emergency meeting to discuss the incident. They were still terribly upset from the incidents of the previous night. They explained that there had been a cardiac arrest on the floor and two other patients, while not arresting, were very sick and needed constant attention. The families of these patients, already upset by the illnesses of their relatives, were deeply disturbed by the screaming and frantic behavior of the Chankoff family. The staff had one request—they wanted the family's physician to tell the family that, in a contest between this patient and any other on the floor, Mr. Chankoff would come last on the queue.

Many of the staff saw Mr. Chankoff's case as hopeless. He was somewhere deep in a permanent coma. Although the family insisted he could communicate with them, could respond to his wife, and even occasionally talk a bit, the nurses reported this as wishful thinking, the fantasy needs of grieving relatives. They were sorry and sympathetic, but unmoved. They felt adamantly that it would be squandering the very scarce resources of the floor staff, especially at night when they are stretched thinnest, to provide attention to Mr. Chankoff when others were in real need. In their eyes, the needs of this hopelessly ill patient did not outweigh the competing needs of others.

Mr. Chankoff's doctor saw things very differently. He explained to the staff that, whatever they might think about Mr. Chankoff's condition, both his wife and two of his children were convinced that he could communicate with them. They were aware of the staff's prognosis but had not lost hope that he would recover. Indeed, during this illness, one of the children had even moved in order to be closer to the hospital and help his mother as she came every day to sit by the bedside.

The doctor stood firm. He felt that his professional duty, as well as his personal sympathies, required him to be the forceful advocate for this family's expressed needs. He also stressed that he felt acutely his role as the family physician to both Mr. and Mrs. Chankoff. He was convinced that if Mr. Chankoff died now, and especially if Mrs. Chankoff felt the slightest complicity in the death of her husband, it would spell the end of her life too. Her only chance of surviving the death of her husband, yet one more in the series of brutal losses she had experienced over her lifetime, would lie in knowing she did "everything possible" to prolong and sustain his life.

"Look," he finally said, exasperated, "I have sympathy for the other patients on the floor, but they are not my patients and not my direct responsibility. My energy has to be directed at the needs of my patients and my patients only." The fact that the health-care staff was being stressed he considered unfortunate, but irrelevant to his role. As to the claim of scarce medical resources from the house staff the night before, he felt his patient deserved no less than any other.

In his view, it was not his job to balance the needs of other patients against his own; it was the job of a physician to stick up for his patients. He allowed that perhaps such conflicting demands would, at some point, need to be mediated by somebody whose job it was to conserve resources. But for now, he saw his role as the diagnosis, treatment, and advocacy for Mr. and Mrs. Chankoff, and was adamant there would be no statement from him to the family that Mr. Chankoff's care would be curtailed.

In his view, the robust doctor-patient relationship eclipsed whatever problems of scarce resources existed. The staff was distressed by his obdurate stance, but respected the steadfast concern and determination from which it sprung: to do the best for his patients. To be sure, there is good reason to respect the doctor's position and honor its place in medical practice, especially in an era of growing scarcity. Our current free market of medical services necessitates the doctor's constant vigilance and advocacy if the "haves" are not to simply overwhelm the "have-nots" in the competitive commerce of health. As long as America has no official plan to deal with scarcity, rationing, and access to care, only the staunch advocacy of the individual physician will guarantee a minimal level of adequate care to those who manage to make it into the health-care system. Destroying that will create more harm than good.

In that context, Mr. Chankoff presented a true dilemma. On one side lay the good of maintaining the physician's loyalty and advocacy for his individual patient; on the other, we could not let the Chankoff family's perceptions and demands to allow some other patient to die or suffer serious harm. I proposed that the nursing supervisor, or the house-staff director, sit with the family and explain the medical facts of life and the needs of other patients for care. Yet nobody was ready to challenge the attending physician and override his decision about care. The situation stayed in an uneasy limbo for the next five weeks, until Mr. Chankoff died.

Mr. Chankoff's case exemplifies why it is wrong to ask doctors to ration at the bedside. Indeed, if there is anything on which ethicists, doctors, and planners agree, it is that doctor rationing—often called the "gatekeeper" function—is precisely the wrong way for us to make these tough calls, for several reasons. First, our system requires that physicians be staunch advocates for their patients. That is a good thing, the best way we know to assure quality care. Questions of allocating scarce resources raise a kind of utilitarian specter that somehow we won't do our all for Aunt Millie, but will instead enter her in some kind of inhuman equation and see what happens. That can only erode and undermine the trust necessary for a healthy doctor-patient relationship. It would be terribly destructive if patients, already compromised and dependent, had to worry that their doctor was also wearing the hat of judge and rationer. When we or our loved ones are sick, we need to know we can count on the doctor to be on our side—firmly and enthusiastically.

Second, it is terribly unfair to most doctors to ask them to make these choices. Unless they are ICU directors with special training in allocation matters, setting rules about scarce resources will never be easy, and it makes doctors tremendously uncomfortable. It creates a terrible dissonance with the primary role as healers. Medicine can be an inhumanly demanding job as is, and we should not put its practitioners in a position where their loyalties to patients are conflicted and compromised.

Third, most doctors and nurses have no special training in making such moral and public policy decisions. There is little tradition of discussing such matters openly in hospitals, and their schooling—although exhaustive—is not geared to provide systematic, informed training about what you do when there is not enough to go around.

But perhaps the most important reason we do not leave such decisions in doctors' hands is a human one. It is simply unrealistic to expect doctors and nurses to check their attitudes and prejudices at the hospital door. If you were to walk into any big-city hospital and listen for an evening to the discussions of the harried house staff, you would hear a variety of acronyms uttered in frustration denoting a menagerie of undesirable patients: the "GOMER's" ("Get Out of My Emergency Room"), the LOLFOF's ("Little Old Lady Found on Floor"); the "rutabagas" (permanently vegetative patients). These labels are in part black humor, that very human way we insulate emotions from the horrific tasks that saving lives demands. But sometimes beneath the humor can lie intolerance and bigotry. Obviously, we cannot count on practitioners with those attitudes to allocate scarce resources impartially, to determine fairly which lives get saved and which don't.

Ethically, allocation questions should involve a straightforward, value-neutral calculation of the needs of one patient versus those of another. But left in individuals' hands, with no guidelines or oversight, other less noble principles can and do come into play. Historically, whole classes of patients have been seen as deserving less humane, aggressive, or scrupulous care—sometimes no care at all. Recent medical history is strewn with examples of egregious, even fatal, medical discrimination against women, old people, poor people, gay people, black people. The infamous Tuskegee Experiment, lasting from 1932 to 1972, where black men were left untreated so doctors could observe the progress of their syphilis; the systematic exclusion of women from research studies assessing new medical treatments; the profound medical indifference in the early years of the AIDS epidemic as it killed tens of thousands of gay men; our nation's chronic indifference to the health of our poorest citizens: ours is not a record to inspire confidence.

It is not that most doctors condone such actions. The overwhelming majority of the colleagues and medical friends I have met in two decades are scrupulous, giving, and fair people. But like all of us, physicians are human, and some have more humanity than others. If history teaches us nothing else, it is that asking mostly white, male, middle-to-upper-income doctors to decide for people who may be poor, black, Hispanic, HIV-positive, gay, pregnant, or simply different than their doctors, risks abuse.

There is a growing consensus that we cannot ask our practitioners to shoulder that burden alone. Our healers, like their patients, are fallible and imperfect. Fallible in that they may not understand what a patient truly wants, and so be unable to fulfill society's consensus that an individual's wishes should be honored where possible. Imperfect, because physicians, like all of us, have their own deeply held personal values. One may feel that an eighty-eight-year-old deserves less aggressive care than an eighteen-year-old; another that a woman is less able to make difficult emotional decisions than her husband; a third that a black gay man deserves less care than a married white father. But those are not the attitudes of society, so we should not allow one practitioner's prejudices or biases to direct care decisions.

We are only beginning to confront the complexities of practicing medicine in an era of scarcity. What is clear is that these questions are becoming more and more pressing as resources shrink. Even if we establish an equitable system for universal access to care, which we must, we will not prevent, and some argue we will even expand, the hard choices we face about scarce resources.

12

AN OUNCE
OF
PREVENTION

GOOD PLANNING

FOR

BAD TIMES

As a practicing bioethicist, I find it rare that a month goes by without my receiving two or three phone calls from people seeking help—either distant family members, friends, or friends of friends. The scenario is always the same: someone, generally a parent, but maybe a relative or close friend, is in the hospital or about to be. Usually, the person calling feels overwhelmed and confused. Often, some procedure is being proposed or urged. And always comes a torrent of questions: What should we do? How do we figure out what's best? Which questions should we ask?

As I talk with them, I try to weave together knowledge about the substance of the question they are facing with my experience about how hospitals work, don't work, and should work. My goal is to point people in the right direction and guide them to the clear avenues of thought that can help them find the "right" answers for them. Equally important, I try to point out the areas where they cannot make a difference or should not assume responsibility.

But beneath this advice lies another truth, one I cannot

always share with the anxious voice on the other end of the phone. It is that by the time I get the call, it may be too late to do the most good. The best health-care planning is preemptive, done in advance without the pressures and emotions of the moment. The best way for any of us to retain control—for ourselves as for those we love—is by thinking ahead, asking the questions, and making the plans *before* they are needed. If we are to guide our own fate, at least where our health care is concerned, we must chart our course ahead of time. If you are reading this book, you are doing just that.

These pages have urged you to think about issues of medical care in advance, and if at all possible to record your preferences and document your specific wishes. Each chapter has contained specific suggestions to follow in times of crisis; at times of great stress it always helps to have something concrete to grasp. By now, you may even know in very explicit terms what you want—and don't want—to see happen to you and your loved ones in the future. That means there are several actions you can and should take to ensure that the care you receive will be as you want it to be. I offer this chapter as your decision-making tool kit, an assortment of tips and strategies to help you take, and keep, control.

Life Planning

In our grandparents' day, the idea of "family planning" was a new one. It was a concept that grew out of technological and medical advances surrounding contraception and childbirth, and was traditionally concerned with the number and spacing of children. In the last decade of this century "family planning" has taken on new facets. For families are not just about children, but include our older parents and ourselves. Given fantastic developments in medical technology over the last decades and the increasing number of medical options at the end of life, such planning should now include what you want to have happen to you at all stages of your life. This is especially important if incapacity intervenes and you can't participate in the decisions when the time comes. Yes, it is "family planning," but it is much broader than that. Perhaps the more descriptive term is "life planning."

In some respects, life planning is not a new idea. We already do it in the spheres of our lives that concern wealth and property: we write wills, buy life insurance, hire estate planners and accountants to plan our bequests and taxes. Yet when it comes to infinitely more personal matters—concerns of life and dignity—we often neglect the most basic planning. Equally important are the quality and control of life, passages from health to illness, the extent of dependence, the nature of suffering, and the many decisions that must be made about medical care. Yet it seems a central irony of our society that most people do not plan for their personal/medical lives as thoroughly as they plan for their finances. We owe it to ourselves and our loved ones to change that.

That simple idea is the basis of "life planning," and the core of the information in this final chapter. The following four-step plan will help you more efficiently and effectively guide your present and your future health-care decisions:

- Gathering information.
- Assessing your own values and beliefs.
- Documenting your wishes about care to serve as a guide if you become incapable of deciding—a living will.
- Appointing a specific person—a health-care "agent" or "proxy"—to decide for you when you can no longer do so.

Step One: Gathering Information

The first step is always to gather information about the sorts of decisions you may face, now and in the future. You began that quest by picking up this book. From here, the next step is to have a talk with your physician. At your next office visit, either for a checkup or for a specific problem, state that you would like to take five minutes to begin a discussion about planning for future health care.

The following questions might help to get the discussion going:

◆   What possible health problems do you see emerging in the future given my present state of health, my medical history, and that of my family?

◆   What paths might my particular condition take that could impair my ability to participate in decisions about my care? Is that likely?

◆   Are there some articles or books I could read about my condition?

◆   How do you feel about honoring any specific instructions I might leave about my care? Would you object to honoring a DNR order or a directive, under some conditions, to terminate care?

◆   Can I appoint someone to make decisions for me? Do you know what the law and the practice are in this state governing those kinds of appointments? Do you know where I can find out?

◆   How do my wishes get communicated to the hospital if I am hospitalized?

◆   Do you see your role as an advocate for my wishes?

◆   Would you be more comfortable following my wishes, documented in a living will, or the specific directions of my designated decider?

◆   How do you feel about removing respirators or feeding tubes from patients whose prognosis is hopeless?

◆   Would you help family members or friends reach that decision if the situation were hopeless, and I had no possibility of returning to a sapient state or of ever relating to and responding to another human being?

Such questions should open up the discussion with your physician, or with the nurse practitioner or physician-assistant who assists her. The questions will not only elicit specific information but will also give you some sense about how your care provider understands her roles and responsibilities and thinks about your rights and about the sorts of ultimate issues you could one day face.

Be prepared for the fact that some doctors find this sort of discussion odd; some may be frankly hostile to the whole dialogue. I remember my experience, some twenty-one years ago, interviewing pediatricians before the birth of my first child—now a common practice. At the time, however, some were startled by the request and others seemed offended. One woman was terrific and interested and supportive of the quest for a compatible pediatrician—and wound up caring for our children over two decades.

There remain physicians who still react to advance planning discussions as improper encroachments on the professional territory of their medical expertise. Happily, however, their numbers are shrinking. These discussions have so permeated the medical world, as well as the popular press, that increasing numbers of doctors are now aware of these issues and know how important these discussions are for you and them alike. Particularly if your doctor trained at one of the growing number of medical schools or teaching hospitals with an ethics program, he probably already understands the need for these discussions.

If your doctor reacts negatively, you have the choice of engaging the doctor in a discussion in order to broaden his outlook, explaining how important these issues are to you and enlisting his support, or finding some other physician whose views may be more in line with your own.

In general, you will likely find that physicians whose medical specialties bring them into frequent contact with such issues—geriatricians, specialists in cancer, newborns, and AIDS—are quite comfortable with these discussions. Many of them even welcome them, knowing that their work is made easier when they know what you want and everyone agrees on what decisions should be made, and how to make them.

Step Two: The Personal Values Inventory

After getting a feel for the medical facts of your own situation with your doctor, the next step is a personal one, to figure out exactly what *you* think, feel, and want to have happen. If there is one theme this book has stressed again and again, it is that most medical decisions are, at root, an amalgam of medical information and personal values and preferences. Decisions about care should be based on the medical facts, of course, but also on your religious beliefs, philosophical principles, collected experience, likes, and dislikes.

The values history form (see page 383) will help you open that dialogue with yourself. It was created by my friend and colleague Joan McIver Gibson, Ph.D., a bioethicist at the Center for Health Law and Ethics and the University of New Mexico School of Law. This excellent guide was created to help you clarify your own feelings and values about the choices you may confront. It is one of the best tools available to help people raise the fundamental questions and expose the bedrock responses that steer and shape medical decisions: How much do you value independence, control, and freedom? Do your religious beliefs require or forbid certain actions? How do you tolerate pain? How do you variously weigh pain, illness, dying, and death? What in life gives you pleasure? Sorrow?

Discussing the questions on the values history form can yield important information not only for you yourself, but for those who might, one day, have to make medical decisions for you if you can no longer do so. Whether they are family or friends, physicians or others, talking about such issues ahead of time helps minimize disagreements. That way, should such decisions need to be made, the burden of responsibility weighs less heavily because others feel more confident about your wishes.

As you continue to grow and change, so will your values and ideas, and so may the values reflected on the values history form. You may want to come back to it every few years, to reconsider and reevaluate your preferences and wishes. The values history can be an important form in preparation for the next two life-planning documents.

Step Three: Your Living Will

The first two steps concerned getting information, both externally and internally. These next two steps, operating in tandem, concern putting your wishes into action through what are termed "advance directives." They let you specify *what* you would want—through a living will (see page 375)—and *who* you want to decide for you—your designated decider, health-care agent, or "proxy." Each of these tools has specific strengths and weaknesses, and you need to know how to use them, alone or in combination, to provide the best solution for your individual situation, location, needs, and wants. Even if you have already heard of these, perhaps even executed such documents, there is much new thinking and information about them, and this chapter may be of help.

Most Americans have by now heard of a living will; it is estimated that one in six persons (approximately 15–20 percent, depending on which survey you read) has signed one. A living will is a set of precise instructions, created when you are capable of making decisions about your health care. It anticipates what future decisions may arise around your health care and states clearly what you want to have happen, to provide a guideline for loved ones and caregivers.

The living will was the first attempt to create a mechanism to control the indiscriminate use of new medical technologies. It grew out of the experience of many individuals who had watched loved ones die tethered to machines and pinioned to hospital beds, and had seen firsthand the horror of the process. It was revolutionary in its time as a way to extend individual wishes beyond the time when the patient was able to participate in discussions and decisions.

Your living will is a completely personal and distinctive document, reflecting your preferences, experiences, and expectations. As such, it is appropriate for you alone. You may, for example, fear the prospect of a painful passing most of all. Perhaps you have watched a spouse or parent go through a protracted and agonized death, or simply feel you have had a long and full life and have no interest in any life-extending or life-sustaining measures. You may have a personal horror of ending your days dependent on a machine, unable to speak or move. To you, quality of life may be more important than its absolute length.

But another person might want to eke out every moment, to struggle against death no matter the cost. Perhaps because of emotional, philosophical, personal, or religious reasons, they want above all to stay until they can stay no more. Still others are most concerned about the economic or emotional burden their illness places on their survivors (although I would argue that financial consideration as a determining factor demonstrates the basic unjustness of our society). Perhaps one person wants more than anything to die at home, among loved and familiar surroundings; another may want to be where she can receive the closest monitoring and the most elaborate care; and a third may care most of all about dying in dignity and peace, wherever that may be.

When it comes to such questions, the wishes and preferences that count most are yours. No wise judge or devout clergy can divine these answers as well as you can for yourself. Nor can an expert physician feed the facts into a computer and calculate precisely what is best. Because these decisions count among the most personal decisions you will ever make, your right to consent or refuse specific treatments in the future is the most important thing you can and must hold on to, and your living will is one tool to help you do just that.

In general, a living will follows a specific form, an "if"

followed by a "then." The "if" usually states something to the effect of "If I am terminally ill" or "If I am so debilitated or demented that I can no longer relate to family and friends" or "If I am in a deep coma or a persistent vegetative state"; and a second element such as the "prognosis for my return to sapient existence is hopeless." The "then" involves the treatments you want to have administered, withheld, or withdrawn. It lists a specific series of interventions and treatments that you would want or would want to refuse, such as antibiotics, dialysis, resuscitation, artificial nutrition and hydration—food and fluid—mechanical ventilation, transfusions, and transplants. In each case, you indicate your desire to include or exclude each one.

It may also include another option, a catchall involving "any other medical treatment or intervention that might extend my life or prolong the process of dying." Most living wills also have an optional section saying that you would accept all measures designed purely for comfort, or that, if at all possible, you would like to live your last days at home or in a hospice.

Not surprisingly, the wording of your living will is all-important. Certain states may have specific requirements for language, demanding specific legal formalities or prohibiting specific uses for the document. For example, some states require that you notarize your living will. Others—Kentucky, Wisconsin, Connecticut, Georgia—do not permit a living will to be used to refuse artificial food or fluid. (That, happily, seems to be changing. In many of the states that have tried to limit these rights, courts have declared such attempts unconstitutional, an infringement of the common-law right we each possess to refuse care.)

Some earlier living wills tended to use vague and general terms. They referred to people being "terminally ill," "hopelessly ill," and rejecting "extraordinary" or "heroic" treatments. Such vague terms are worse than useless; they can, in fact, sow such confusion and doubt that when the time comes to apply them, nobody has a clue what to do. The newer, and better, living wills offer a "menu" of specific interventions among which you can choose. The best ones of all are concise, specific, short, and crystal clear.

Most people think of living wills as a way to set limits on certain kinds of life-sustaining interventions. They can do that, certainly, and that is what the great majority of people use them for. But they can also be used to do just the opposite, if you prefer; this tool is equally powerful to request and encourage care and say nothing about refusing it. This purpose, however, is always tempered by the basic medical appropriateness of a given intervention: a patient cannot demand what doctors deem to be wrong treatment. It is a tool to make your preferences known if you cannot do so when the time comes—no more and no less. A good living will is also an excellent discussion guide to use with your family or with someone who you expect to act as your health-care agent.

There are two good reasons to have these specific discussions even if you will appoint a health-care agent. First, they help ensure that your agent really knows what you want and will be able to carry out your wishes. Second, they give your agent support to make hard decisions that may permit death, reducing any guilt or regret. If you have only had vague and general discussions with your agent and that person then has to decide to forgo life-sustaining care, he may be more comfortable and more willing if he is certain that it reflects your wishes. If you really care about "stopping" care, the firmest basis for that decision is always your clear wishes.

Living wills are also critical if you have very specific things you do—or don't—want. My friend Jerry, age seventy-nine, is a very precise person, an ex–newspaper journalist without a shred of sentimentality. He has had a number of heart attacks and absolutely refuses to have surgery. He was also on a ventilator once in his life, for two days, which he describes as the single worst experience in his life. He is adamant that he never wants to repeat that experience for any reason: "Lying there, tied down with that tube, I nearly lost my mind from claustrophobia. It was the single worst thing that ever happened to me—or that I could ever *imagine* happening to me." He is not afraid of death, which he knows is approaching, but is quite fearful of the process of dying. Jerry, an independent, energetic man, is utterly determined: he does not want a ventilator for any length of time, and above all does not want to be resuscitated, no matter what others' perceptions of its utility may be.

Given his specific experience and his fierce personal value of staunch independence, Jerry has made his family promise he will never be forced to undergo such an experience again. He filled out a living will and gave copies to his wife and children, the staff of the admitting room, and the emergency room of his local hospital. He appointed his wife his proxy, giving her specific instructions about the sort of care he will not accept. He has spoken with all of his friends, urging them to support his wife as she makes the hard decisions and asking them to remind her if need be that this is what he wants.

As of this writing, forty-two states and the District of Columbia have specific living will laws permitting you to state wishes to accept or refuse specific treatments under specific circumstances. In all other states, it is assumed by lawyers that the common law of the state permits a patient to fill out a living will, which will be respected, even though the terms and conditions have not been set by statute.

Limits to Living Wills

In the last five years, living wills have become very popular among Americans, particularly older Americans. There is no doubt that the living will is the life-planning tool that is, at least for now, most commonly known to medical professionals and hospitals. In many places it is the most likely to be immediately recognized and respected when difficult care decisions arise. But these documents are not foolproof and, in this case, what you don't know can hurt you. For what you are not likely to hear about in the popular press, on television, or in the magazines are the very real—and very significant—limitations of living wills.

Despite the popular perception, a living will is an imperfect invention, with at least three serious problems. First, it is a static document, circumscribed by form and language. So, for example, your living will might refuse a ventilator. But, aside from my friend Jerry, who really does not want a ventilator for even one minute no matter what the medical payoff, most people would accept a limited time of ventilation if it might mean years of extended life. A living will that simply refuses a ventilator makes no such contextual distinctions.

The second problem is that a living will is a time-bound document, reflecting what you once thought about a specific option at a specific time in the past. It cannot reflect changes that have occurred since it was written, nor explain with certainty what you would now decide were you faced with the current situation.

In addition, it cannot adapt to new medical advances, nor can it respond to nuances of situations that you did not foresee when you wrote it. In the worst case, that rigidity can lead caregivers to discount a living will because its exact language does not fit precisely with the situation at hand.

That was exactly what happened in a well-known legal case a few years ago in New York. Tom Wirth was a forty-seven-year-old man, dying of AIDS, who had executed a living will. In it, he clearly stated that in the event of an "illness, disease, or injury," or if he should "experience extreme mental deterioration such that there is no reasonable expectation of recovering or regaining a meaningful quality of life," he would no longer want certain kinds of care, including a ventilator and antibiotics.

A few months later, he contracted pneumocystis pneumonia, a common, life-threatening illness for AIDS patients. As his condition declined, his friend, John Evans, produced his living will, stating the clear wishes the man had expressed before his illness. He explained that Wirth had expressed the view that he had fought long enough and was in fact prepared to die, as attested to by the living will. The hospital's job, said Evans, was to honor it.

The hospital attorneys, however, disputed the interpretation of the document. They argued that in the course of AIDS, any particular bout of pneumonia may just be another intermittent and treatable condition. Hence, his condition was not one in which there was "no reasonable expectation of recovering or regaining a meaningful quality of life." The rigid interpretation of the legal language had created a loophole through which the hospital and doctor could drive, if not a truck, then certainly a respirator. The debate went to court, where the judge, taking refuge in the ambiguity, ordered the continuation of antibiotics, the very treatment Mr. Wirth had earlier refused.

In principle, law and ethics decree that specific living wills made out by people who are capable of expressing their wishes should be honored. But because of the lack of clarity in Tom Wirth's document, the court's refusal to let his friend describe what he meant when he filled it out, and the rigid interpretation of the word "terminal," Tom Wirth ended up having to endure the further pain and suffering of treatment that he might not—indeed, said his friend, definitely did not—want.

Many living will forms use the words "terminal illness" or "condition" to describe the situation that would trigger its provisions. Many conditions, however, such as a permanent or persistent vegetative state, end-stage amyotrophic lateral sclerosis (Lou Gehrig's disease), or even end-stage Alzheimer's disease, are not considered medically "terminal" conditions. That is, they won't kill you themselves, or at least not yet; one might go on living, as Nancy Cruzan did, in a persistent vegetative state for years. You may want to strike out this language in the document, removing that limiting precondition to make sure the document will be honored when you most need it.

Far more seriously, a living will can be absent. You may have written the best, most explicit, most ironclad living will possible; but it only works if it is brought to the right place at the right time. But in the rushed reality of a modern teaching hospital, when life-and-death decisions are made often within minutes, the chances that the exact right piece of paper will surface at just the right time to do what you want are next to nil.

My files contain cases where physicians have placed a person on a respirator to save a life, then found out days later that the person had specifically requested that never happen—all because the patient's living will didn't surface at the moment treatment was begun. This is hardly the physicians' fault; they were just doing their job in an emergency. The problem was nobody had the living will at the right place and the right time.

Its third drawback is that a living will is passive. A mere piece of paper, it will never stand up on its own to argue your position, advocate for your right to refuse care, or challenge a doctor about to perform a procedure. It is all too easily ignored when the escalator of providing care is running and the language has some ambiguity.

For all of these reasons, a living will may be necessary but it is not always sufficient. Ideally, it should only be one leg of your life-planning strategy in certain locations and circumstances, and generally is best used as a backup.

Step Four: Designating a Decider

The fourth step reflects the most current thinking about life planning, the next step beyond a living will. As discussed, however detailed the living will, it cannot anticipate every circumstance. Something more is needed, and that next step is the designated decider, or health-care agent. Where living wills establish *what* you want to decide, appointing an agent establishes *who* you want to decide. This may be termed a health-care agent appointment, a "proxy appointment," or a "durable power of attorney (DPA) for health-care decision making" (see page 378). Whatever its name, such a document has broad powers, translating your confidence and trust in another person into the legal power for them to decide for you, if you cannot decide for yourself. Under most circumstances, your agent has the same power to consent to or refuse care that you would if you were capable of deciding. Your designated decider is there when the discussions are being held and decisions being made. He is your surrogate, a living, thinking person to interpret your wishes, advocate for your preferences, and discuss the medical risks and benefits of a given option at the time that a decision must be made.

The person making decisions for you must be someone you yourself trust to act when you cannot. In all likelihood, you will choose a person you know, who shares a relationship of some long duration, who knows your values and lifestyle, and can present them accurately, conveying your views and expectations if you cannot. In general, if you have someone available whom you trust, this is an important way to extend your wishes beyond your ability to express them.

The designated decider, proxy, or health-care agent is particularly important in our time and culture. American society is very wary of letting others decide for an individual, even when we know that the individual is clearly incapable of deciding for himself. In part this is due to our society's deep respect for the individual; in part this is because we are the world's most litigious culture; and in part this is because we are just beginning to grapple with the thorny issues posed by new medical technology and practices. With so many factors at work, the players in health-care decisions welcome whatever help the patient can provide, particularly when that help legally and clearly appoints a surrogate decider for the patient.

This book has spotlighted many of the bedside phantoms

now at work in the medical system. The more players jockeying to control your care, the more important it is for you to choose someone you trust to make your wishes heard. Your written proxy, or DPA, or health-care agent appointment, gives that person the power to wade into the welter of competing interests and take control on your behalf. Your signature on that piece of paper gives him or her legal standing in the hospital, hospice, or nursing home to stand up for you among all the players who attend, often invisibly, by the bed.

As of this writing, twenty-four states clearly permit you to designate a health-care decider. Like living wills, the details of designating deciders vary state to state. In your state, the person you choose may be termed a "proxy," a health-care agent, or a surrogate. Some states, like New York, have created a specific health-care proxy form. Others accomplish the same thing by means of what is called durable power of attorney for health-care decisions.

No matter what name is used, it is important that whatever form you use include the critical element of legal language that makes it most effective under your state's law. If your state has a form, you are better off using it. These are usually brief, often a single page. They are specific to your state's laws and familiar to doctors and hospitals.

Starting in December 1991, for the first time, a federal law, the Patient Self-Determination Act (see page 374), requires all hospitals and nursing homes to explain in detail what their particular state permits, and alert patients to their rights to execute living wills, appoint a health-care agent/decider/proxy, or do both.

More information about health-care agents is contained in the helpful, free booklet *Health Care Power of Attorney*. This publication, stock number D13895, is available from the American Association of Retired Persons, 109 K Street, N.W., Washington, D.C. 20049. In addition, you may find free information and counseling from your local office of senior affairs, your state department on aging, agencies providing legal services for the elderly, and Choice In Dying, Inc.—the national council for the right to die, 250 West Fifty-seventh Street, New York, NY 10107; telephone (212) 246-6973. Your attorney should also be able to offer assistance.

Combining Life-Planning Tools

Until the last few years, many experts recommended that people execute both of the documents discussed. But in fact, each of these has its own advantages and disadvantages:

	Advantages	Disadvantages
Living will	• Concrete, detailed • Legally valid • Widely accepted and understood	• Overly restrictive • Passive • May be absent
DPA's/proxy	• More flexible in many circumstances • Can assertively advocate and persuade • Present in discussions	• Not as widely recognized in some places • Not as familiar to caregivers • Cedes control to another's judgment

There is no doubt that, if you live in a state where health-care agents are recognized, these are the more powerful and flexible way to go—*for most, but not all, people.* That is because, in general, you do better to have a person on your side than merely a piece of paper. But for certain people in specific circumstances, a living will may be a better solution than a designated decider.

Life-Planning Checklist

A living will is preferable if you:

◆ Have no one to appoint as your decider.

◆ Live in a state whose law does not permit the designation of a decider.

◆ Have very specific and concrete feelings about specific kinds of care that you would want, or want to refuse, in specific circumstances.

◆ Travel a lot and need a document that can be carried on your person.

◆ Want to appoint an agent who travels often and have no ready alternative decider.

A designated decider is preferable if you:

◆ Have a trusted person to designate as your decider.

◆ Live in a state that permits health-care agents.

◆ Feel comfortable that your decider will choose as you would wish in all important circumstances.

◆ Trust that your decider will choose wisely whether or not she knows your express wishes.

As designated deciders have become more common, and as the very real limitations of living wills have become clear, deciders have received greater emphasis, with correspondingly less focus on living wills. Indeed, some ethicists, and most especially some lawyers, feel that, if you have designated a decider, living wills can work against your interests.

Those who argue this position worry that in the risk-averse world of hospitals, there is a very real potential for conflict between the terms of the living will and what your decider might decide. In that way, living wills can create confusion and contradiction if caregivers interpret their provisions differently than your designated decider.

If you live in a state that allows a designated decider, you will likely do better not to execute a separately existing living will. Instead, use the living will to structure your discussion with and support your agent. Let the agent have a copy for reference and state clearly on the living will and on the proxy appointment that the living will is to be used *only if* a) the agent is unavailable, or b) the agent chooses to use the document as a reference.

The use of health-care agent designations, or DPA's, or proxy designations is newer than the use of living wills. There are yet *no* legal cases that present the positions, arguments, and outcome of a contest between a living will and a proxy. In some hospitals having both documents, if the living will is not clearly subordinate, triggers a different level of scrutiny. The more levels of review, the more chances phantoms have to state their positions and argue for their concerns rather than yours.

But even given the general superiority of agent appointments, remember that there are very real and good reasons for going through the process and thinking about the issues that a living will raises. First, for anybody to serve as your knowledgeable advocate, he must fully understand your wishes. Your living will can help. The very act of considering and filling out a living will helps structure the conversations and cover the issues you should discuss with your designated decider. It becomes a way to help ensure that your decider has a deep understanding of your wishes and values.

I tell patients to examine and consider the clauses of a living will as an exercise in communication with their agent. It provides an excellent checklist of the sorts of medical interventions that the agent may likely face in the future; discussing those issues will prepare him to do your bidding when the time comes. The sample living will at the end of this book has been specifically drafted to help raise the range of issues you need to think about, including artificial feeding and hydration, resuscitation, and antibiotics.

Second, having your living will in reserve will give your designated decider the concrete ammunition necessary to go in and do battle on your behalf with the other actors in the medical system—if and only if she decides she needs it. It is one thing for her to say she knows what you want; it is far more powerful if she can point to it in writing, a specific, clear, and unambiguous document, signed by you.

Life Planning in a Mobile Society

We Americans are a peripatetic people. Perhaps your job takes you into different states frequently; you may be retired, spending winters in Florida and summers in New York, with a family member attending school in another state nine months out of the year. In all these cases, moving from place to place can raise particular life-planning issues. People who spend substantial time in different locales are more likely than most to face the problems that come when medical-care decisions arise in different states.

They may, for example, have designated a decider, or proxy, in New York, which permits it, using a New York form, but find themselves facing illness and accident, physicians and hospitals, in Missouri, which recognizes only a living will. Or perhaps their living will, perfectly legal in Illinois, is not recognized at all when they fall sick in Pennsylvania (it may only be useful as a common-law documentation of the individual's wishes). Even with careful life planning, any of us could find ourselves in the situation that the legal language we used in an advance directive does not comply fully with the laws or regulations of a state where something befalls us. What then—are we helpless prisoners of our paperwork?

The real answer is: maybe. These life-planning tools are new enough that nobody knows how they will play out in different states, especially where laws, standards, and practices conflict. Again, having both documents executed may be the best way to ensure that your wishes are respected—but prudence dictates that you always establish a hierarchy with either the agent or the living will at the top.

Life Planning and Lawyers

Even though life-planning tools are legal documents, you probably don't need a lawyer to fill them out and make them valid. In the last few years, lawyers have formed a new subspecialty of the law, called elder law. Lawyers who describe themselves in this way specialize in the legal problems that most often affect elderly persons. In addition to the usual wills, trusts, probate, estate, and tax planning, they write living wills, durable powers of attorney, and instructions to govern the use of orders not to resuscitate.

"Life planning" or "health-care planning" is a key part of what these lawyers charge for. In addition to living wills and proxy documents, they may also counsel older people, helping them arrange their affairs and transfer their assets so that a future need for long-term care will be covered by Medicaid.

Most people, however, don't need an attorney to make a living will, or fill out a health-care proxy form or durable power of attorney for health-care decision making, or to express their wishes regarding resuscitation. If you need professional help, it is probably not from a lawyer but rather from a doctor, or some other capable health-care provider. That person can help you to think about the future technological interventions that may be suggested and the immediate and long-term risks and benefits of each.

Your next step is to contact Choice In Dying, Inc.—the national council for the right to die, 250 West Fifty-seventh Street, New York, New York 10107; (212) 246-6973. Without charge they will send you one set of the living will form and the durable power or proxy form most appropriate to the specific laws of your state. These forms are written to take into account the particular phrases or text necessary to make the document most legal and effective under your state regulations. This organization is also the nation's single best source of information on the law of each specific state. Allow a four-to-six-week period for delivery, due to the heavy demand for their materials.

In general, what you do need to know are the kinds of issues we have discussed: what you actually want and don't want, and what sort of flexibility you would want your agent to have under what circumstances. You should also know what is allowed in your own state. Remember it is best to discuss these issues with a health-care professional to be sure that you understand the medical intervention and the various contexts in which they can be used. Discussion of these issues should be a part of your ongoing medical relationship.

In some cases, having a lawyer draw up a living will makes things worse! To be sure, some lawyers prepare excellent living wills. But some write documents so long, complex, and convoluted as to defy mere mortals, let alone hospital personnel, to interpret them. Using a complex, twenty-page form from lawyers tends only to create problems, not solve them. Each complexity of language and condition makes it less clear to physicians how to apply it, and opens greater chances for loopholes and disputes. When drafting a living will, less is usually more. The best living will is clear and simple, stating specifically and unambiguously what event triggers it, and what specific treatments you would accept or refuse.

Although you probably do not need a lawyer to fill out forms, there is one special kind of situation when you definitely need a lawyer's help. If you are facing a long, protracted illness with a possible prognosis of several years' deterioration and think you may be eligible—or would like to arrange your assets to ensure eligibility—to receive public funding through Medicaid for long-term care, then legal advice is critical. In such circumstances, it is important to integrate your estate planning with smart health-care planning. There are many rules and regulations addressing how you spend and transfer assets in order to be eligible eventually for public assistance to support long-term care. A lawyer is absolutely essential in such circumstances, for it is her job to maximize her client's benefit to the degree legally permissible. In this, as in most complex arenas of our society, our lawmakers have given a bonus to those who are savvy enough to know about the issues, and to hire someone who can maximize future benefits.

But remember, that is the exception that proves the rule. For most of you, most of the time, the general forms in your state will be sufficient for your health-care planning needs.

Put Yourself on Tape

Some people use one other life-planning tool, a video- or audiotape supplement to the standard advance directives. These have one major purpose: to give an emotional and human grounding to your standard living will. As we have seen, a living will is simply a piece of paper, conveying information with little passion or emotion. A designated decider is more helpful, often simply because he brings these more human factors into the discussion, making them effective advocates for your wishes.

A tape is the messenger of your human presence into the debate at a time when you cannot do so in person. This book has demonstrated that medical decisions rest on religious values, philosophical commitments, personal history, values, emotions, and intellect. A tape allows you to state your own feelings in your own language, infusing your full emotional tone into the dry words of the written documents. Its value is not as a legal or official document, but a human one. By speaking with your voice, stating your reasons and feelings on continuation or cessation of care, such a tape can carry significant emotional weight.

Tapes are simple to make. I prefer video to a simple audiotape, as they make it much easier for care providers to relate to the patient they see before them than does a disembodied taped voice they may never have heard. Simply sit down, facing the camera or tape recorder, and talk normally, in a relaxed way.

A sample tape might run:

> Hello, my name is ——. I am fifty-four years old, and it is December 12, 1991. I am making this tape of my own free will, and expect that what I am about to say will be seen as a true reflection of my wishes and as binding on my health-care providers. These issues are important to me, and I very much want to express my wishes so that, if I should be incapacitated, whoever is making decisions about my health care—and possibly my life—will have the most information to know what I in fact want.

It is less important you follow these exact words than that your taped supplement include:

◆ A short discussion of why you feel as you do. Perhaps you saw a parent or grandparent suffer and don't want that, or have strong religious beliefs, or are terrified by hospitals. Give whatever information you feel will help people understand why you want what you want.

◆ Refer people to your health-care agent or your living will for the details of what you want or don't. The specifics you mention on the tape should best be read exactly from your living will, so there is no room for error, doubt, or ambiguity. A tape that conflicts with what is on paper or the guidelines you have given your decider is worse than no tape at all.

◆ Talk about your personal feelings. Remember, the idea is to impart aspects of you that the paper can't. The tape is your chance to make clear the emotions, beliefs, and values behind your decisions.

◆ Keep it short. An effective, complete taped supplement can be done in less than five minutes. Keeping it succinct and to the point means there is a greater chance everybody will watch it when the time comes.

• Finally, remember that this is best as a supplement, not a substitute, for your official advance directives. Don't bother making such a tape until your legal, formal advance directives are complete and signed.

Life Planning: The Best for Everybody

Every person, of whatever age, who writes a will should also execute a living will or appoint a health-care agent, or in certain circumstances do both. For many people, especially those who are already sick, the process of life planning is a way to feel more in control. When facing hard circumstances, most people find it much easier to decide ahead of time, rather than inflicting such agonizing choices on a beloved spouse, parent, or child; or worse, leaving the decisions to the vagaries of the medical care system.

Your explicit life planning saves your loved ones the anguish, guilt, and responsibility of feeling unsure, or worrying that they are doing the wrong thing in what may be their final moments with you. In such moments, it is agony enough to face life-and-death decisions about those we love; to endure a lifetime of regret that we let a loved one die too soon, or forced him to endure undue pain and suffering, is a burden none of us should ever have to carry. If you have thought and acted in advance, if you have made your wishes clear with a living will or empowered a trusted person to decide with a proxy form, neither you nor your family member should ever face that. Used properly, life planning can be a precious parting gift to ourselves and to those we love most.

EPILOGUE

On February 8, 1991, Hennepin County Medical Center in Minneapolis, Minnesota, filed a lawsuit in the Fourth Judicial District Court seeking to resolve a dispute between the hospital, its caregivers, its ethics committee, and the family of Mrs. Helga Wanglie. In this action the hospital asked the court to appoint a conservator to represent the patient and to decide whether or not it was appropriate to continue treating Mrs. Wanglie.

At that point Mrs. Wanglie had been in the hospital since December 14, 1989, on which date she had fallen and broken her hip. The initial hip fracture had been treated successfully. However, respiratory failure and a later cardiopulmonary arrest had left Mrs. Wanglie with irreversible brain damage. The physicians and the ethics committee all agreed that continued treatment was not in the best interest of the patient. The family maintained that Mrs. Wanglie would want care continued for both personal and religious beliefs that they, too, shared. The hospital based its position on the proposition that a family cannot demand that the treating physicians continue to provide medical care and treatment that "is not in the patient's best personal medical interest" or is "futile."

The Wanglie case represents the first time that any health-care provider or institution had sued to discontinue care. The logic of the treating doctors, and the ethics committee that had consulted on the case, was clear and simple. These medical professionals stated that the care they were providing was "futile," as it could neither restore Mrs. Wanglie to her previous level of health nor offer her any chance for improvement in the future. As Mrs. Wanglie was in a persistent vegetative state and was respirator-dependent, continued care could only support organ function, prolong the process of dying, and postpone her moment of death. They argued that this was an inappropriate use of medicine and a violation of their most basic ethic of "do no harm."

This case, or one like it, had seemed inevitable for years. If it had not first surfaced in a suit brought by the Hennepin County Medical Center, it might have emerged in a case instituted by a private advocacy organization for pregnant women or by advocates for the dying. The hypothetical arguments these groups could raise would begin with reference to the enormous cost of caring for those in persistent vegetative states, the shrinking health-care dollar, and the need of poor pregnant women and children for adequate preventive health care. At the time that the suit was filed the cost of caring for Mrs. Wanglie had exceeded $800,000.

Advocates in the future arguing to terminate care might argue that patients in this class could be assumed to oppose their continued care—as most of us would if we were in the state—and that, therefore, without the specific informed consent of the patient the care was an assault and battery and should be stopped. They could argue: Can we as a society justify the expenditure of funds to support those in the twilight zone of life while we ignore the needs of those who are struggling and in need? And they might conclude by citing the American commitment to "life" and the "pursuit of happiness," and, by asserting that these rights protect the vigorous and the striving against the claim to resources of the moribund and vegetative.

The lawyers in the Wanglie case were careful to avoid monetary argument. They wanted to establish the principle that care for a patient like Mrs. Wanglie is "futile" and is therefore neither legally nor morally mandatory. My illustrative cases, however, present the unacknowledged subtext of the Wanglie case. America is the only civilized country that does not grant its citizens a right to health care. It is also the only country that has yet to engage its population and its political and governmental entities in a discussion about rationing health care; one entails the other. Given the explosion in medical technology and the demands on government coffers, some discussion of conflicting agendas is inevitable and necessary. The mindless adherence to technologically possible but morally problematic care ignores the real economic costs of that care and the neglected health of many who are young, old, and in between.

But open discussion of appropriate care for those in a persistent vegetative state is prevented by present realities and past horrors. Politically powerful groups ranging from religious organizations to single-issue lobbies see every life as an absolute that must be maintained no matter what the level of technological support required and money expended. Others remember the degradation of society that resulted from the effort of Nazi Germany to judge the value of lives—the retarded, the mentally ill, Jews and Gypsies, among others—and to do away with the least valued. Some are concerned that even considering withdrawal of technological medical support revives these old antihumanitarian thoughts and the possibility of vicious and discriminatory actions.

Supporters of more restricted use of medical life supports, however, appeal not to the value of a patient's life, but rather to the quality of that life. They argue that a life without the ability to relate to others, to experience pleasure or even pain, to experience the beauty of surroundings, to respond to music, to sense the stimulation of taste and smell, is a life so devoid of human characteristics that it is disrespectful to the person that *was* to insist that the person who *is* be continued on life supports.

Depending on the individual's personal religious and moral convictions, one or another of these arguments will make the most sense. But there is no doubt which one is the most politically explosive, at least for the moment, and that is the position that condones the termination of care. It remains to be seen whether those who argue to limit technology will begin to gain adherents to their position; that is one issue for the next decade.

This is not the only issue looming, however. Many discussions in the near future will involve the world of reproductive technologies. In October of 1991, Mrs. Arlette Schweitzer gave birth to twins for her daughter, who was born without a uterus and could therefore not gestate her own children. Mrs. Schweitzer had the eggs of her daughter, which had been fertilized in the laboratory by her son-in-law's sperm, implanted in her womb. Two of these fertilized eggs grew to maturity and were born on October 18 at six pounds seven ounces and four pounds one ounce, respectively.

This case, as others before it, raises questions about the rights and liabilities of the genetic and the gestational mother, and how society should view their competing claims should they arise. In media interviews Mrs. Schweitzer was quoted as saying how surprised she was that anyone would be interested in her behavior. She said that she had done in the past, and would continue to do in the future, many things to help her daughter and her other children. This was just one more loving and supportive act of assistance.

But consider for a moment how the issue might seem if the daughter needed not only the womb, but also the eggs of the mother. Would we be as willing to accept the commonplace nature of the act if the child were the genetic daughter of the grandmother and the grandmother's son-in-law, the genetic half sister of the legal mother? Should we insist that the daughter adopt the child once born? What if the genetic mother were not the grandmother of the child but rather a stranger who had been hired for the job? And what if this stranger changed her mind and decided that she wanted to keep the baby? That, of course, has already happened in a case in New Jersey called the Baby M case. What should be the kinds of rules that govern these cases?

Legislatures and courts will grapple with these issues in the next few years. And for these issues an analysis that focuses on individual values and preferences will be the starting point of the discussion. Values of society, consequences for community, and theories of democracy will be central.

The issues explored in this book have involved individual choice and the control of decisions about health, life, and death. The issues in any succeeding volume will, of necessity, deal with life, death, health care, equity, and justice. As individuals become more comfortable with and more competent in addressing individual care decisions, the more abstract topics of rationing and access to care will inevitably move to the top of the medical ethics agenda.

I realize that this is not a "quick fix" book. Whereas there are some guides and charts included, the real value of the book, I suspect, comes from providing a framework and the language to rescue life-and-death choices from the shadows. I know that some of the cases are upsetting both in the stories they tell and in the fears they must raise in anyone even remotely facing a similar quandary. But I hope that new skills affecting insights, analyses, and personal advocacy will justify those moments of discomfort. Doctors are the experts on medicine, but you are the expert on yourself and the protector of those you love.

APPENDIXES

In the following pages you will find an example of a living will, a durable power of attorney, and a values history form.

Please note that there may be a new development in state law that may require a slightly different format. Please check at a local organization or contact: Choice In Dying, Inc.—the national council for the right to die, 250 West Fifty-seventh Street, New York, NY 10107; (212) 246-6973.

At a Glance: The Patient Self-Determination Act

The Patient Self-Determination Act took effect on December 1, 1991 and governs all health-care facilities funded by Medicare or Medicaid. In essence, the Act requires medical facilities to:

◆ Provide written information to each individual concerning

(i) an individual's rights under state law (whether statutory or as recognized by the courts of the state) to make decisions concerning such medical care, including the right to accept or refuse medical or surgical treatment and the right to formulate advance directives . . . , and

(ii) the written policies of the provider or organization respecting the implementation of such rights;

◆ Document in the individual's medical record whether or not the individual has executed an advance directive;

◆ Not condition the provision of care or otherwise discriminate against an individual based on whether or not the individual has executed an advance directive;

◆ Ensure compliance with requirements of state law . . . respecting advance directives at facilities of the provider or organization; and

◆ Provide (individually or with others) for education for staff and community on issues concerning advance directives.

The Act also requires the federal Department of Health and Human Services to mount a national Public Education Campaign and to develop materials explaining patients' rights, to be distributed by medical facilities.

Based on material published by Choice In Dying, Inc.—the national council for the right to die.

LIVING WILL

To my family, friends, loved ones, doctors and all concerned with my care, I   , being of sound mind, make this statement as a directive to be followed if I become unable to make or communicate decisions regarding my medical care.

IN 1–3, FOR EACH SECTION, CHOOSE THE SENTENCE (a) (b) OR (c) WHICH EXPRESSES YOUR WISHES; THEN CHECK AND INITIAL IT. IN ADDITION, READ (d) IN EACH SECTION; IF YOU DECIDE TO REFUSE FOOD AND FLUIDS, CHECK AND INITIAL (d). THE TREATMENTS YOU MIGHT WANT TO REFUSE ARE:

    DIAGNOSTIC PROCEDURES
    CARDIOPULMONARY RESUSCITATION
    INTUBATION
    MECHANICAL RESPIRATION
    ANTIBIOTICS
    DIALYSIS
    SURGERY
    BLOOD TRANSFUSIONS
    OTHER DRUGS NOT FOR COMFORT

1. If my doctors determine that I have a condition or illness that is incurable or irreversible and from which my doctors do not expect me to survive, I direct my doctors:

_____ [ ] (a) To use all appropriate medically accepted treatments and interventions.

_____ [ ] (b) To withhold or withdraw only the following treatments or interventions:

    _____

    _____

    _____

_____ [ ] (c) To withhold or withdraw all treatments or interventions which are not designed solely for my comfort.

_____ [ ] (d) I expressly refuse artificial food and fluids by any technology.

375

2. If I am irreversibly in a deep coma or persistent vegetative state, I direct my doctors:

_____ [   ] (a) To use all appropriate medically accepted treatments and interventions.

_____ [   ] (b) To withhold or withdraw only the following treatments or interventions:

    _____

    _____

    _____

_____ [   ] (c) To withhold or withdraw all treatments or interventions which are not designed solely for my comfort.

_____ [   ] (d) I expressly refuse artificial fluids and foods by any technology.

3. If I am irreversibly demented and am unable to recognize or respond to family and friends, and contract an illness or condition, whether or not such illness or condition is in itself life threatening, I direct my doctors:

_____ [   ] (a) To use all appropriate medically accepted treatments and interventions.

_____ [   ] (b) To withhold or withdraw only the following treatments or interventions:

    _____

    _____

    _____

_____ [   ] (c) To withhold or withdraw all treatments or interventions which are not designed solely for my comfort.

_____ [   ] (d) I expressly refuse applicable artificial food and fluids by any technology.

These directions express my legal right to refuse or consent to treatment. Therefore I expect my family, friends, loved ones, doctors and everyone concerned with my care to regard themselves legally and morally bound to act in accord with my wishes.

I understand that I may cancel or change this Living Will at any time.

IN WITNESS WHEREOF, I have hereunto set my hand and seal this _____ day of _____, 1990.

_____
DECLARANT

The foregoing, consisting of three pages, including this one, was signed, sealed and declared by the above named declarer, as and for Living Will, in our presence and hearing, and we thereupon on request, in presence and the presence of each other, subscribed our names as witnesses thereto this day of   ,   , 1990.

_____ RESIDING AT _____

_____   _____

_____ RESIDING AT _____

_____   _____

Developed by the Division of Law and Ethics and the Bioethics Committee at Montefiore Medical Center.

HEALTH CARE PROXY
(DURABLE POWER OF ATTORNEY)

(1) I, _____

hereby appoint _____

      (name, home address and telephone number)

_____

_____

as my health care agent to make any and all health care decisions for me, except to the extent that I state otherwise. This proxy shall take effect when and if I become unable to make my own health care decisions.

(2) Optional instructions: I direct my proxy to make health care decisions in accord with my wishes and limitations as stated below, or as he or she otherwise knows. (Attach additional pages, if necessary).

_____

_____

(Unless your agent knows your wishes about artificial nutrition and hydration [feeding tubes], your agent will not be allowed to make decisions about artificial nutrition and hydration. See instructions on reverse for samples of language you could use.)

(3) Name of substitute or fill-in proxy if the person I appoint above is unable, unwilling or unavailable to act as my health care agent.

      (name, home address and telephone number)

_____

_____

(4) Unless I revoke it, this proxy shall remain in effect indefinitely, or until the date or conditions stated below. This proxy shall expire (specific date or conditions, if desired):

_____

(5) Signature _____

Address _____

Date _____

Statement by Witnesses (must be 18 or older)

I declare that the person who signed this document is personally known to me and appears to be of sound mind and acting of his or her own free will. He or she signed (or asked another to sign for him or her) this document in my presence.

Witness 1 _____

Address _____

Witness 2 _____

Address _____

About the Health Care Proxy

This is an important legal form. Before signing this form, you should understand the following facts:

1. This form gives the person you choose as your agent the authority to make all health care decisions for you, except to the extent you say otherwise in this form. "Health care" means any treatment, service or procedure to diagnose or treat your physical or mental condition.

2. Unless you say otherwise, your agent will be allowed to make all health care decisions for you, including decisions to remove or withhold life-sustaining treatment.

3. Unless your agent knows your wishes about artificial nutrition and hydration (nourishment and water provided by a feeding tube), he or she will not be allowed to refuse those measurements for you.

4. Your agent will start making decisions for you when doctors decide that you are not able to make health care decisions for yourself.

You may write on this form any information about treatment that you do not desire and/or those treatments that you want to make sure you receive. Your agent must follow your instructions (oral and written) when making decisions for you.

If you want to give your agent written instructions, do so right on the form. For example, you could say:

> *If I become terminally ill, I do/don't want to receive the following treatments.* . . .
> *If I am in a coma or unconscious, with no hope of recovery, then I do/don't want.* . . .
> *If I have brain damage or a brain disease that makes me unable to recognize people or speak and there is no hope that my condition will improve, I do/don't want.* . . .

Examples of medical treatments about which you may wish to give your agent special instructions are listed below. This is not a complete list of treatments about which you may leave instructions.

- artificial respiration
- artificial nutrition and hydration (nourishment and water provided by feeding tube)
- cardiopulmonary resuscitation (CPR)
- antipsychotic medication
- electric shock therapy
- antibiotics
- psychosurgery
- dialysis
- transplantation
- blood transfusions
- abortion
- sterilization

Talk about choosing an agent with your family and/or close friends. You should discuss this form with a doctor or another health care professional, such as a nurse or social worker, before you sign it to make sure that you understand the types of decisions that may be made for you. You may also wish to give your doctor a signed copy. You do not need a lawyer to fill out this form.

You can choose any adult (over 18), including a family member or close friend, to be your agent. If you select a doctor as your agent, he or she may have to choose between acting as your agent or as your attending doctor; a physician cannot do both at the same time. Also, if you are a patient or resident of a hospital, nursing home or mental health facility, there are special restrictions about naming someone who works for that facility as your agent. You should ask the staff at the facility to explain those restrictions.

You should tell the person you choose that he or she will be your health care agent. You should discuss your health care wishes and this form with your agent. Be sure to give him or her a signed copy. Your agent cannot be sued for health care decisions made in good faith.

Even after you have signed this form, you have the right to make health care decisions for yourself as long as you are able to do so, and treatment cannot be given to you or stopped if you object. You can cancel the control given to your agent by telling him or her or your health care provider orally or in writing.

Filling Out the Proxy Form

Item (1) Write your name and the name, home address and telephone number of the person you are selecting as your agent.

Item (2) If you have special instructions for your agent, you should write them here. Also, if you wish to limit your agent's authority in any way, you should say so here. If you do not state any limitations, your agent will be allowed to make all health care decisions that you could have made, including the decision to consent to or refuse life-sustaining treatment.

Item (3) You may write the name, home address and telephone number of an alternate agent.

Item (4) This form will remain valid indefinitely unless you set an expiration date or condition for its expiration. This section is optional and should be filled in only if you want the health care proxy to expire.

Item (5)   You must date and sign the proxy. If you are unable
to sign yourself, you may direct someone else to sign
in your presence. Be sure to indicate your address.

Two witnesses at least 18 years of age must sign your proxy. The
person who is appointed agent or alternate agent cannot sign as a
witness.

New York State Department of Health

VALUES HISTORY
INSTRUCTIONS

Section one allows you to record both written and oral instructions you might already have prepared. If you have not yet written or talked about these issues, you may want to leave this section and come back to it when you have completed section two.

Section two asks a number of questions about your attitude toward your health; feelings about doctors and nurses; thoughts about independence and control; personal relationships; your overall attitudes to life, illness, dying, and death; your religious beliefs; your living situation; feelings about finances; and even wishes concerning your funeral. There are many ways to approach these questions. You may want to write down your own thoughts before talking with anyone else, or you might prefer to start by asking the important people in your life to come together and talk about your—and their—answers to these questions.

Often, these deep and intimate topics are difficult to consider and painful to talk about. The goal of the values history form is to help spur and support those conversations when it is easier to have them—before a medical crisis occurs.

As you continue to grow and change, so will your values and ideas, and so may the values reflected in the values history form. You may want to come back to this form every few years, to reconsider and reevaluate your preferences and wishes. The values history can be an important form to complete in preparation for the living will and health care proxy.

VALUES HISTORY FORM

NAME: _____

DATE: _____

If someone assisted you in completing this form, please fill in his or her name, address, and relationship to you.

Name: _____

Address: _____

_____

Relationship: _____

The purpose of this form is to assist you in thinking about and writing down what is important to you about your health. If you should at some time become unable to make health care decisions for yourself, your thoughts as expressed on this form may help others make a decision for you in accordance with what you would have chosen.

The first section of this form asks whether you have already expressed your wishes concerning medical treatment through either written or oral communications and if not, whether you would like to do so now. The second section of this form provides an opportunity for you to discuss your values, wishes, and preferences in a number of different areas, such as your personal relationships, your overall attitude toward life, and your thoughts about illness.

Section 1

A. Written Legal Documents

Have you written any of the following legal documents?
_____

If so, please complete the requested information.

Living Will

Date written:_____

Document location:_____

Comments: (e.g., any limitations, special requests, etc.)_____

_____

_____

_____

_____

Durable Power of Attorney

Date written:_____

Document location:_____

Comments: (e.g., whom have you named to be your decision maker?)

_____

_____

_____

Durable Power of Attorney for Health Care Decisions

Date written:_____

Document location:_____

Comments: (e.g., whom have you named to be your decision maker?)

_____

_____

_____

Organ Donations

Date written:_____

Document location:_____

Comments: (e.g., any limitations on which organs you would like to donate?) _____

_____

_____

B. Wishes Concerning Specific Medical Procedures

If you have ever expressed your wishes, either written or orally, concerning any of the following medical procedures, please complete the requested information. If you have not previously indicated your wishes on these procedures and would like to do so now, please complete this information.

Organ Donation

To whom expressed:_____

If oral, when?_____

If written, when?_____

Document location:_____

Comments:_____

_____

_____
_____
_____

Kidney Dialysis

To whom expressed:_____

If oral, when?_____

If written, when?_____

Document location:_____

Comments:_____

_____
_____
_____
_____
_____

Cardiopulmonary Resuscitation (CPR)

To whom expressed:_____

If oral, when?_____

If written, when?_____

Document location:_____

Comments:_____

_____
_____
_____
_____

Respirators

To whom expressed:_____

If oral, when?_____

If written, when?_____

Document location:_____

Comments:_____

_____

_____
_____
_____
_____
_____

Artificial Nutrition
To whom expressed:_____
If oral, when?_____
If written, when?_____
Document location:_____
Comments:_____
_____
_____
_____
_____
_____

Artificial Hydration
To whom expressed:_____
If oral, when?_____
If written, when?_____
Document location:_____
Comments:_____
_____
_____
_____
_____

C. General Comments

Do you wish to make any general comments about the information you provided in this section?_____
_____
_____

_____

_____

_____

Section 2
A. Your Overall Attitude Toward Your Health

1. How would you describe your current health status? If you currently have any medical problems, how would you describe them?

_____

_____

2. If you have current medical problems, in what ways, if any, do they affect your ability to function?_____

_____

_____

3. How do you feel about your current health status?_____

_____

_____

4. How well are you able to meet the basic necessities of life—eating, food preparation, sleeping, personal hygiene, etc.?_____

_____

5. Do you wish to make any general comments about your overall health?_____

_____

_____

_____

B. Your Perception of the Role of Your Doctor and Other Health Caregivers

1. Do you like your doctors?_____

_____

2. Do you trust your doctors?_____
_____
_____

3. Do you think your doctors should make the final decision concerning any treatment you might need?_____
_____
_____

4. How do you relate to your caregivers, including nurses, therapists, chaplains, social workers, etc.?_____
_____
_____

5. Do you wish to make any general comments about your doctor and other health caregivers?_____
_____
_____
_____
_____

C. Your Thoughts About Independence and Control

1. How important is independence and self-sufficiency in your life?
_____
_____
_____

2. If you were to experience decreased physical and mental abilities, how would that affect your attitude toward independence and self-sufficiency?_____
_____
_____
_____

3. Do you wish to make any general comments about the value of independence and control in your life?
_____
_____
_____

D. Your Personal Relationships

1. Do you expect that your friends, family and/or others support your decisions regarding medical treatment you may need now or in the future?_____

_____

_____

_____

2. Have you made any arrangements for your family or friends to make medical treatment decisions on your behalf? If so, who has agreed to make decisions for you and in what circumstances?

_____

_____

_____

_____

3. What, if any, unfinished business from the past are you concerned about (e.g., personal and family relationships, business and legal matters)?_____

_____

_____

_____

4. What role do your friends and family play in your life?_____

_____

_____

_____

5. Do you wish to make any general comments about the personal relationships in your life?_____

_____

_____

_____

E. Your Overall Attitude Toward Life

1. What activities do you enjoy (e.g., hobbies, watching TV, etc.)?

_____

_____

_____

2. Are you happy to be alive?_____

_____

3. Do you feel that life is worth living?

_____

4. How satisfied are you with what you have achieved in your life?

_____

_____

_____

5. What makes you laugh/cry?_____

_____

_____

_____

_____

6. What do you fear most? What frightens or upsets you?_____

_____

_____

_____

_____

7. What goals do you have for the future?_____

_____

_____

_____

8. Do you wish to make any general comments about your attitude toward life?

_____

_____

_____

_____

F. Your Attitude Toward Illness, Dying, and Death

1. What will be important to you when you are dying (e.g., physical comfort, no pain, family members present, etc.)?_____

_____

_____

2. Where would you prefer to die?

_____

_____

3. What is your attitude toward death?_____

_____

_____

4. How do you feel about the use of life-sustaining measures in the face of: terminal illness?_____

_____

permanent coma?_____

_____

irreversible chronic illness (e.g., Alzheimer's disease)?_____

_____

5. Do you wish to make any general comments about your attitude toward illness, dying, and death?_____

_____

_____

_____

G. Your Religious Background and Beliefs

1. What is your religious background?_____

_____

2. How do your religious beliefs affect your attitude toward serious or terminal illness?_____

_____

_____

3. Does your attitude toward death find support in your religion?

_____

_____

4. How does your faith community, church or synagogue view the role of prayer or religious sacraments in an illness?

_____

_____

_____

5. Do you wish to make any general comments about your religious background and beliefs?_____

_____

_____

_____

H. Your Living Environment

1. What has been your living situation over the last 10 years (e.g., lived alone, lived with others, etc.)?_____

_____

_____

2. How difficult is it for you to maintain the kind of environment for yourself that you find comfortable? Does any illness or medical problem you have now mean that it will be harder in the future?_____

_____

_____

_____

3. Do you wish to make any general comments about your living environment?

_____

_____

_____

_____

I. Your Attitude Concerning Finances

1. How much do you worry about having enough money to provide for your care?_____

_____

_____

2. Would you prefer to spend less money on your care so that more money can be saved for the benefit of your relatives and/or friends?

_____

_____

_____

3. Do you wish to make any general comments concerning your finances and the cost of health care?_____

_____

_____

_____

_____

J. Your Wishes Concerning Your Funeral
1. What are your wishes concerning your funeral and burial or cremation?

_____

_____

_____

_____

_____

_____

2. Have you made your funeral arrangements? If so, with whom? _____

_____

_____

_____

3. Do you wish to make any general comments about how you would like your funeral and burial or cremation to be arranged or conducted?

_____

_____

_____

_____

_____

Optional Questions

1. How would you like your obituary (announcement of your death) to read?

_____

_____

_____

_____

_____

_____

_____

_____

_____

_____

2. Write yourself a brief eulogy (a statement about yourself to be read at your funeral)._____

_____

_____

_____

_____

_____

_____

_____

_____

_____

_____

_____

Developed by Joan McIver Gibson, Ph.D.

Suggestions for Use

After you have completed this form, you may wish to provide copies to your doctors and other health caregivers, your family, your friends, and your attorney. If you have a living will or durable power of attorney for health care decisions, you may wish to attach a copy of this form to those documents.

INDEX

Adkins, Janet, 169, 171
adolescent medicine, 298–302
  see also pediatric medicine
advance directives, 38, 121–124, 257–261, 374
  see also living wills; proxies
ageism, 203–207
AIDS (Acquired Immune Deficiency Syndrome), 15, 24, 108, 172, 221, 312
  living wills and, 352–353
  patients' confidentiality and, 28–29, 293–298, 300–301
  teenagers and, 292–298, 300–301
American Academy of Pediatrics, 249, 251
American Association of Retired Persons, 356
American Bar Association Commission on the Legal Problems of the Elderly, 207, 235–236
American Society for Health-care Risk Management (ASHRM), 58
Arras, John, 4
assisted suicide, 166–167, 169–171, 173
autonomy:
  definition of, 90
  in nursing homes, 226–228
  of patients, 90–95, 98–102, 110–111, 123–124, 148–151, 170, 198, 212–215
  of senior citizens, 192–193, 196–197, 202, 212–215, 217, 220, 226–229, 237
  of teenagers, 285, 287, 299, 302

Baby Doe, 246–249, 252–253, 275
Baby Faye, 76
Baby Jane Doe, 24, 78–80, 250–253
Baby M, 371
Barnard, Christian, 314

beneficence, 198–199, 201, 241
"best interest" standard, 127–129, 137–142, 242, 275–280
Beth Israel Hospital (Boston), 182–183, 185
bioethicists, roles of, 1–10, 23, 29, 40–48, 85, 103–104
bisexuality, 27–30
brain death, 157–160, 314
Brown v. Board of Education, 291

California Natural Death Act, 72
Caplan, Arthur, 224
cardiopulmonary resuscitation (CPR),
  see resuscitation
Cardozo, Benjamin, 115
care, refusal of, *see* refusal of care
Carey v. Population Services, 291
Caro, Francis G., 218
Center for Health Law and Ethics, University of New Mexico, 346
children:
  abuse of, 266–267
  caregivers for, 265, 272, 276–277
  courts and, 265, 269–275
  neglect of, 265–266, 268
  as property, 263, 274, 302
  refusal of care for, 267–272
  societal values and, 271–275
Choice In Dying, Inc., 122–124, 357, 361–362, 373, 374
church, community support by, 221–222
clinical bioethics, *see* bioethicists, roles of
Collopy, Bart, 90
confidentiality:
  AIDS risk and, 28–29, 293–298, 300–301
  in treating teenagers, 299–301
Conroy, Claire, 73

Index